# 用英语说中国

## INTRODUCE CHINA IN ENGLISH

### 古今名人

**Eminent Persons**

| 主编 | 浩 瀚 | 李生禄 | | |
|---|---|---|---|---|
| 编委 | 齐 齐 | 宋美盈 | 王亚彬 | 李 硕 |
| | 李庆磊 | 刘雷雷 | 马 兰 | 蔡 丹 |
| | 姚 青 | 李林德 | 潘永亮 | 王应铜 |
| | 赵秀丽 | 尹晓洁 | 韩 磊 | 刘梓红 |
| | 徐 萍 | 马 迅 | 徐光伟 | 赵修臣 |
| | 李明亚 | 陈伟华 | 李 红 | |
| 策划 | 北京浩瀚英语研究所 | | | |

科学技术文献出版社

Scientific and Technical Documents Publishing House

北京

(京)新登字 130 号

## 内 容 简 介

  古老的中华民族文化辉煌灿烂，经久不衰。历史上的名人名家更是千古流芳，为世人所景仰。这些大人物杰出的思想和伟大的成就已成为我国民族文化中浓墨重彩的一笔。
  本书纵览古今，从政治、文化、科技等领域向读者朋友们介绍了 69 位杰出的历史人物及其成就。力求能使今人了解他们，并以此励志奋进。
  本书最适合具有中级以上英语水平的读者参阅。

---

  科学技术文献出版社是国家科学技术部系统惟一一家中央级综合牲科技出版机构，我们所有的努力都是为了使您增长知识和才干。

# 前言 Foreword

从春秋战国的连年烽火到清朝末年的乱世苍凉,从南昌起义的第一声枪响到新中国冉冉升起的五星红旗,两千多年,古老的中华民族一路走来。这一路,带来了恢宏壮丽的文明史迹,也带来了时代更迭的嗟吁慨叹,而透过历史的长镜头,我们最容易关注的是那一个个个性丰满、搏浪弄潮的身影。

从先秦诸子的思想光芒到儒家思想的大一统,再到近现代学者的"反孔"呼声,从秦皇汉武的霸主雄风到唐宗宋祖的风骚国度,再到康乾盛世的荣光万丈,大浪淘尽多少风流人物!

了解他们是在追忆历史,评述他们是在传播文化。

基于此,我们精心编辑了这本书,希望能使广大读者朋友通过本书了解这些响当当的人物,提高英语阅读能力,并能通过本书提供的给养丰富文化交流的底蕴。

此外,我们也希望通过本书浅显易懂的描述,能使外国友人初步了解这些赫赫有名的人物,增进对汉语言文化的认识深度。

本书共分为六章,分别从思想政治,文化科技等方面向读者展示了著名的人物及其事迹。在编写形式上,我们采用了英语为主,汉语为辅的思路,通过整篇的英文概述,配加相关的英汉互译句子、重点单词释义,力求能够达到篇章会意的水平;另外,文章又补充了各种中文的轶事趣文,以便给读者营造一个轻松的阅读氛围。

时间不止,俊杰辈出,数风流人物还看今朝!

谨以此鼓励广大学习者奋发向上,立志图强!

本书每部分内容分栏为:

**流畅精句**:选择了贴切、简单实用的语句,采用英汉对照的形式,让你脱口而出。

**精彩片段**:采用典型的具有代表性文章段落,介绍详细具体,一目了然,可让你获得英语学习和景点了解的双重丰收。

**文化链接**:用汉语讲述相关知识背景,可以让你更深层地了解中国文化艺术。

**妙词连珠**:鲜活、亮丽词汇,为你脱口而出打下坚实基础。

用英语说中国,不仅让中国走向世界,也让世界更多地了解中国。

# 目 录

## Chapter 1　Ancient Thinkers　思想先哲

Unit 1　Confucius
　　　　孔子 ·················································································· [1]
Unit 2　Mencius
　　　　孟子 ·················································································· [6]
Unit 3　Lao Zi
　　　　老子 ·················································································· [10]
Unit 4　Zhuang Zi
　　　　庄子 ·················································································· [16]
Unit 5　Mo Zi
　　　　墨子 ·················································································· [19]
Unit 6　Xun Zi
　　　　荀子 ·················································································· [23]
Unit 7　Han Fei
　　　　韩非 ·················································································· [26]
Unit 8　Dong Zhongshu
　　　　董仲舒 ··············································································· [29]
Unit 9　Wang Chong
　　　　王充 ·················································································· [32]
Unit 10　Zhu Xi
　　　　　朱熹 ················································································ [36]
Unit 11　Sun Wu
　　　　　孙武 ················································································ [40]

1

# Chapter 2
## Famous Statesmen 著名政治家

| | | |
|---|---|---|
| Unit 1 | Emperor Qin Shihuang 秦始皇 | [45] |
| Unit 2 | Emperor Liu Bang 刘邦 | [49] |
| Unit 3 | Emperor Wu of Han 汉武帝 | [53] |
| Unit 4 | Cao Cao 曹操 | [57] |
| Unit 5 | Emperor Li Shimin 李世民 | [61] |
| Unit 6 | Empress Wu Zetian 武则天 | [65] |
| Unit 7 | Emperor Zhao Kuangyin 赵匡胤 | [71] |
| Unit 8 | Genghis Khan 成吉思汗 | [75] |
| Unit 9 | Emperor Zhu Yuanzhang 朱元璋 | [80] |
| Unit 10 | Emperor Kangxi 康熙 | [84] |
| Unit 11 | Guan Zhong 管仲 | [89] |
| Unit 12 | Shang Yang 商鞅 | [92] |
| Unit 13 | Zhuge Liang 诸葛亮 | [98] |
| Unit 14 | Wang Anshi 王安石 | [104] |
| Unit 15 | Mao Zedong 毛泽东 | [108] |
| Unit 16 | Zhou Enlai | |

周恩来 ·································································· [115]

## Chapter 3 — National Heroes 民族英雄

| Unit 1 | Su Wu |
| | 苏武 ···························································· [122] |
| Unit 2 | Yang Ye |
| | 杨业 ···························································· [127] |
| Unit 3 | Yue Fei |
| | 岳飞 ···························································· [131] |
| Unit 4 | Wen Tianxiang |
| | 文天祥 ························································· [137] |
| Unit 5 | Qi Jiguang |
| | 戚继光 ························································· [141] |
| Unit 6 | Shi Kefa |
| | 史可法 ························································· [148] |
| Unit 7 | Zheng Chenggong |
| | 郑成功 ························································· [151] |
| Unit 8 | Lin Zexu |
| | 林则徐 ························································· [156] |
| Unit 9 | Sun Yat-sen |
| | 孙中山 ························································· [159] |

## Chapter 4 — Famous Scientists 著名科学家

| Unit 1 | Cai Lun |
| | 蔡伦 ···························································· [164] |
| Unit 2 | Zhang Heng |
| | 张衡 ···························································· [168] |
| Unit 3 | Hua Tuo |
| | 华佗 ···························································· [170] |
| Unit 4 | Zu Chongzhi |
| | 祖冲之 ························································· [176] |
| Unit 5 | Shen Kuo |

　　　　　沈括 ············································································· [179]
Unit 6　Li Shizhen
　　　　　李时珍 ········································································· [182]
Unit 7　Xu Guangqi
　　　　　徐光启 ········································································· [185]
Unit 8　Tsien Hsue-shen
　　　　　钱学森 ········································································· [188]

# Chapter 5
## Eminent Literati 文化名人

Unit 1　Qu Yuan
　　　　　屈原 ············································································· [193]
Unit 2　Zhang Qian
　　　　　张骞 ············································································· [198]
Unit 3　Sima Qian
　　　　　司马迁 ········································································· [202]
Unit 4　Wang Xizhi
　　　　　王羲之 ········································································· [207]
Unit 5　Xuanzang
　　　　　玄奘 ············································································· [211]
Unit 6　Li Bai
　　　　　李白 ············································································· [216]
Unit 7　Du Fu
　　　　　杜甫 ············································································· [220]
Unit 8　Bai Juyi
　　　　　白居易 ········································································· [225]
Unit 9　Su Shi
　　　　　苏轼 ············································································· [229]
Unit 10　Lu You
　　　　　陆游 ············································································· [233]
Unit 11　Xin Qiji
　　　　　辛弃疾 ········································································· [236]
Unit 12　Zheng He
　　　　　郑和 ············································································· [239]

Unit 13　Cao Xueqin
　　　　　曹雪芹 ·················································· [243]
Unit 14　Yan Fu
　　　　　严复 ···················································· [246]
Unit 15　Liang Qichao
　　　　　梁启超 ·················································· [250]
Unit 16　Lu Xun
　　　　　鲁迅 ···················································· [257]
Unit 17　Guo Moruo
　　　　　郭沫若 ·················································· [263]
Unit 18　Lin Yutang
　　　　　林语堂 ·················································· [267]
Unit 19　Mao Dun
　　　　　茅盾 ···················································· [271]

# Chapter 6　Famous Chinese Women　巾帼风范

Unit 1　Wang Zhaojun
　　　　王昭君 ··················································· [278]
Unit 2　Princess Wencheng
　　　　文成公主 ················································· [282]
Unit 3　Li Qingzhao
　　　　李清照 ··················································· [287]
Unit 4　Qiu Jin
　　　　秋瑾 ····················································· [291]
Unit 5　Soong Ching-ling
　　　　宋庆龄 ··················································· [294]
Unit 6　Bing Xin
　　　　冰心 ····················································· [297]

# 1 思想先哲
## Ancient Thinkers

## Unit 1 孔子 Confucius

### Key Sentences 流畅精句

1. To govern is to keep straight. If you take a lead in doing so, who will dare to act otherwise?
   政者,正也。子率以正,孰敢不正。(《论语·颜渊》)
2. Good government should make people nearby live happily and those far away desire to come.
   近者悦,远者来。(《论语·子路》)
3. Is humanity far away? So long as I want it, it is right here by me.
   仁远乎哉？我欲仁,斯仁至矣。(《论语·述而》)
4. Do not do to others what you would not like yourself.
   己所不欲,勿施于人。(《论语·颜渊》)
5. When you see a virtuous man, think of emulating him; when you see a immoral man, examine yourself.
   见贤思齐焉,见不贤而内自省也。(《论语·里仁》)
6. The superior man is always calm and at ease; the inferior man is always worried and full of distress.
   君子坦荡荡,小人长戚戚。(《论语·述而》)

7. It is desirable for a superior man to be slow in word and prompt in action.
   君子欲讷于言而敏于行。(《论语·里仁》)
8. To spread what you have heard on the way is to throw your virtue away.
   道听途说,德之弃也。(《论语·阳货》)
9. The superior man seeks to enable the good wishes of others, not their bad ones. The inferior man does just the contrary.
   君子成人之美,不成人之恶。小人反是。(《论语·颜渊》)
10. Men who differ in their ways cannot take counsel with each other.
    道不同,不相为谋。(《论语·卫灵公》)
11. A man who reviews the old so as to find out the new is qualified to teach others.
    温故而知新,可以为师矣。(《论语·为政》)
12. When three of us are walking together, I am sure to have a teacher. I'd select his merits to follow, and his bad qualities to correct myself.
    三人行,必有我师焉:择其善者而从之,其不善者而改之。(《论语·述而》)

## Wonderful Paragraph
精彩片段

### Paragraph 1

## Confucius 孔子生平

Confucius, whose given name is Qiu, styled himself Zhongni (551-479B.C.), was born in Zouyi, the State of Lu (now to south-eastern Qufu, a city in Shandong Province). As founder of the Confucianism, he was a great philosopher and educator in the end years of the Spring and Autumn Period. His forefathers were nobles in the State of Song, later the whole family was moved to the State of Lu. When Confucius was very young, his father died, so the family began to decline. He developed a firm and persistent character owing to the early years' experience of frustrations.

## Paragraph 2

## 孔子的思想
## Confucius' Thought

Confucius was the first thinker in China's intellectual history to consider moral standard as the first and highest criterion of man's behaviour and government. The core of morality, according to him, is humanity (humaneness or benevolence). "To be humane is to be a man," he said. This shows that in his view it is the quality of humanity that makes a man a man. He pointed out that humanity meant to "love other men"; to "help others to be established when one wishes to be established oneself; and help others to be successful when one wishes to be successful oneself"; and "not to impose on others what one does not desire oneself".

## Paragraph 3

## 关于《论语》
## About the Analects

The Analects is a book compiled after discussions by his disciples, and probably his disciples' disciples, who had taken notes of what their master and his main disciples had talked about.

The book is faithful and reliable because it is based on the notes taken by the students of what their teacher had said. At the same time, it is only natural if there are in it some repetitions and inconsistency in wording, because it is a collection of the notes taken by different students.

In the book there are all together about 490 sayings of Confucius and his main disciples. These are divided into 20 sections, in about 12700 words. They discuss a wide range of subjects: morality and rites, government and law, education and learning, knowledge and practice, music and poetry, the gentleman's qualities and the small man's weaknesses, the will of Heaven and destiny, the mean, the way of self cultivation, and the right attitude toward ghosts and spirits. In addition, there are a few entries describing Confucius' personality and lifestyle. In size it is a small book, but it contains immeasurable wisdom. It was like a torch that lit up the path of the Chinese people for centuries, because, in spite of its limitations, it distinguished between right and wrong. The Chinese people's appreciation of the book and Confucius is poetically expressed in the following two lines written by a scholar of the Song Dynasty: "Had Heaven not produced Zhongni (Confucius), there would be eternal night."

## Cultural Links
文化链接

### 孔庙四大明碑

洪武碑,立于洪武四年(1371年),是朱元璋"为祀岳、镇、海、渎,免祀杂神,专崇孔子"之御碑。碑文道:"朕奋起布衣,以安民为念,训将练兵,平定华夷,大统以正,永为治之道,必本于礼。"又说:"孔子善明先王之要道,为天下师。"其政治用意,不言而喻。

永乐碑,为朱元璋第四子朱棣所立,永乐十五年(1417年)重修曲阜孔庙,朱棣便亲自写下了这幢御制孔子庙碑文,赞扬孔子"参天地、赞化育、明王道、正彝伦,使君君、臣臣、父父、子子、夫夫、妇妇,各得以尽其份"。命有司维修孔庙,"撤其旧而新之"。以期"作我士,世有才贤,佐我大明,於万斯年"。同时炫耀朱元璋尊孔之盛举。

成化碑,明宪宗御制重修孔子庙碑。成化四年(1468年)立,龟趺螭首,碑文说"天不生孔子……万古如长夜","天生孔子,实所以为天地立心,为生民立命,为往圣继绝学,为万艺开太平者也","孔子之道在天下,如布制菽粟,民生日用不可暂缺。"

弘治碑,立于弘治十七年(1504年),因碑文中有"金元入主中国,纲常扫地之时"一语,招惹清乾隆皇帝不悦,遂将碑亭拆掉,只剩龟趺孤碑了。

## Vocabulary 妙词连珠

on humanity 论仁
loving and understanding 爱人、知人
poverty and low position 富贵、贫贱
on the rites 论礼
essence of the rites 礼之本
the rites and harmony 和为贵
the foundation of humanity 仁之本
filial piety and reverence 孝与敬
on self-cultivation 论修身
four worries 四种忧虑
examining oneself three times daily 三省吾身
amending faults 有过应改
on the gentleman and the small man 论君子与小人
rectification of names 正名
on teaching and learning 论教与学
inferring three corners after being shown one 举一反三
on knowledge and practice 论知与行
diligent in duties and careful in speech 慎言敏行

talking and doing 言与行
personality and words 人与言
on literature 论文艺
on the way and the mean 论道与中庸
loyalty and reciprocity 忠恕
the mean 中庸
going too far and falling short 过犹不及
simplicity and refinement 文质彬彬
heaven, destiny and ghosts and spirits 天命、命运与鬼神
destiny, the rites and words 命, 礼, 言
about confucius himself 关于孔子本人
being established at thirty 三十而立
blaming neither heaven nor man 不怨天, 不尤人

# Unit 2  Mencius
孟子

## Key Sentences
流畅精句

1. All men have the mind which cannot bear (to see the suffering of others).
   人皆有不忍人之心。(《孟子·公孙丑上》)

2. There is no man who is not good; there is no water that does not flow downwards.
   人无有不善,水无有不下。(《孟子·告子上》)

3. If a ruler honors the worthy and employs the competent so that offices are occupied by the wisest, then scholars throughout the world will be delighted to stand in his court.
   尊贤使能,俊杰在位,则天下之士皆悦,而愿立于其期矣。(《孟子·公孙丑上》)

4. The compass and square are the ultimate standards of the circle and the square. The sage is the ultimate standard of human relationships.
   规矩,方圆之至也;圣人,人伦之至也。(《孟子·离娄上》)

5. In a state the people are the most important; the spirits of the land and grain are the next; the ruler is of slight importance.
   民为贵,社稷次之,君为轻。(《孟子·尽心下》)

6. The great man does not insist that his words be necessarily truthful or his actions be necessarily resolute. He acts only according to righteousness.
   大人者,言不必信,行不必果,惟义所在。(《孟子·离娄下》)

7. One weakness of a man is to consider himself as the teacher of others.

人之患在好为人师。(《孟子·离娄上》)

8. I can distinguish words. And I am skillful in nourishing my strong, moving vital force.

我知言,我善养吾浩然之气。(《孟子·公孙丑上》)

9. Neither riches nor honors can tempt him, neither poverty nor a low social position can change his noble mind, neither threat nor force can bend his will, such a person is great man.

富贵不能淫,贫贱不能移,威武不能屈,此之谓大丈夫。
(《孟子·滕文公下》)

## Wonderful Paragraph
精彩片段

### Paragraph 1

### The Second Sage
亚圣

One cannot discuss Confucianism without at least mentioning the man the Chinese call "The Second Sage", Meng Tzu, or, in Latinized form, Mencius (c. 372—289B. C.). Mencius, like Confucius and Mo Tzu before him, concerned himself entirely with political theory and political practice; he spent his life bouncing from one feudal court to another trying to find some ruler who would follow his teachings. Like Confucius and Mo Tzu before him, he was largely unsuccessful in his endeavor.

### Paragraph 2

### Mencius' Thought
孟子的思想

As a philosopher, Mencius' main doctrine is the Goodness of human nature. He advocated "Nourishing the moving force," and put forth the idea of "Heaven and man combine into one". Compare with Confucius, in the viewpoint of human nature, Mencius took a big step forward. Mencius declared definitely that human nature is "originally good". Moreover, he built his entire philosophy on this tenet, and presented a series of concepts: (1) Man possesses the innate knowledge of the good and "innate ability" to do good; (2) If one "develops his mind to the utmost", he can "serve Heaven" and "fulfil his destiny"; (3) Evil is not inborn but due to man's own failures and his inability to avoid evil external influences; (4) Serious efforts must be made to recover men's original nature; (5) The end of learning is none other than to "seek for the lost mind".

## Cultural Links
文化链接

### 后天教育至关重要

孟轲认为人的本性虽然具有仁、义、礼、智的"善端",但还必须通过教育,加强道德修养,尽量去扩充和发展这些"善端"。他主张只要人们不断地探索内心的"善端",就会通过对人性的了解而达到对天命的认识。

孟轲最强调的是内心的道德修养;但他同时也不否认后天环境对人性的影响。他认为后天的环境可以改变先天的心性,后天的恶习,可以使人丧失善性。孟轲认为教育的作用比政治的作用更有效果。他说:"善政不如善教之得民也。善政民畏之,善教民爱之,善政得民财,善教得民心"。为了争取民心,他提出要注意培养"明人伦"的君子或大丈夫。他说:"教以人伦,父子有亲,君臣有义,夫妇有别,长幼有序,朋友有信"(《滕文公上》)。

## Vocabulary 妙词连珠

human nature is originally good 人性本善
practice humanity with virtue 以德行仁
he who exerts his mind to utmost knows his nature 尽心知性
skillful in nourishing vital force 善养浩气
sage 贤明的,明智的,审慎的;圣人
Latinize 拉丁化
bounce (使)反跳,弹起,(指支票)被银行退票,弹跳
feudal 封建的,封建制度的,封地的,领地的
endeavor 努力,尽力
doctrine 教条,学说
nourish 滋养,使健壮,怀有(希望、仇恨等)
tenet 原则
innate 先天的,天生的
destiny 命运,定数
commiseration 怜悯,同情

righteousness 正直,公正,正义
revolt 反叛,背叛
mandate 批准,颁布
humane 仁慈的
violence 猛烈,强烈,暴力,暴虐,暴行,强暴
rectifiable 可纠正的,可矫正的
sensible 有感觉的,明智的,有判断力的
muddled 混乱的,乱七八糟的
insincere 虚假的
artifical 人造的,虚伪的
sincerity 诚挚,真实,真挚
resolute 坚决的
exhaust 用尽,耗尽,抽完,使精疲力尽
altruism 利他主义,利他
neglect 忽视,疏忽,漏做
fragrant 芬芳的,香的
virtue 德行,美德,贞操,优点,功效,效力,英勇
uprightness 垂直,正直

# Unit 3  老子 Lao Zi

## Key Sentences
流畅精句

1. The Tao that can be told is not the eternal Tao. The name that can be named is not the eternal name. The nameless is the origin of Heaven and Earth. The named is the mother of all things.
   道可道,非常道;名可名,非常名。无名,天地之始;有名,万物之母。(《老子·一章》)

2. Man models himself after Earth. Earth models itself after Heaven. Heaven models itself after Tao. Tao models itself after Nature.
   人法地,地法天,天法道,道法自然。(《老子·二十五章》)

3. By acting without action, all things will be in order.
   为无为,则无不治。(《老子·三章》)

4. The tranquil is the ruler of the hasty.
   静为躁君。(《老子·二十六章》)

5. No action is undertaken, and yet nothing is left undone. An empire is often brought into order by having no activity. If one undertakes activity, he is not qualified to govern the empire.
   无为而无不为。取天下常以无事。及其有事,不足以取天下。(《老子·四十八章》)

6. The humble is the basis of honor. The low is the foundation of height.
   贵以贱为本,高以下为基。(《老子·三十九章》)

7. Reversion is the action of Tao. Weakness is the function of Tao.
   反者道之动,弱者道之用。(《老子·四十章》)

8. It is often the case that things gain while received depreciation and lose while received appreciation.

    物,或损之而益,或益之而损。(《老子·四十二章》)

9. He who knows does not talk. He who talks does not know.

    知者不言,言者不知。(《老子·五十六章》)

10. The roots are deep and the stalks are firm, which is the way of long life and everlasting vision.

    深根、固柢,长生、久视之道。(《老子·五十九章》)

11. Heaven's net is indeed vast. Though its meshes are wide, it misses nothing.

    天网恢恢,疏而不失。(《老子·七十三章》)

12. The Sage discards the extremes, the extravagant, and the excessive.

    圣人去甚,去奢,去泰。(《老子·二十九章》)

13. The Sage knows himself but does not show himself. He loves himself but does not exalt himself.

    圣人自知不自见,自爱不自贵。(《老子·七十二章》)

## Wonderful Paragraph
精彩片段

### Paragraph 1

# L老子
## ao Zi

Lao Zi (also spelled Lao Tzu, or Lao Tse) was a famous Chinese philosopher who is believed to have lived in approximately the 4th century B. C. , during the Hundred Schools of Thought and Warring States Periods. He is credited with writing the seminal Taoism work, the Tao Te Ching. He became a popular deity in Taoist religion's pantheon. His most famous follower, Zhuang Zi, wrote a book that had one of the greatest influences on Chinese Literati, through the ideas of individualism, freedom, carefreeness, and, even if the author never speaks about it, art, which may well be the cornerstone of Chinese art.

**Paragraph 2**

# 老子生平
## Lao Zi's life

Little is known about Lao Zi's life. His historical existence is strongly debated as is his authorship of the Tao Te Ching. Regardless, he has become an important culture hero to subsequent generations of Chinese people. Tradition says he was born in Ku Prefecture (苦县) of the state of Chu (楚), which today is Luyi County (鹿邑) of Henan province, in the later years of Spring and Autumn Period.

According to the tradition, Lao Zi was an older contemporary of Confucius and worked as an archivist in the Imperial Library of the Zhou Dynasty (1122 BC-256 BC). Confucius intentionally or accidentally met him in Zhou, near the location of modern Luoyang, where Confucius was going to browse the library scrolls. According to these stories, Confucius, over the following months, discussed ritual and propriety, cornerstones of Confucianism, with Lao Zi. The latter strongly opposed what he felt to be hollow practices. Taoist legend claims that these discussions proved more educational for Confucius than the contents of the libraries.

Afterwards, Lao Zi resigned from his post, perhaps because the authority of Zhou's court was diminishing. Some accounts claim he travelled west on his water buffalo through the state of Qin and from there disappeared into the vast desert. These accounts have a guard at the westernmost gate convincing Lao Zi to write down his wisdom before heading out into the desert. Until this time, Lao Zi had shared his philosophy in spoken words only.

## 思想先哲
## Ancient Thinkers

### Paragraph 3

## 老子的著作与思想
## Lao Zi's Work and Thought

Lao Zi's famous work, the Tao Te Ching, has been widely influential in China. The book is a mystical treatise covering many areas of philosophy, from individual spirituality to techniques for governing societies.

If we refer to this book, we can draw in few lines what and how Lao Zi was thinking. He emphasized a specific "Tao", which often translates as "the Way," and widened its meaning to an unnameable inherent order or property of the universe: "The way Nature is." He highlighted the concept of wu-wei, or "action through inaction." This does not mean that one should sit around and do nothing; but that one should avoid explicit intentions, strong will, and proactive action and then reach real efficiency by following the way things spontaneously increase or decrease. Actions taken in accordance with Tao (Nature) are easier and more productive than actively attempting to counter the Tao. Lao Zi believed that violence should be avoided when possible, and that military victory was an occasion to mourn the necessity of using force against another living thing, rather than an occasion for triumphant celebrations. Lao Zi also indicated that codified laws and rules result in society becoming more difficult to manage.

As with most other ancient Chinese thinkers, his way to explain his ideas often uses paradoxes, analogies, reuse and appropriation of ancient sayings. Using ellipsis, repetition, symmetries, rhymes, rhythm, his writings are poetical, dense and often obscure. They often served as a starting point for cosmological or introspective meditations. Many of the aesthetic theories of Chinese art are widely grounded in his ideas and those of his most famous follower: Zhuang Zi.

Although Lao Zi does not have as deep an influence as Confucius does in China, he is still widely respected by the Chinese. Confucius and Lao Zi are the best-known Chinese philosophers in the Western world.

# 用英语说中国——古今名人
## Introduce China in English—Eminent Persons

### Paragraph 4

## 老子的名字
## Lao Zi's Names

The name Lao Zi is an honorific title. Lao means "venerable" or "old." Zi translates literally as "boy," but it was also a term for a rank of nobleman equivalent to viscount, as well as a term of respect attached to the names of revered scholars. Thus, "Lao Zi" can be translated roughly as "the old master."Lao Zi's personal name was Lǐ ěr（李耳）, his courtesy name was Boyang, and his posthumous name was Dān（聃）, which means "Mysterious."

Lao Zi is also known as：Elder Dan（老聃）, Senior Lord（老君）, Senior Lord Li（李老君）, Senior Lord Taishang（太上老君）, Taoist Lord Lao Zi（老子道君）. In the Li Tang Dynasty, in order to create a connection to Lao Zi as the ancestor of the imperial family, he was given a posthumous name of Emperor Xuanyuan（玄元皇帝）, meaning "Profoundly Elementary"; and a temple name of Shengzu（圣祖）, meaning "Saintly/Sagely Progenitor."

### Cultural Links
### 文化链接

### 贝肯鲍尔欣赏老子

世界杯开赛后,"足球皇帝"贝肯鲍尔俨然成了"空中飞人"。为了方便他在12个赛场之间奔波,赞助商阿联酋航空公司为他提供了一架直升机。德国媒体将这架专机命名为"空中老子"。

贝肯鲍尔欣赏老子,这在德国并不算新闻。早在青少年时期,喜欢读书的他就涉猎了老子的著作,"千里之行,始于足下"成了当时他最喜爱的格言。当他称雄足坛后,仍不忘老子的忠告,"胜人者有力,自胜者强"。他带领德国队夺得大力神杯后却突然"隐退",很多人表示不解。在接受《明镜》周刊采访时,他引用老子的一句话:"功成身退,天之道也。"几十年来,老子的《道德经》一直放在他随身携带的公文箱内。

# Ancient Thinkers

## Vocabulary 妙词连珠

Tao models itself after nature 道法自然
letting nature take its own course 无为而治
Reversion is the action of Tao 反者道动
approximately 近似地,大约
seminal 种子,精液的,生殖的
Tao Te Ching 道德经
deity 神,神性
Literati 文人,文学界
contemporary 同时代的人
archivist 案卷保管人
browse 浏览,吃草,放牧
propriety 适当
diminishing 逐渐缩小的
buffalo [动]( 印度,非洲等的) 水牛 <美>[动]美洲野牛

treatise 论文,论述
spirituality 精神性,灵性
inherent 固有的,内在的,与生俱来的
explicit 外在的,清楚的,直率的,(租金等)直接付款的
spontaneously 自然地,本能地
triumphant 胜利的,成功的,狂欢的,洋洋得意的
paradox 似非而是的论点,自相矛盾的话
ellipsis 省略,省略符号
cosmological 宇宙哲学的,宇宙论的
introspective (好)内省的,(好)自省的,(好)反省的
meditation 沉思,冥想
courtesy name 字

# Unit 4  Zhuang Zi 庄子

## Key Sentences
流畅精句

1. The future cannot be waited for; the past cannot be sought again. When good order prevails in the world, the sage seeks for accomplishment. When disorder prevails, he may preserve only his own life. At the present time, the best one can do is to escape from punishment.
   来世不可待,往世不可追也。天下有道,圣人成焉;天下无道,圣人生焉。方今之时,仅免刑焉。(《庄子·人间世》)

2. Form without Tao cannot have existence. Existence without virtue cannot have manifestation.
   形非道不生,生非德不明。(《庄子·天地》)

3. The sage harmonizes the right and wrong and rests them in natural equalization. This is called following two courses at once.
   圣人和之以是非而休乎天钧,是之谓两行。(《庄子·齐物论》)

4. The "this" is also the "that". The "that" is also the "this". The "this" has a standard of right and wrong, and the "that" also has a standard of right and wrong.
   是亦彼也,彼亦是也。彼亦一是非,此亦一是非。(《庄子·齐物论》)

5. The growing of things is like the galloping of a horse. There is no movement when it is not changeable and no time when it is not shifting.
   物之生也,若骤若驰,无动而不变,无时而不移。(《庄子·秋水》)

6. I work with my mind and not my eyes.
   以神遇,而不以目视。(《庄子·养生主》)

7. What is to be done? What is not to be done? Things are transformed of themselves.
何为乎？何为乎？夫固将自化。(《庄子·秋水》)

## Wonderful Paragraph
## 精彩片段

### Paragraph 1

# Zhuang Zi
# 庄子

Confucius was followed by Mencius, and Lao Zi by Zhuang Zi. In those cases, the first was the real teacher and either wrote no books or wrote very little, and the second began to develop the doctrines and wrote long and profound discourses. Zhuang Zi (c. 369-286B. C.) was separated from Lao Zi's death by not quite two hundred years, and was strictly a contemporary of Mencius. Yet the most curious thing is that although both these writers mentioned the other philosophers of the time, neither was mentioned by the other in his works.

### Paragraph 2

# Lao—Zhuang
# "老庄"

It has been customary to speak of Lao Zi and Zhuang Zi together as Lao-Zhuang. Zhuang Zi's chief doctrines were based upon the sayings of Lao Zi. While Lao Zi emphasized difference between glory and disgrace, strength and weakness, and advocated the tender values and non-action, Zhuang Zi identified them all. Lao Zi aimed at reform, whereas Zhuang Zi's goal was absolute spiritual emancipation and peace, achieved through knowing the capacity and limitations of one's own nature, nourishing it and adapting it to the universal process of transformation. He abandoned selfishness of all descriptions, be it fame, wealth, preferred to move in the realm of "great knowledge" and "profound virtue", and travel beyond the mundane world. All these make him all the more Taoistic. His conception of the Way of Heaven is colored by pantheism. He pit the principle of nature and spontaneity against artificiality, and the theory of relativism against dogmatism.

## Cultural Links 文化链接

### 庄子故里

　　庄子故里在商丘市民权县顺河集东北三里的清莲寺村。庄子故里有一古井,相传为庄子取水处,至今仍被周围百姓称作"庄子井"。作为庄子的邻里,庄子生时的故事至今仍在当地百姓中流传。庄子故里不远处的唐庄村东有庄子墓。庄子墓只有孑然一冢,没有其他,墓前所立一镌刻有"庄周之墓"四字的墓碑为清乾隆五十四年所立。据传,"庄子将死,弟子欲厚葬之。庄子曰:吾以天地为棺椁,以日月为连璧,星辰为珠玑,万物为赍送。吾葬具岂不备也? 何以如此!"(见《庄子·列御寇》)。庄子墓葬虽然简陋,由于他是世代敬仰和世界闻名的文哲大师,所以每年仍吸引许多海内外游客前来拜谒。2000 年,前国家邮政部在这里举行了"庄子"纪念邮票首发式。

## Vocabulary 妙词连珠

| | |
|---|---|
| Tao operates in all things 道通万物 | profound 深刻的,意义深远的,渊博的,造诣深的 |
| All things are one 万物一齐 | |
| all things change 物无不变 | mundane 世界的,世俗的,平凡的 |
| Travel beyond the mundane world 逍遥游世 | pantheism 泛神论 |
| | spontaneity 自发性 |
| Nature is inaction 自然无为 | artificiality 人工,不自然,不自然之物,人造物 |
| emancipation 释放,解放 | |
| description 描写,记述,形容,种类,描述 | relativism 相对论,相对主义 |
| | dogmatism 教条主义 |
| realm 领域 | |

# Unit 5  墨子 Mo Zi

## Key Sentences 流畅精句

1. Mo Zi was a great philosopher in the early Warring States Period and a founder of the Mohist School.
   墨子是战国初年的伟大思想家,墨家学派的创始人。

2. In his early years, Mo Zi studied Confucianism, later he founded Mohism, and finally he became an opposition faction of the Confucianism. His thoughts were mainly reflected in the book Mo Tse.
   墨子早年曾学习儒术,后创立了墨家,成为儒家的反对派,其思想主要反映在《墨子》一书中。

3. The core of Mo-thought is "discriminate love".
   墨子思想的核心是"兼爱"。

4. Mo Zi puts forward the thought of non-aggressiveness and opposes war of any kind.
   墨子提出了"非攻"思想,反对一切战争。

5. Mo Zi spreads the thought that there is no fate to oppose the idea of fate.
   墨子宣扬"非命"思想,反对"天命"观。

6. He also puts forward the proposals to eliminate rites, music and funerals as an opposition of the rites, and music culture and elaborate funeral of Confucianism, while expostulating on saving expenditure in order to lighten the people's burden.
   他还提出了"非乐"、"节用"、"节葬"的主张,反对儒家的礼乐文化和厚葬风尚,劝诫统治者节约用度,以减轻人民的负担。

7. Mo Zi's opinions typically reflect the class standing of minor producers.
   墨子的主张典型地反映了他所持的小生产者的阶级立场。
8. The Mohism, founded by Mo Zi, is a party of compact organization and strict discipline with moral principles and sacrifice spirits, which earned the school a reputation of chivalrous Mo.
   墨子创立的墨家是一个组织严密、纪律严明、富于道义感和牺牲精神的团体,故有"墨侠"之称。

## Wonderful Paragraph
精彩片段

*Paragraph 1*

# 墨子及其思想
# Mo Zi and His Thought

Mo Zi (Mo-tse:468—376B.C.) was China's first true philosopher. Mo Zi pioneered the argumentative essay style and constructed the first normative and political theories. He formulated a pragmatic theory of language that gave classical Chinese philosophy its distinctive character. Speculations about Mo Zi's origins highlight the social mobility of the era. The best explanation of the rise of Mohism links it to the growth in influence of crafts and guilds in China. Mohism became influential when technical intelligence began to challenge traditional priestcraft in ancient China. The "Warring States" demand for scholars perhaps drew him from the lower ranks of craftsmen. Some stories picture him as a military fortifications expert. His criticisms show that he was also familiar with the Confucian priesthood.

The Confucian defender, Mencius, complained that the "words of Mo Zi and Yang Zhu fill the social world". Mo Zi advocated utilitarianism (using general welfare as a criterion of the correct Tao guiding discourse) and equal concern for everyone. The Mohist movement eventually spawned a school of philosophy of language (called Later Mohists) which in turn influenced the mature form of both Taoism (Zhuang Zi) and Confucianism (Xun Zi).

The core Mohist text has a deliberate argumentative style. It uses a balanced symmetry of expression and repetition that aids memorization and enhances effect. Symmetry and repetition are natural stylistic aids for Classical Chinese, which is an extremely analytic language (one that relies on word order rather than part-of-speech inflections). Three rival accounts of most of the important sections survive in the Mo Zi.

## Cultural Links 文化链接

### 墨 子

墨家是先秦诸子百家中的"显学",《墨子》一书是中国思想百花园中的奇葩。可是,在《墨子》中,甚至其姓氏与国籍都没有明确的交代。关于他的姓氏,最通行的说法是姓墨名翟,亦有史家认为墨子姓翟名乌。钱穆在《先秦诸子系年考辨》中认为,墨子这类贱者古时根本没有姓氏,所谓"墨"乃古刑之名,墨子盖为刑徒。关于墨子的国别,有的说鲁国,有的说宋国,更有奇者,说"墨"即"黑","翟"通"狄",疑他为印度人。

墨子自称"贱人","北方之鄙人",擅长于器械发明。这说明墨子本是地位低下之人。墨子早年虽"学儒者之业,受孔子之术",但嫌其烦扰害事而弃之不继。他主要靠自学成才,并强调实用知识而非词章文采。所以,《墨子》的文风生硬、呆板、乏味而重复。"言之无文,行而不远",这大概是《墨子》失传的一个原因。

## Vocabulary
妙词连珠

| | |
|---|---|
| pragmatic 实事求是；实用主义 | priesthood 教士，僧侣，神父 |
| highlight 使显著；使突出 | utilitarianism 功利主义；实利主义 |
| mobility 可动性；易变性 | discourse 演说；演讲；论文 |
| craft 行会；手工艺 | core 核心部分 |
| guild（互动性的）团体；协会 | symmetry 对称 |
| influential 有影响有，有势力的 | memorization 记住，默记 |
| priestcraft 祭司 | inflections 变形 |

# Unit 6  荀子  Xun Zi

## Key Sentences
## 流畅精句

1. Xun Zi's view on nature is unprecedented.
   荀子的自然观是前无古人的。
2. He thinks the change of the natural world is under the control of objective laws, which have no relations with man.
   他认为自然界的变化是客观规律使然，与人事之间没有任何关系。
3. He rejects the thought of correspondence between man and universe.
   他否定了天人感应的思想。
4. As for the relation between man and nature, he affirms the dominant and positive power of man before nature, and puts forward the thought of "controlling fatality and making use of it"—for the first time, man's will is set above the natural world scientifically.
   在人与自然的关系上，他肯定了人在自然界面前的主导作用和能动作用，并提出了"制天命而用之"的思想，第一次将人的意志科学地树立在自然界之上。
5. Xun Zi believed that even human beings are the products of nature.
   荀子认为就连人类也是自然界的产物。

## Wonderful Paragraph
## 精彩片段

### Paragraph 1

## 荀子及其思想
## Xun Zi and His Thought

Xun Zi (c. 313-238 B.C.), whose given name was Kuang and courtesy name Qing, was born in the State of Zhao and was a key figure in the Confucius school. When studying in the State of Qi, he became one of the celebrated scholars at the Jixia Academy. In his late years, he dedicated himself in teaching disciples and writing books, one of which is Xun Zi, an epitome of his thoughts. Politically, he inherited the Confucian thought of li (rites) and considers li as not merely a moral standard but a necessity of governing the country. He also called upon the practice of the "royal regulations" which emphasizes li and fa (standards): the purpose of li is to educate while that of fa is to rule. The practice of them combined means to restrain the evil in human nature.

Xun Zi epitomized the academic thoughts of the Pre-Qin period. The Book of Xun Zi was the crystallization of his thoughts. As for his political thought, he chiefly inherits Confucian thought of rites and etiquette, which he considers as a sort of basic social system that may regulate social relations. As for the theory of human nature, Xun Zi thinks the nature of man is evil, which should be normalized and restricted by "rites and morality", so he values moralization and study after a man's birth. The first article in The Book of Xun Zi is "Encouraging Learning". Xun Zi's epistemology is a theory of reflection of materialism, he puts forward a proposition of "achieving calmness by modesty and concentration". By "modesty" he means freedom from prejudice in the process of getting insight into the objective world. "Concentration" means focusing on what you are doing with full attention. "Calmness" means observing calmly and maintaining an objective attitude. His epistemology has some rationality.

## Cultural Links
文化链接

### 青出于蓝而胜于蓝

"青取之于蓝而青于蓝"这句名言,最早就是荀子说的。后来,这句话演变为"青出于蓝而胜于蓝"这句谚语,用以比喻学生胜过先生,后人胜过前人。"劝学"是《荀子》三十二篇中的第一篇。作者在这篇文章中,比较全面地论述了学习目的、意义、态度和方法,对人们具有深刻的启迪作用。文章中有这样一段话:"学不可以已。青,取之于蓝,而青于蓝;冰,水为之,而寒于水。"意思是:学习是不应当停止和废弃的。青色是从蓝色的染料里提取出来的,可是它比蓝色还要青;冰是水结成的,可是它比水还要凉。在这里,荀子以青与蓝,冰与水的关系作比喻,说明学生只要通过坚持不懈地刻苦学习,就能够有所提高,学生一定要有志气超过自己的老师,一代要比一代强。

## Vocabulary 妙词连珠

| | |
|---|---|
| dedicate 献(身)致力,题献(一部著作给某人) | etiquette 礼节 |
| epitome 摘要 | restrict 限制,约束,限定 |
| inherited 通过继承得到的,遗传的、继承权的 | materialism 唯物主义 |
| rite 仪式,典礼,习俗,惯例,礼拜式,教派 | rationality 合理性,惟理性 |
| crystallization 结晶化 | objective laws 客观规律 |
| | key figure 关键人物 |
| | restrain 阻止,约束 |
| | epistemology 认识论 |

# Unit 7　Han Fei
韩非

## Key Sentences
流畅精句

1. "Fa" mainly emphasizes the authority and justice of the law: that is, "the high-rank official should be punished if he breaks the law; awarding should be granted to the common folk."
   所谓"法",主要强调法律的权威性和公正性,即"刑过不避大夫,赏善不遗匹夫"。
2. "Shu", refers to the autocratic emperor's conspiratorial method or art of vindicating his authority.
   所谓"术",即专制君主维护其权力的阴谋权术。
3. "Shi", that refers to power, is to use the feudalistic state establishments.
   所谓"势",即权势,是关于如何运用封建国家机器的理论。
4. The Legalist thought of combination of fa, shu and shi provides the theoretical foundation for building a new autocratic feudalistic centralization of state power.
   法、术、势相结合的法家思想,为建立新兴的封建专制集权政权,提供了理论支持。
5. But Han Fei believes in the evil nature of man, thus considering the relationship between people as a relationship of pure interests, exaggerating the opposition between people, and obliterating the commune element between people.
   但韩非从性恶论出发,把人与人之间的关系看成是一种纯粹的利害关系,夸大了人际关系中的对立成分,抹杀了人际关系中的同一性。

6. Furthermore, he publicizes violent repression and denies the role of the moralization, all of which has become the theoretical basis for despotic rule.

他进而提出了非道德主义，公开宣扬暴力镇压，否定了道德教化的作用，成为暴政的理论基础。

## Wonderful Paragraph
精彩片段

### Paragraph 1

## 韩非及其思想
## Han Fei and His Thought

Han Fei (c. 280—233 B. C.), a native of the State of Han and a former student of Xun Zi, synthesized the thoughts of the Legalist School of the pre-Qin period. His doctrines served as the theoretical basis for the State of Qin's unification of China and the establishment of a feudal and autocratic empire. Han Fei's entire work is collected in Han Fei Zi, a book containing 55 chapters. Han Fei adopted and developed a progressive social and historical view put forward by earlier legalists (Shang Yang, for instance) and further proposed his notions of social development and historical evolution. He pointed out that "one does not have to follow ancient practices in order to govern" and "as conditions in the world change, different principles should be applied accordingly." He also held that the impetus of social development lies in the material foundation and inner conflicts of the society.

Han Fei believes in the thought of historical development, thinking that "in ancient times, people contest in morality; in mediaeval times, in resourcefulness and nowadays, in effort." He also proposes political reform in order to make the country rich and the army strong, which manifests the spirits of defiance and innovation. He is the one who advocates the idea of ruling by law—an idea put forward by the Legalist School in early days, which he fuses with the thought of "rule by shu (method or art of conducting)" and "rule by shi (power or authority)" of the School of Huang Lao. Later, by systematic alteration, he builds a new system of the Legalist thought which combines fa, shu and shi.

## Cultural Links
文化链接

### 韩非子寓言——巧还清白

晋文公的时候,有一次,他的家臣端一碗烤肉给文公吃,肉上有几根头发缠绕着。文公勃然大怒,把厨师叫来训斥说:"你想噎死我吗? 为什么把头发缠在烤肉上!"厨师连忙下跪,不断地磕头请罪说:"小人该死,罪有三条:其一,在磨刀石上磨过的厨刀,锋利得像干将宝剑,切肉,肉断,可是却没有把头发割断;其二,拿铁锥贯穿肉块,竟然没发现这几根头发;其三,很小心地把肉块送进炽热的炉子里,炭火红通通,肉都烤熟了,而没有把头发烧掉。小人失职,甘愿受罚。"晋文公恍然大悟,召集所有家臣,一个个进行讯问,终于查出了陷害厨师的人,并且把这个人杀掉了。

## Vocabulary
妙词连珠

| | |
|---|---|
| synthesize 综合,合成 | mediaeval 中古的,中世纪的 |
| theoretical 理论的 | resourcefulness 足智多谋 |
| autocratic 独裁的,专制的 | defiance 挑战,蔑视,挑衅 |
| notion 概念,观念,想法,意见,打算,主张,(复数)＜美语＞小饰物 | innovation 改革,创新 |
| | fuse 熔合,结合 |
| | the evil nature of man 性恶论 |
| evolution 进展,发展,演变,进化 | commune element 同一性 |
| impetus 推动力,促进 | obliterate 消除;毁迹 |

# 思想先哲 Ancient Thinkers

# Unit 8 董仲舒 Dong Zhongshu

## Key Sentences 流畅精句

1. Dong Zhongshu's Confucian system is one that mixes the theory of Yin and Yang with Wu Xing (that means five elements) theory.
   董仲舒的儒学体系是阴阳五行化的儒学。
2. Remolding Confucianism with Yin and Yang theory and Wu Xing theory, Dong builds a philosophical system of teleology in which there is an interaction between nature and man.
   用阴阳五行学说改造儒学的结果,使董仲舒建立了天人感应的目的论哲学体系。
3. He interpreted the relationship between nature and man by applying a theory of "heterodoxy of natural disasters".
   他用"灾异说"来解释天与人之间的关系。
4. He also proposes "moral is more vital than punishment," emphasizing the function of moralization.
   他还主张"任德不任刑",强调道德教化的作用。
5. He advocates the moral system of "Three Cardinal Guides and Five Constant Virtues", which have a far-reaching influence on the formation and development of traditional Chinese morality.
   他提出了"三纲五常"的道德体系,对传统道德的形成与发展有深刻的影响。

用英语说中国——古今名人
Introduce China in English—Eminent Persons

## Wonderful Paragraph
精彩片段

### Paragraph 1

### D董仲舒
  ong Zhongshu

Dong Zhongshu (Wade-Giles Tung Chung-shu) (179 -104B. C.) was a Han Dynasty scholar who is traditionally associated with the promotion of Confucianism as official ideology of the Chinese imperial state.

Born in Guangchuan (in modern Hebei), he later entered the imperial service during the reign of the Emperor Jing and rose to high office under the Emperor Wu. His relationship with the emperor was uneasy, though. At one point he was thrown into prison and nearly executed for writings that were considered seditious, and he may have cosmologically predicted the overthrow of the Han Dynasty and its replacement by a Confucian sage, the first appearance of a theme that would later sweep Wang Mang to the imperial throne.

### Paragraph 2

### D董仲舒的思想
  ong Zhongshu's Thought

Dong Zhongshu's thought integrated Yin Yang cosmology into a Confucian ethical framework. He emphasized the importance of the Spring and Autumn Annals as a source for both political and metaphysical ideas, following the tradition of the Gongyang Commentary in seeking hidden meanings from its text.

The only work that has survived to the present that is attributed to Dong Zhongshu is the Luxuriant Dew of the Spring and Autumn Annals in 82 chapters. However, it bears many marks of multiple authorship. Its authenticity has been called into question by Chinese literati (Zhu Xi, Cheng Yanzuo) and researchers in Japan (Keimatsu Mitsuo, Tanaka Masami), and the West. Scholars now reject as later additions all the passages that discuss five elements theory, and much of the rest of the work is questionable as well. It seems safest to regard it as a collection of unrelated or loosely related chapters and shorter works, most more or less connected to the Gongyang Commentary and its school, written by a number of different persons at different times throughout the Former Han and into the first half of the Later Han.

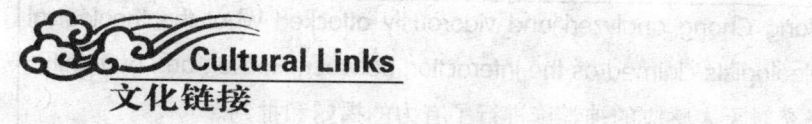

## Cultural Links 文化链接

### "天人三策"

董仲舒自幼熟读儒家经典。据说,为了刻苦攻读,他三年不出门,以致不知春夏秋冬。武帝早已微知其名,一次亲阅其试卷,被其惊人的论点、严谨的逻辑和优美的语言所折服。在其试卷上批了"贤良之首"四个大字,并命速传董仲舒进宫当面策问,即天子面试。

策问的当天,武帝就天道、人世、治乱等三个方面的问题,进行了三次策问,董仲舒一一从容作答,史称"天人三策"。"天人三策"主要是说,君主受命于天,就要奉行天道。天道,就是使国家走向大治的途径。而儒家的仁义礼乐,是推行天道的具体方法。国家的治乱关键在于国君。国君首要的是用人。用人得当,方法正确,国家就会大治。反之,国家就会大乱。他建议"罢黜百家,独尊儒术"。

武帝被他的君权神授、天下一统的宏大理论所振奋。后来,"罢黜百家,独尊儒术"成为汉朝推行新政的指导思想。

## Vocabulary 妙词连珠

ideology 意识形态
seditious 煽动性的,妨害治安的
cosmological 宇宙哲学的,宇宙论的
ethical 与伦理有关,民族的
metaphysical 纯粹哲学的,超自然的

authenticity 确实性,真实性
frustration 挫败,挫折,受挫
stimulus-response 刺激物,促进因素
treatise 论文,论述

# Unit 9　Wang Chong 王充

## Key Sentences
流畅精句

1. Wang Chong analyzed and vigorously attacked what the theological teleologists claimed as the interaction between Heaven and humanity.
   王充对天人感应的神学论进行了有力的揭露和批判。
2. Heaven, he claimed, is natural so that it is not will-driven and emotional.
   他指出天是一种物质实体,没有意志和情感,天是自然之天。
3. Furthermore, Wang Chong criticized the prevailing superstitious ideas and practices, especially the belief of life after death.
   王充还批判了当时流行的各种迷信思想和迷信活动,特别是对"人死为鬼"之说的批判最为彻底。
4. He held that human beings are born with original vigor and human beings are unique only because they have physical bodies and consciousness.
   他认为人禀元气而生,人之所以为人,是因为人有形体,有知觉,是形体和精神的结合体。
5. The illusion of ghosts and spirits are just hallucinations caused by frustration, illness and madness.
   同时指出人之所以产生鬼的观念,是由于人处在困、病、狂三种状态下容易产生见鬼的幻觉。

## 思想先哲
## Ancient Thinkers

## Wonderful Paragraph
## 精彩片段

### Paragraph 1

### W 王充
### ang Chong

Wang Chong (27—c. 97) was a Chinese philosopher during the Han Dynasty who developed a rational, secular, naturalistic, and mechanistic account of the world and of human beings. His main work was the Lun-Heng (论衡).

Unusually for a Chinese philosopher of the period, Wang Chong spent much of his life in non-self-inflicted poverty; indeed, he was said to have studied by standing at bookstalls. A superb memory, however, allowed him to become very well-versed in the Chinese classics, and he eventually reached the rank of District Secretary, a post which he soon lost as a result of his combative and anti-authoritarian nature.

### Paragraph 2

### W 著作及思想
### orks and Thought

Also unusual is the fact that Wang cannot be placed in any particular school of Chinese philosophy. Rather, he reacted to the state that philosophy had reached in China by his day. Taoism had long before degenerated into superstition and magic, and Confucianism had been the state religion for some 150 years. Confucius and Lao Zi were worshipped as gods, omens were seen everywhere, belief in ghosts was almost universal, and feng shui had begun to rule people's lives. Wang's response to all this was derision, and he made it his vocation to set out a rational, naturalistic account both of the world and of the human place in it. He was also a friend of Ban Gu, the historian who contributed to the Book of Han (Han Shu).

At the centre of his thought was the denial that Heaven has any purpose for us, whether benevolent or hostile. To say that Heaven provides us with food and clothing is to say it acts as our farmer or tailor—an obvious absurdity. We humans are insignificant specks in the universe and cannot hope to effect changes in it, and it is ludicrous arrogance to think that the universe would change itself just for us.

Wang insisted that the words of previous sages should be treated critically, and that they were often contradictory or inconsistent. He criticized scholars of his own time for not accepting this, as well as what he called the popular acceptance of written works. He believed that the truth could be discovered, and would become obvious, by making the words clear, and by clear commentary on the text. One example of Wang Chung's rationalism is his argument that thunder must be created by fire or heat, and is not a sign of the heavens being displeased. He argued that repeatable experience and experiment should be tried before adopting the belief that divine will was involved.

He was equally scathing about the popular belief in ghosts. Why should only human beings have ghosts, he asked, not other animals? We're all living creatures, animated by the same vital principle. Besides, so many people have died that their ghosts would vastly outnumber living people; the world would be swamped by them. "People say that spirits are the souls of dead men. That being the case, spirits should always appear naked, for surely it is not contended that clothes have souls as well as men." (Lun-Heng)

## Cultural Links
文化链接

### 王充破佛

一日,王充路过街头,见围满了人,便挤了进去。只见一个道人盘腿而坐,面前放着一尊金佛,黄绫上写着"如来算命"四个篆字。那道人口里念念有词:"各人吉凶祸福,佛祖了如指掌。要说出事由,佛祖明示祥、歹:祥者佛祖点头,歹者佛祖不动。"

王充问:"我想做生意,不知能否赚钱?"只见那老道拿起金戒尺,在佛像前后左右绕了几绕,佛像当即频频点头,老道双手合十说:"恭喜,恭喜,日后定发财!"并要了王充三两纹银。

次日,王充带了个泥塑金佛又到街上,对那老道佯笑曰:"请试试这个如来菩萨灵不灵。"老道一愣,慌忙拿起那尊小金佛溜了。

原来,佛像是铁制的,佛像的头可以动。那金戒尺则一头是铁,一头是磁石。那道人如要佛像点头,便握铁质的一端,使磁石的一端在佛像头部绕动,佛像哪有不点头之理,反之则一摇不摇。王充在众人面前破了那道人的骗人机关。

## Vocabulary 妙词连珠

rational 理性的,合理的,推理的
secular 长期的
naturalistic 自然的,自然主义的,博物学的
mechanistic 机械论学说的,机械论的
combative 好战的,杀气的,好斗的
degenerate 退化
superstition 迷信

omen 预兆,征兆
derision 嘲笑
benevolent 慈善的
absurdity 荒谬,谬论
ludicrous 可笑的,滑稽的,愚蠢的
arrogance 傲慢态度,自大
superb 极好的
divine 神的,神圣的,非凡的,超人的,非常可爱的

# Unit 10  Zhu Xi 朱熹

## Key Sentences 流畅精句

1. He held that the universe has two aspects: the formless and the formed.
   在宇宙观上,朱熹持理气论。
2. The formless, or li is, a principle or a network of principles that is supreme natural law and that determines the patterns of all created things.
   无形的,或者"理"是指决定世间万物形状的最高自然法则。
3. Thus in reality the human nature embodies the conflicts between "Heaven's laws" and "human desires", and they can never coexist.
   所以,现实人性中存在着"天理"与"人欲"的对立,天理与人欲不能共存。
4. Zhu Xi's idea of putting ethical principles over physical desires bears some features of rationalism, but it also has a negative side of suppressing individuality.
   朱熹以伦理来主宰物欲的理欲观,明显具有一种理性主义的特征,也有压抑人的个性的一面。

## Wonderful Paragraph 精彩片段

*Paragraph 1*

### Zhu Xi 朱熹

Zhu Xi (Wade-Giles: Chu Hsi) (1130 — 1200) was a Song Dynasty

(960—1279) Confucian scholar who became one of most significant Neo-Confucianism in China. He taught at the famous White Deer Grotto Academy for some time. During the Song Dynasty, Zhu Xi's teachings were considered to be orthodoxy. Zhu Xi and his fellow scholars added two additional Chinese classic texts: the Great Learning, and the Doctrine of Mean to the Confucian canon. Their writings were not widely recognized in Zhu Xi's time; however, they later became accepted as standard commentaries on the Confucian classics.

Zhu Xi considered the earlier philosopher Xun Zi to be a heretic for departing from Confucius's beliefs about innate human goodness. Zhu Xi contributed to Confucian philosophy by articulating what was to become the orthodox Confucian interpretation of a number of beliefs in Taoism and Buddhism. He adapted some ideas from these competing religions into his form of Confucianism.

He argued that all things are brought into being by two universal elements discussed by Confucius and Mencius: vital (or physical) force (qi), and law or rational principle (li). Li is also called Tai Ji or Tai Chi, which means Great Ultimate. According to Zhu Xi, Tai Ji causes qi movement and change in the physical world, resulting in the division of the world into the two energy modes (yin and yang) and the five elements (fire, water, wood, metal, and earth).

According to Zhu Xi's theory, every physical object and every person contains aspects of li or Tai Ji. What is referred to as the human soul, mind, or spirit is defined as the Great Ultimate (Tai Ji), or the supreme regulative principle at work in a person. Zhu Xi argued that the fundamental nature of humans was morally good; even if people displayed immoral behaviour, the supreme regulative principle was good.

According to Zhu Xi, vital force (qi) and rational principle (li) operated together in mutual dependence. These are not entirely non-physical forces, but resulted in the creation of matter. When their activity is rapid the yang energy mode is generated, and when their activity is slow, the yin energy mode is generated. The yang and yin constantly interact, gaining and losing dominance over the other. This results in the structures of nature known as the five elements.

He did not hold to traditional ideas of God or Heaven (Tian), though he discussed how his own ideas mirrored the traditional concepts. He encouraged an agnostic tendency within Confucianism, because he believed that the Great Ultimate was a rational principle, and discussed it as an intelligent and ordering will behind the universe. He did not promote the worship of spirits and offerings to images. Although he practiced some forms of ancestor worship, he disagreed that the souls of ancestors existed, believing instead that ancestor worship is a form of rememberance and gratitude.

### Paragraph 2

## 治学之道及创办学院
## On Teaching, Learning and the Creation of an Academy

Zhu Xi very much focused his energies on teaching, claiming that learning is the only way to sagehood. He wanted to make the pursuit of sagehood attainable to all men. He lamented more modern printing techniques and the proliferation of books that ensued. This, he believed, made students less appreciative and focused on books, simply because there were more books to read than before. Therefore, he attempted to redefine how students should learn and read. In fact, disappointed by local schools in China, he established his own academy, White Deer Grotto Academy, to instruct students properly and in the proper fashion.

### Cultural Links
### 文化链接

## 朱熹讨诗

朱熹是南宋时期的大学问家。有一次他脚上生了疮，疼痛难忍，于是就请了一个很有名气的道士给他针灸。还真是"一针就灵"，疼痛大减。连续几针,便可行走。朱老夫子为表达谢意,便挥笔写下一首赞美诗赠与道士。送走道士,朱熹的脚又疼痛起来。他暗忖,自己名重一时,赠出去的诗背离事实,倘误传开来,贻害他人。于是顾不上足疾,一瘸一拐地撑上把赠诗讨回来方安心。

## Vocabulary 妙词连珠

| | |
|---|---|
| White Deer Grotto Academy 白鹿书院 | immoral 不道德的,邪恶的,放荡的 |
| orthodoxy 正统的 | dominance 优势,统治 |
| commentary 注释,解说词 | compatible 谐调的,一致的,兼容的 |
| heretic 异教徒,异端者 | pursuit 追击 |
| innate 先天的,天生的 | proliferation 增殖,繁殖 |
| articulating 清晰明白地说 | redefine 重新定义 |
| regulative 调整的,调节的 | individuality 个性主义 |

# Unit 11 孙武 Sun Wu

## Key Sentences 流畅精句

1. Sun Wu's The Art of War, composed of 13 articles, was the first systematic book on military strategies and tactics in ancient China and one of the earliest works on military strategies and tactics in the world.
   《孙子兵法》共13篇,是中国古代第一部系统的兵书,也是世界上最早的系统精辟地论述战略战术问题的军事学著作。
2. Tao refers to political strategies, which require the monarch and his people to make concerted efforts to support the war.
   "道"即政治,要求君民和衷共济,上下同心同德。
3. Tian and Di refer to the natural conditions in warfare.
   "天"与"地"是自然条件,在战争中起重要作用。
4. Jiang refers to the qualities of the military commander, in which "zhi (wit), xin (credibility), ren (benevolence), yong (courage), yan (strictness)" are a must.
   "将"指将帅的素质,孙子提出将帅必须具备"智信仁勇严"5种品质。
5. Fa refers to the relevant rules and regulations during warfare.
   "法"是制度规范。
6. Decrees must be issued and the systems of penalties and rewards must be applied to reinforce these rules and regulations and to heighten morale.
   要建立健全法令制度,运用赏罚的手段来加强法纪,激励士气。

思想先哲
Ancient Thinkers

## Wonderful Paragraph
## 精彩片段

### Paragraph 1

### S 孙武
### un Wu

Sun Wu (544—496 BC) was a Chinese author of The Art of War (兵法), an immensely influential ancient Chinese book on military strategy. He is also one of the earliest realists in international relations theory. The name Sun Tzu is an honorific title bestowed upon Sun Wu, the author's name. The character wu, meaning "military", is the same as the character in wu shu, or martial art. Sun Wu also has a courtesy name, Chang Qing (长卿).

### Paragraph 2

### A 历史形象
### s a Historical Figure

The only surviving source on the life of Sun Tzu is the biography written in the 2nd century BC by the historian Sima Qian, who describes him as a general who lived in the state of Wu in the 6th century BC, and therefore a contemporary of one of the great Chinese thinkers of ancient times—Confucius. According to tradition, Sun Tzu was a member of the landless Chinese aristocracy, the shi, descendants of nobility who had lost their dukedoms during the consolidation of the Spring and Autumn Period. Unlike most shi, who were traveling academics, Sun Tzu worked as a mercenary. According to tradition, King Helü of Wu hired Sun Tzu as a general approximately 512 BC after finishing his military treatise, The Art of War. After his hiring, the kingdom of Wu, previously considered a semi-barbaric state, went on to become the most powerful state of the period by conquering Chu, one of the most powerful states in the Spring and Autumn Period. Sun Tzu suddenly disappeared when King Helü finally conquered Chu. Therefore his date of death remained unknown.

The historicity of Sun Tzu is discussed extensively in the introduction to Lionel Giles' 1910 translation of The Art of War available as a Project Gutenberg online text. In Giles' introduction to his translation, he expands on the doubt and confusion which has surrounded the historicity of Sun Tzu.

In 1972 a set of bamboo engraved texts were discovered in a grave near Linyi in Shandong. These have helped to confirm parts of the text which were already known and have also added new sections. This version has been dated to between 134-118 BC, and so rules out older theories that parts of the text had been written much later.

Sun Bin, also known as Sun the Mutilated, allegedly a crippled descendent of Sun Tzu, also wrote a text known as the Art of War. A more accurate title might be the Art of Warfare since this was more directly concerned with the practical matters of warfare, rather than military strategy. At least one translator has used the title The Lost Art of War, referring to the long period of time during which Sun Bin's book was lost. There is, however, no commonality between the content or writing style in Sun Bin and Sun Tzu.

The Art of War has been one of the most popular combat collections in history. Ancient Chinese have long viewed this book as one of the entrance test materials, and it is one of the most important collections of books in the Chinese literature. It is said that Mao Zedong and Joseph Stalin both read this book while in war.

*Paragraph 3*

## 孙武著作
## Books Written by Sun Wu

The Art of War is a Chinese military treatise written during the 6th century BC by Sun Wu. Composed of 13 chapters, each of which is devoted to one aspect of warfare, it has long been praised as the definitive work on military strategies and tactics of its time.

The Art of War is one of the oldest and most famous studies of strategy and has had a huge influence on Eastern military planning, business tactics, and beyond. First translated into a European language in 1782 by French Jesuit Jean Joseph Marie Amiot, it had been credited with influencing Napoleon, the German General Staff, and even the planning of Operation Desert Storm. Leaders as diverse as Mao Zedong, Vo Nguyen Giap, and General Douglas MacArthur have claimed to have drawn inspiration from the work.

The Art of War has also been applied, with much success, to business and managerial strategies.

## Cultural Links 文化链接

### 孙武演阵

有一天,孙武去见吴王阖闾,吴王问他能不能训练女兵,孙武说:"可以。"于是吴王便拨了一百多位宫女给他。

孙武把宫女编成两队,用吴王最宠爱的两个妃子为队长,然后把一些军事的基本动作教给她们,并告诫她们要遵守军令,不可违背。不料孙武开始发令时,宫女们觉得好玩,都一个个笑了起来。孙武以为自己说话没说清楚,便重复一遍,等第二次再发令,宫女们还是只顾嘻笑。这次孙武生气了,便下令把队长拖去斩首,理由是队长领导无方。吴王听说要斩他的爱妃,急忙向他求情,但是孙武说:"君王既然已经把她们交给我来训练,我就必须依照军队的规定来管理她们,任何人违犯了军令都该接受处分,这是没有例外的。"结果还是把队长给杀了。

宫女们见他说到做到,都吓得脸色发白。第三次发令,没有一个人敢再开玩笑了。

# Introduce China in English—Eminent Persons

## Vocabulary 妙词连珠

immensely 无限地，广大地，庞大地
bestow 给予，安放
aristocracy 贵族，贵族政府
dukedom 公爵领地，公爵爵位
mercenary 唯利是图的
procedure 程序，手续
combat 战斗，格斗，战斗，搏斗
allegedly 依其申述
accurate 正确的，精确的
commonality 公共，平民
diverse 不同的，变化多的
managerial 管理的

# 2 著名政治家
## *Famous Statesmen*

## Unit 1 秦始皇 Emperor Qin Shihuang

### Key Sentences
流畅精句

1. He had been the King of the pre-Qin State for 5 years and the First Emperor of the Qin Dynasty for 12 years. When he died he was at his 49.
   他在秦王位历时5年,帝位12年,终年49岁。
2. After Ying Zheng had unified China, he ordered that the highest ruler of the country should be called "Emperor" and he himself should make all the important decisions of the country.
   嬴政统一天下后,规定最高统治者称皇帝,国家一切重大事务由皇帝决定。
3. The Great Wall was the crystallization of wisdom and hard labor of the working people of China.
   万里长城是中国古代劳动人民血汗和智慧的结晶。
4. The disaster known as "burning books and burying intellectuals in pits" devastated the Chinese culture for generations.
   "焚书"和"坑儒"事件的发生,严重地摧残了文化。
5. After his death First Emperor Ying Zheng was buried in Lishan Hill, now in Lintong County, Shaanxi Province.
   嬴政死后葬于骊山,在今陕西省临潼县境内。

## Wonderful Paragraph

### Paragraph 1

# Qin Shi Huang 秦始皇

Qin Shi Huang ( November or December 260 B. C.—September, 210 B. C. ), personal name Zheng, was king of the State of Qin from 247 B. C. to 221 BC, and then the first emperor of a unified China from 221 B. C. to 210 B. C., ruling under the name First Emperor.

Having unified China, he and his prime minister Li Si passed a series of major reforms aimed at cementing the unification, and they undertook some Herculean construction projects, most notably the precursor version of the current Great Wall of China. For all the tyranny of his autocratic rule, Qin Shi Huang is still regarded today as some sort of a colossal founding father in Chinese history whose unification of China has endured for more than two millennia (with interruptions).

### Paragraph 2

# Naming Conventions 名字的由来

Qin Shi Huang was born in the Chinese month zheng yue(正月), the first month of the year in the Chinese calendar (in the 3rd century BC the Chinese year started before the Winter solstice, and not after as it does today), and so he received the name Zheng (政), both characters being used interchangeably in ancient China. In ancient China, people never joined family name and given name together as is customary today, so it is anachronistic to refer to Qin Shi Huang as "Ying Zheng". The given name was never used except by close relatives, therefore it is also incorrect to refer to the young Qin Shi Huang as "Prince Zheng", or as "King Zheng of Qin". As a king, he was referred to as "King of Qin" only. Had he received a posthumous name after his death like his father, he would have been known by historians as "King NN. (posthumous name) of Qin", but this never happened.

After conquering the last independent Chinese state in 221 BC, Qin Shi Huang was now the king of a state of Qin ruling over the whole of China, which was unprecedented. Wishing to show that he was no more a simple king like the kings of old during the Warring States Period, he created a new title, huangdi (皇帝), combining the word huang (皇) which was used to call the legendary Three Huang who ruled at the dawn of Chinese history, and the word di (帝) which was used to call the legendary Five Di who ruled immediately after the Three Huang. These Three Huang and Five Di were considered perfect rulers, of immense powers, and very long lives. The word huang also meant "big", "great". The word di also referred to the Supreme God in Heaven, creator of the world. Thus, by joining these two words, which no one had ever done before, Qin Shi Huang created a title on par with his feat of uniting the seemingly endless Chinese realm, in fact uniting the world (people at that time believed their empire encompassed the whole world, a concept referred to as all under heaven).

This word huangdi was rendered in most Western languages as "emperor", a word with also a long history going back to Roman Empire, and which Europeans deemed superior to the word "king". Qin Shi Huang adopted the name First Emperor (Shi Huangdi, literally "commencing emperor"). He abolished posthumous names, by which former kings were known after their death, judging them inappropriate and contrary to filial piety, and decided that future generations would refer to him as the First Emperor (Shi Huangdi), his successor would be referred to as the Second Emperor (Er Shi Huangdi, literally "second generation emperor"), the successor of his successor as the Third Emperor (San Shi Huangdi, literally "third generation emperor"), and so on, for ten thousand generations, as the imperial house was supposed to rule China for ten thousand generations ("Ten thousand years" is equivalent to "forever" in Chinese, and it also means "good fortune").

# 用英语说中国——古今名人
## Introduce China in English—Eminent Persons

### Cultural Links 文化链接

#### "世界第八大奇迹"

1973年3月29日，这是一个值得永远纪念的日子。当时，上级号召打井抗旱，西扬村决定把井打在村南160米的柿树林畔，这里地处骊山冲击扇前缘，历经山洪泥石淤积。3月24日动工，挖到3米多深时，发现下面是红烧土、烧结硬块和炭屑灰烬，大家以为碰上了老砖瓦窑。继续往下打，在5米多深处的井壁西侧，阴暗的光线下终于露出了"兵马俑"宁静的面容，村民们正诧异间，恰好公社干部房树民来检查打井进度，他下到井底仔细观察，发现出土的砖块与秦始皇陵附近发现的秦砖一模一样，他急忙告诉大家停止打井，匆匆赶往县城文化馆报告，就这样，兵马俑被发现了。

秦兵马俑博物馆位于西安临潼县秦始皇陵东1.5公里处，是秦始皇陵的从葬坑，被誉为"世界第八大奇迹"，1987年由联合国教科文组织列入"世界人类文化遗产"目录。

### Vocabulary 妙词连珠

cementing 胶接，溶接，粘合
unification 统一，合一，一致
Herculean 力大无比的，巨大的
notably 显著地，特别地
precursor 先驱
tyranny 暴政，苛政，专治
autocratic 独裁的，专制的
winter solstice 冬至
interchangeably 可替交地
anachronistic 时代错误的
posthumous 死后的，身后的，作者死后出版的，遗腹的
unprecedented 空前的
immense 极广大的，无边的，<口>非常好的
par 同等，(股票等)票面价值;票面的，平价的，平均的，标准的
seemingly 表面上地
realm 领域
encompassed 关入笼或栏内
inappropriate 不适当的，不相称的
filial 子女的，孝顺的，当作子女的
piety 虔诚，孝行

# Unit 2  Emperor Liu Bang
刘邦

## Key Sentences
流畅精句

1. Liu Bang became the King of Han, which marks the beginning of the Western Han Dynasty.
   刘邦做了汉王,西汉纪元由此开始。
2. The next step he took was to fight Xiang Yu, a former ally now a rival to rule the country.
   这以后,刘邦和他原来的同盟者项羽为争夺天下展开了激烈的斗争。
3. Liu Bang was a native of Pei county. Born into a humble family, he somehow managed to become a petty official in his youth.
   刘邦是沛县人,出身微贱,原来是当地的一名小吏。
4. Later some of his friends killed the official of Pei county and invited Liu Bang to be their leader.
   后来他的朋友杀了沛县的官吏起来造反,就把他接回去当了首领。
5. Before he defeated Xiang Yu, Liu Bang had proclaimed himself emperor in the 2nd month of 202 BC, which marked the formal beginning of the Western Han Dynasty.
   打败项羽之前,刘邦在公元前202年2月登上了皇位,西汉皇朝从此建立。
6. Liu Bang attributed his success to his ability to make use of able men.
   刘邦认为自己成功的主要原因是善于用人。

# Introduce China in English—Eminent Persons

## Wonderful Paragraph

### Paragraph 1

# L 刘邦
### iu Bang

Emperor Gao (256 BC or 247 BC-June 1, 195 BC), commonly known inside China as Gaozu (高祖), personal name Liu Bang, was the first emperor of the Chinese Han Dynasty, ruling over China from 202 BC until 195 BC, and one of only a few dynasty founders who emerged from the peasant class (the other major example being Zhu Yuanzhang, founder of the Ming Dynasty). Before becoming an emperor, he was also called Duke of Pei (沛公) after his birthplace. He was also created as the Prince of Hàn by Xiang Yu, the Grand Prince of Western Chu following the collapse of Qín Dynasty, and was called so before becoming emperor.

### Paragraph 2

# E 早年生涯
### arly Life

Liu Bang was born into a peasant family in Pei (present Pei County in Jiangsu Province). When he was young, he did not like farm work, and was evidently living a rogue's life. Not surprisingly, he was not the favorite son of his peasant father.

After he grew up, Liu Bang served as a patrol officer in his county. Once he was responsible for transporting a group of prisoners to Mount Li in present Shaanxi province. During the trip many prisoners fled. Fearful that he would be punished for the prisoners' flight, Liu Bang released the remaining prisoners and fled himself, becoming the leader of a band of brigands. On one of his raids, he met a county magistrate who became impressed with his leadership skills and gave his daughter Lü Zhi to him in marriage.

著名政治家
Famous Statesmen

**Paragraph 3**

## C 楚汉之争
## hu-Han Contention

Now considering the whole former Qín Empire under his domination, Xiang Yu realigned the territories of not only the remaining parts of Qín but also the rebel states, dividing the territories into 19 principalities. Xiang Yu did not honor the promise by Xin, Prince Huai of Chu, who would soon himself be assassinated by Xiang's orders. Instead, he gave Guanzhong to the princes of three Qins. Liu Bang was only awarded the Principality of Han (modern Sichuan, Chongqing, and southern Shaanxi).

In Hanzhong, Liu Bang focused his efforts on developing agriculture methods and training an army, through which he reinforced his resource accumulation and military power. Before long, Liu broke out of his principality, deposed the kings of three Qins and occupied Guanzhong, where he launched a war now known as the Chu-Han War, against Xiang Yu.

Although Xiang Yu was far superior in military ability to Liu Bang, he was at a political disadvantage. Xiang Yu kept defeating Liu in the battlefield, but each of his victories drove more people to support Liu. When Xiang Yu finally was defeated, he could not recover and committed suicide.

The war lasted five years (206—202 BC) and ended with Liu Bang's victory. Having defeated Xiang Yu, Liu proclaimed himself emperor and established the Han Dynasty in 202 BC and made Chang'an (present city of Xi'an) his capital city. Liu became historically known as Emperor Gao of Han.

### Cultural Links
文化链接

## 鸿门宴

秦末,刘邦与项羽各自攻打秦王朝的部队,刘邦先破咸阳(秦始皇的都城),但刘邦兵力不及项羽,项羽大怒,派当阳君击关,项羽入咸阳后,到达戏西,而刘邦则在霸上驻军,一场恶战在即。刘邦说服了项羽的部下项伯,项伯答应为之在项羽面前说情,并让刘邦次日前来向项羽谢罪。

鸿门宴上,虽不乏美酒佳肴,但却暗藏杀机,项羽的亚父范增,一直主张杀掉刘邦,在酒宴上,一再示意项羽发令,但项羽却犹豫不决。范增召项庄舞剑为酒宴助兴,趁机杀掉刘邦,项伯为保护刘邦,也拔剑起舞,掩护了刘邦,在危急关头,刘邦部下樊哙带剑拥盾闯入军门,怒目直视项羽,项羽见此人气度不凡,只好问来者为何人,当得知为刘邦的参乘时,即命赐酒,樊哙立而饮之,项羽命赐猪腿后,又问能再饮酒吗,樊哙说,臣死且不避,一杯酒还有什么值得推辞的。樊哙还乘机说了一通刘邦的好话,项羽无言以对,刘邦乘机一走了之。后人将鸿门宴喻指暗藏杀机。

## Vocabulary 妙词连珠

| | |
|---|---|
| Duke of Pei 沛公 | domination 控制,统治,支配 |
| the Grand Prince of Western Chu 西楚霸王 | realign 重新排列,再结盟 |
| rogue 流氓,无赖 | principality 公国,侯国 |
| patrol 巡逻 | depose 免职,废(王位),作证,宣誓作证 |
| brigand 土匪,强盗,歹徒(常指流窜帮中的一员) | assassinate 暗杀,行刺 |
| raid 袭击,搜捕 | accumulation 积聚,堆积物 |
| magistrate 文职官员,地方官员 | proclaim 宣布,声明,显示,显露 |

# Unit 3　Emperor Wu of Han
汉武帝

## Key Sentences
流畅精句

1. Politically, he continued the policy of consolidating the authority of the central government by reducing the power of local vassals.
   在政治上,汉武帝继续父辈强干弱枝的治国方略,削弱了地方诸侯的力量,使权力集中到中央政府。
2. By establishing a system of monopoly over salt, iron and minting, the imperial court kept a firm hold on the country's economy.
   在经济上,他建立了盐铁专营、货币官铸等制度,朝廷因此得以掌控国家的经济命脉。
3. Following the proposal of Dong Zhongshu, he advocated Confucianism as the national orthodox ideology.
   在思想上,他采纳学者董仲舒的意见,以儒学为国家惟一的正统学术。
4. He initiated extensive cultural exchanges with the west by opening up lines of transport between China and countries to the west.
   他派人开辟了中国和西域各国的交通线,由此开始了大规模的中西文明的经济交流。
5. He also developed close ties with minority nationalities in the southwest, southeast and northeast.
   他在位时还使西汉与西南、东南以及东北少数民族的关系更加密切。
6. In 89 BC, he issued a decree reflecting critically on his over-expansion of the country.
   公元前89年,他下诏对自己扩张政策的过错进行反思。

# 用英语说中国——古今名人
## Introduce China in English—Eminent Persons

## Wonderful Paragraph
### 精彩片段

**Paragraph 1**

# E 汉武帝
## mperor Wu of Han

Emperor Wu of Han (156 BC—87 BC), personal name Liu Che, was the sixth emperor of China emperor of the Chinese Han Dynasty, ruling from 141 BC to 87 BC. A military campaigner, Han China reached its greatest expansion under his reign, spanning from Kyrgyzstan in the west, Northern Korea in the Northeast, to Northern Vietnam in the south. He was best known for his role in expelling the nomadic Xiongnu from the boundary of China. The Han people named themselves after him.

Emperor Wu dispatched his envoy Zhang Qian in 139 BC to seek an alliance with the Yuezhi of modern Uzbekistan. Zhang returned in 123 BC and Emperor Wu then sent many missions per year to Central Asia.

During the end of his reign, his power was severely weakened. Open war broke out between rival families of the Empress Wei and the Li clan. The Li family killed most of Empress Wei's family and forced Empress Wei to commit suicide; during this time, Wu was forced to flee. In the end, Wu was too weak to even name his own successor, who was chosen two days before Wu's death.

**Paragraph 2**

# E 武帝与匈奴
## mperor Wu and Xiongnu

During the "Taoism era", China was able to maintain peace with Xiongnu by paying tribute and marrying princesses to them. During this time, the dynasty's goal was to relieve the society of harsh laws, wars, and conditions from both the Qin Dynasty, external threats from nomads, and early internal conflicts within the Han court. The government reduced taxation and assumed a subservient status to neighboring nomadic tribes. This policy of the government's reduced role over civilian lives (休养生息) started a period of stability, which was called the Rule of Wen and Jing (文景之治), named after the two Emperors of this particular era. However, under Emperor Wu's leadership, the most prosperous period (140—87 BC) of the Han Dynasty, the Empire was able to fight back. At its height, China incorporated the present day Qinghai, Gansu, and northern Vietnam into its territories.

## Cultural Links 文化链接

### 秦皇汉武

汉武帝即位后,开拓西部疆域,建立丰功伟业,使西汉进入鼎盛时期。西汉帝国的强大,使中原人不再被称为"秦人",而通称"汉人"、"汉族"了。历史上把"秦皇汉武"并称,正是因为秦始皇和汉武帝先后完成了统一中国、稳固发展的伟大事业。

## Vocabulary 妙词连珠

| | |
|---|---|
| expansion 扩充,开展,膨胀,扩张物,辽阔,浩瀚 | envoy 外交使节,特使 |
| | alliance 联盟,联合 |
| spanning [数](尤指树形子图)生成的 | Uzbekistan 乌兹别克斯坦 |
| | clan 部落,氏族,宗族,党派 |
| Kyrgyzstan 吉尔吉斯斯坦 | flee 逃避,逃跑,逃走 |
| Vietnam 越南 | successor 继承者,接任者,后续的事物 |
| expel 驱逐,开除,排出,发射 | |
| nomadic 游牧的 | harsh 粗糙的,荒芜的,苛刻的,刺耳的,刺目的 |
| boundary 边界,分界线 | |
| dispatched 分派,派遣派遣,急件 | territory 领土,版图,地域 |

nomad 游牧部落的人，流浪者，游    incorporated 组成公司的，
  牧民游牧的                              合成一体的
subservient 屈从的，有帮助的，有
  用的，奉承的

# Unit 4　Cao Cao
### 曹操

## Key Sentences
### 流畅精句

1. Cao Cao was regarded to become "a capable minister in times of peace or an unscrupulous schemer in times of turmoil."
   曹操曾被人称为"治世之能臣、乱世之奸雄"。
2. Cao Cao indeed became a capable official in the Eastern Han government, being strict and impartial in implementing the law.
   曹操曾经是东汉政府里一个能干的官员,他执法严明,颇有政绩。
3. Over the next seven years he wiped out Yuan Shao's remaining forces and united northern China.
   此后他又花了七年时间消灭了袁绍的残余势力,统一了中国的北方。
4. In actual history, however, he was a phenomenal strategist and statesman despite certain negative aspects of his personality.
   不过就史实而言,曹操虽然有残忍阴险的一面,但也不失为一位杰出的军事家和政治家。
5. It is also worthwhile to note that Cao Cao and his two sons, Cao Pi and Cao Zhi, were all accomplished writers, known as the "Three Caos" in Chinese literary history.
   此外值得一提的是,曹操和他的儿子曹丕、曹植都是在中国文学史上有着重要地位的作家,史称"三曹"。

## Wonderful Paragraph

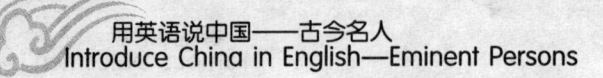

精彩片段

### Paragraph 1

# Cao Cao 曹操

Cao Cao (155-220), zi Mende, was a regional warlord who rose to become the self-appointed Imperial Secretarist under Han Xian Di and the de facto ruler of Northern China during the last years of Eastern Han Dynasty. He laid down foundations for what was to become the Kingdom of Wei under his son Cao Pi. Although generally remembered as a cruel and suspicious character, Cao Cao was also a brilliant ruler, strategist and poet.

Historical interpretation Cao Cao was the son of a court official of the Han Dynasty. He held positions at this court until an attempted coup by general Dong Zhuo brought down the dynasty. Dong Zhuo was not able to consolidate his hold on the empire and China fell into civil war and anarchy. Cao Cao was part of the Alliance against the Dong Zhuo-controlled Han Dynasty. He quickly gained fame by winning several battles against the Han which earned him the name the "Hero of Chaos" (枭雄).

In the resulting chaos Cao Cao emerged as the Cao Cao Unification of the North, winning a critical battle (the Battle of Guandu) at the Huang He (Yellow River). He assumed effective rule of Northern China and assumed the title of Imperial Secretarist. The last Han emperor would remain a figurehead until the abdication in 220. Cao Cao extended his control northward, past the Great Wall of China, into northern Korea, and southward to the Han River. His attempt to extend his domination south of the Yangtze River was dashed as his forces were defeated by the coalition of Liu Bei (who later founded the Kingdom of Shu in southwestern China) and Sun Quan (who later founded the Kingdom of Wu in southeastern China) at the naval Battle of Red Cliff in 208.

In 213, he was titled Wei Gong (Duke of Wei) and given ten cities as his domain. This area was named the "State of Wei". In 216, Cao Cao was promoted to King of Wei (魏王).

Cao Cao died some time after the defeat and death of the general Guan Yu of Shu. Cao Cao's death was possibly the result of a brain tumor, as he had complained often of painful headaches. A number of his most loyal followers, including his cousin and general Xiahou Dun as well as his bodyguard Xu Chu, died soon after as well, as if following their master into the afterlife. He was posthumously given the title of Wei Wudi (魏武帝, Martial Emperor of Wei). His eldest surviving son Cao Pi inherited his position as Imperial Secretarist and the title Wei Wang (King of Wei). Within one year Cao Pi seized the imperial throne and proclaimed himself to be the first Emperor of the Wei Dynasty - usually referred as the Kingdom of Wei.

*Paragraph 2*

## 曹操的艺术成就
## Cao Cao in Art

While the historical record indicates Cao Cao was a brilliant ruler and poet, in classical Chinese literature he is traditionally represented as a cunning and deceitful general. Cao Cao is also a character in the Chinese classic Romance of the Three Kingdoms, where he is cast as the cunning and capable villain, as he is in Chinese opera, where his character's white makeup is meant to reflect his wicked heart. This is likely due to a subsequent Confucianist interpretation of events which would have attributed his failure to unify China to flaws in his character.

*Paragraph 3*

## 座右铭
## Quotation

"I would rather betray the world, than let the world betray me"
——Cao Cao, Romance of the Three Kingdoms

用英语说中国——古今名人
Introduce China in English—Eminent Persons

## Cultural Links
文化链接

### "说曹操,曹操到"

史载汉献帝在李傕与郭汜火拼时曾一度脱离险境,然而李郭二人合兵后继续追拿汉献帝,有人献计推荐曹操,说他平剿青州黄巾军有功、可以救驾,然而信使未出时联军已经杀到,眼看走投无路之际夏侯敦奉曹操之命率军"保驾"成功,后将李郭联军击溃,曹操被加封官爵。故有"说曹操,曹操到"之说。

## Vocabulary
妙词连珠

warlord 军阀,军阀式首脑
self-appointed 自己作主的
de facto 事实上的,实际的
strategist 战略家
consolidate 巩固
anarchy 无政府状态,政治混乱
Hero of Chaos 枭雄
the Battle of Guandu 官渡之战
figurehead 装饰船头的雕像,破浪神,有名无实的领袖

abdication 退位,让位
posthumous 死后的,身后的,作者死后出版的,遗腹的
depict 描述,描写
treacherous 背叛的,背信弃义的,奸诈的,叛逆的
cunning 狡猾的,巧妙的
deceitful 欺诈的
villain 坏人,恶棍
flaw 缺点,裂纹,瑕疵,一阵狂风

# Unit 5  Emperor Li Shimin
## 李世民

## Key Sentences
### 流畅精句

1. In his childhood, Li Shimin was gifted and intelligent. He was a man of deep thought, farsighted, and decisive. He could also condescend to the lower ranking people.
  李世民幼聪睿,玄鉴深远,临机果断,能屈节下士。
2. Li Shimin was one of the outstanding statesmen among all the emperors and kings in the Chinese history, esteemed as a model of reasonable and enlightened ruler.
  李世民是历代帝王中杰出的政治家之一,被以后的封建统治者奉作有道明君的典范。
3. Therefore he promoted the examination system of selecting officials, and composed Records of Surnames and Families.
  他又健全扩大科举制度,撰修《氏族志》。
4. The marriage of Princess Wencheng to Songtsam Gambo, the Chief of the Tubo nationality, now Tibetan nationality, became the historical symbol of the intimate unity between Han and the minority nationalities, which gave impetus to the cultural and economic progress of the Tibetan and other minority nationalities.
  以文成公主嫁吐蕃王松赞干布,成为汉藏两族人民亲密团结的历史象征,推动了藏族地区经济文化的进步。

5. In the years of Zhenguan reign, the country experienced a period called "Zhenguan's Prosperity", which means a period with a relatively clear politics, stable and untied society, booming economy and strong power. China then was considered as the most powerful and prosperous country in the world of that time.
贞观时期,政治比较清明,社会相对统一安定,经济繁荣,国力强盛,史称"贞观之治",使中国成为当时世界上最富强昌盛的封建国家。

## Wonderful Paragraph
精彩片段

### Paragraph 1

# 唐太宗
# Emperor Taizong of Tang

Emperor Taizong of Tang (599—649), born Li Shimin, was the second emperor of the Tang Dynasty of China from 626 to 649. He encouraged his father, Emperor Gaozu of Tang China ! Li Yuan, to start the uprising that established the Tang dynasty, and many now consider Taizong to have been the co-founder of the dynasty. In 630, Taizong's General Li Jing conquered the once mighty Eastern Turkic Khanate and allowed Tang to become the major political and military power of the region. Accordingly, leaders of bordering tribes convened at Chang'an (Xi'an) the same year and asked for Taizong to take on the title of Heavenly Khan (天可汗). Under his reign, the famous rule of Zhenguan (贞观之治) took place (his era name was Zhenguan). At the time, it was said that there was no need for the people to lock doors at night and that items left on the road remain untouched by others. The prosperity of the era and the leadership of Taizong and his renowned officials epitomizes the peak of traditional rulership that future generations would strive to emulate. His posthumous name was Wenwu-dasheng-daguang Xiao Huangdi (文武大圣大广孝皇帝 "Filial Emperor who is Civil and Martial, Greatly Holy, and Greatly Expansive").

著名政治家
Famous Statesmen

Paragraph 2

# Early Achievements
# 早期成就

Taizong was born in Wugong (武功, in present-day Shaanxi) as the second son of Li Yuan, and was of one-quarter Xianbei (a people related to modern-day Turks) blood. The most capable and militarily inclined of Li Yuan's many sons, Taizong showed his promise at an early age, helping to rescue Emperor Yang from a Turkic ambush and besiegment at the age of 16. In 616, the 18-year-old Taizong followed his general-father to his garrison-post at Jinyang, Shanxi, where he instigated his father to stage a military coup against the autocratic and fast crumbling Sui regime. Leading the troops with his elder brother Li Jiancheng, the rebel army took the capital Chang'an in September 617, thereafter putting a puppet emperor on the throne before Li Yuan himself proclaimed the establishment of a new dynasty, the Tang, in 618.

After the establishment of Tang, Taizong was appointed the Prince of Qin (秦王) by his father. In the succeeding campaigns to augment the power of the new dynasty, Taizong made numerous contributions, intensifying the heated sibling rivalry between him and his two brothers-Li Jiacheng, the heir apparent, and Li Yuanji, a younger brother.

Taizong is credited with creating the custom of Door gods, colorful block prints and carvings placed by the doors of temples, homes, businesses, etc. to ward off evil spirits.

## Cultural Links
文化链接

### 唐朝书家——李世民

我国书法史上,以行书刻碑的首创人物是唐太宗李世民。《温泉铭》便是行书入碑的代表作。李世民是我国历史上一位杰出的帝王,他不仅将封

# Introduce China in English—Eminent Persons

建社会推向鼎盛时期,而且身体力行地倡导书法,促使唐代书法成为我国书法史上辉煌的一页。他亲自为王羲之写传记,不惜重金搜购大王墨迹三千六百纸。

李世民常与虞世南论书,并云:"吾临古人之书,殊不学其形势,唯求其骨力,而形势自生。"这反映了唐太宗的书法观,亦是相当开放的。唐太宗书法师承魏晋,《书小史》称其"工隶书、飞白,得二王法,尤善临古帖,殆于逼真。"《晋祠铭》为其书法杰作,当时各国使节都将精拓本带回去,广泛宣传。

## Vocabulary 妙词连珠

Uprising 起义,升起
co-founder 共同创办人,共同创始人
prosperity 繁荣
epitomize 摘要,概括,成为……的缩影
emulate 仿效
inclined 倾向……的
ambush 埋伏,伏兵
besiegment 被困,围攻者
instigate 鼓动
autocratic 独裁的,专制的
crumble 弄碎,粉碎,崩溃
puppet 傀儡,木偶
intensify 加强,强化
sibling 兄弟,姐妹,同胞,同属
rivalry 竞争,竞赛,敌对,敌对状态
heir 继承人,后嗣
Door gods 门神

# Unit 6　Empress Wu Zetian
武则天

## Key Sentences
流畅精句

1. Driven by ambition, she defeated her concubine-rivals using unscrupulous means.
   野心勃勃的武则天通过一系列不甚光明的手段击败了后宫中的对手。
2. Emperor Gaozong made her his empress in AD 655 in spite of the opposition of the courtiers.
   唐高宗在公元655年不顾大臣的反对而改立她为皇后。
3. Wu Zetian took control of state power upon Gaozong's death in AD 683.
   公元683年唐高宗病死,武则天控制了政权。
4. She claimed the throne in her own right in AD 690 and renamed the dynasty Zhou.
   武则天在公元690年正式称帝,改国号为周。
5. She thus became the first and only woman emperor in Chinese history.
   由此,她成为中国历史上惟一的女皇帝。
6. She died at the age of 82 that same year, leaving behind a legendary image of questionable moral character and a scandalous personal life.
   同年,82岁的武则天病逝。这位传奇女性的个人品德及私生活颇有惹人争议之处。

用英语说中国——古今名人
Introduce China in English—Eminent Persons

## Wonderful Paragraph
精彩片段

### Paragraph 1

# W 武则天
# u Zetian

Wu Zetian (624—705), personal name Wu Zhao, was the only woman in the history of China to assume the title of Emperor. Ruling China first through puppet emperors from 665 to 690, not unprecedented in Chinese history, she then broke all precedents when she founded her own dynasty in 690, the Zhou, and ruled personally under the name Emperor Shengshen (圣神皇帝) from 690 to 705. Her rise and reign has been criticized harshly by Confucian historians but has been viewed under a different light after the 1950s.

### Paragraph 2

# R 掌权之路
# oad to Power

She entered Emperor Taizong's harem most probably in 638 (other possible date: 636), and was made a cairen(才人), i. e. one of the nine concubines of the fifth rank. Emperor Taizong gave her the name Mei, meaning "charming, beautiful". Thus, today Chinese people refer to her as Wu Meiniang (武媚娘) when they write about her youth, whereas they refer to her as Wu Zetian or as Empress Wu when they write about her time in power.

In 649, Taizong died, and, as was customary for concubines, Wu Meiniang had to leave the imperial palace and enter a Buddhist nunnery where she had her hair shaved. Not long afterwards, most probably in 651, she was reintegrated into the imperial palace by Emperor Gaozong, son of Taizong, who had been struck by her beauty while visiting and worshipping in the nunnery. By the early 650s Wu Zetian was a concubine of

Emperor Gaozong, and she was titled zhaoyi（昭仪）, i. e. the highest ranking of the nine concubines of the second rank. Wu Zetian soon had the concubine née Xiao out of the way. The fact that the emperor had taken one of the concubines of his father as his own concubine, and what's more a nun, if traditional history is to be believed, was found to be utterly shocking by Confucian moralists.

In the year 654, Wu Zetian's baby daughter was killed. Empress Wang was suspected of killing the girl out of jealousy and was persecuted. Soon after that, she succeeded in having the emperor create for her the extraordinary title of chenfei（宸妃）, which ranked her above the four concubines of the first rank and immediately below the empress consort. Then eventually, in November 655, the empress née Wang was demoted and Wu Zetian was made empress consort.

## Paragraph 3

# R统治期间
ule

After Emperor Gaozong started to suffer from strokes from November 660 on, she began to govern China from behind the scenes. She was even more in absolute control of power after she had Shangguan Yi（上官仪）executed and the demoted crown prince Li Zhong forced to commit suicide in January 665, and henceforth she sat behind to the now silent emperor during court audiences and took decisions. She reigned in his name and then, after his death, in the name of subsequent puppet emperors, only assuming power herself in October 690, when she proclaimed the Zhou Dynasty, named after her father's nominal posthumous fief as well as in reference to the illustrious Zhou Dynasty of ancient Chinese history from which she claimed the Wu family was descended. In December 689, ten months before she officially ascended the throne, she had the government create the character Zhao, an entirely new invention, created along with 11 other characters in order to show her absolute power, and she chose this new character as her given name, which became her taboo name when she ascended the throne ten months later. On ascending the throne, she proclaimed herself Emperor Shengshen, the first woman ever to use the title emperor which had been created 900 years before by the first emperor of China Qin Shi Huang. Indeed she was the only woman in the 2100 years of imperial China ever to use the title emperor and to sit on the throne (instead of merely ruling from behind the throne), and this again utterly shocked Confucian elites.

Traditional Chinese political theory did not allow a woman to ascend the throne, and Empress Wu was determined to quash the opposition and promote loyal officials within the bureaucracy. Her regime was characterized by Machiavellian cleverness and brutal despotism. During her reign, she formed her own Secret Police to deal with any opposition that might arise. She was also supported by her two lovers, the Zhang brothers. She gained popular support by advocating Buddhism but ruthlessly persecuted her opponents within the royal family and the nobility. In October 695, after several additions of characters, her imperial name was definitely set as Emperor Tian Jinlun Shengshen (天金轮圣神皇帝), a name which did not undergo further changes until the end of her reign. On February 20, 705. Her power ended that day, and she had to step down while Emperor Zhongzong was restored, allowing the Tang Dynasty to resume on March 3, 705. Empress Wu died nine months later, perhaps consoled by the fact that her nephew Wu Sansi, son of her half-brother and as ambitious and intriguing as she, had managed to become the real master behind the scenes, controlling the restored emperor through his empress consort with whom he was having an affair.

*Paragraph 4*

# E 评价
## valuation

Although short-lived, the Zhou dynasty, according to some historians, resulted in better equality between the sexes during the succeeding Tang Dynasty. Considering the events of her life, literary allusions to Empress Wu can carry several connotations: a woman who has inappropriately overstepped her bounds, the hypocrisy of preaching compassion while simultaneously engaging in a pattern of corrupt and vicious behavior, and ruling by pulling strings in the background.

## Cultural Links 文化链接

### 广元女儿节

在旧中国的历史上,妇女地位低下,唯独唐代在武则天当皇帝的那些年,妇女的地位才有所改变,特别是武则天的故乡——广元,妇女们终于有了扬眉吐气的日子,甚至还有了一个自己的节日,那就是每年正月二十三日的"女儿节"。

武则天正月二十三在利州出生。后来她做了皇帝,治理国家有方,使得生产发展、社会安定、人民乐业,赢得了黎民百姓的敬仰。广元人民更为这块土地上孕育了这位中国历史上惟一的女皇帝而自豪,为了纪念武则天,每逢正月二十三这天,广元的妇女、姑娘们身着节日新装到皇泽寺、黑龙潭、上西坝一带的嘉陵江畔游玩。当地人称作:"正月二十三,妇女游河湾。"这一天,家里的事就由男人们来承担。这是妇女们最开心的一天,在那开心的日子里,谁也不记得男尊女卑了。正如鲁迅先生所说:"武则天当皇帝,谁敢说男尊女卑!"朝代更替,时间流逝,而正月二十三妇女游河湾的习俗却一代一代一延续下来。

## Vocabulary 妙词连珠

| | |
|---|---|
| puppet 傀儡,木偶 | utterly 完全地,绝对地,彻底地 |
| precedent 先例 | persecut 迫害 |
| concubine 妾,情妇,姘妇 | consort(尤指)君王或女王的配偶 |
| reintegrate 再重新完整,复兴 | demote 使降级,使降职 |
| nunnery 女修道院,尼姑庵 | henceforth 自此以后,今后 |

nominal 名义上的,有名无实的   brutal 残忍的,兽性的
fief 封地,采邑              despotism 专制
ascend 攀登,上升            intrigue 阴谋,诡计;密谋,私通
quash 取消

著名政治家
Famous Statesmen

# Unit 7 赵匡胤 Emperor Zhao Kuangyin

## Key Sentences
流畅精句

1. In early AD 960, word spread of a Kintan invasion. The Later Zhou court sent Commander Zhao Kuangyin of the imperial army to resist the Khitan troops. They took up position in Chenqiao post station (southeast of present-day Fengqiu, Henan province).
   公元960年初,传言契丹进犯,后周派朝延御林军统帅赵匡胤领兵出征,驻扎在陈桥驿(今河南封丘东南)。

2. At night, Zhao's generals rushed into his quarters and asked him to assume the throne.
   到了晚上,将士们涌到赵匡胤的住地,要求他来做皇帝。

3. They draped a yellow (imperial color) robe on Zhao before he could say anything and knelt down before him to pay imperial homage.
   赵匡胤还没来得及说话,将士们就把预先备好的黄袍披到他身上,并像朝见皇帝那样向他跪拜。

4. Zhao's attempts to decline were in vain and he eventually led the imperial army back to Kaifeng, where he accepted the "abdication" of the Later Zhou emperor.
   推托一番之后,赵匡胤率军回到开封,接受了后周皇帝的"禅让"。

5. Zho kept blaming himself throughout the whole process and cried profusely with regret. Yet this drama was very likely to have been enacted by no one other than himself.
   尽管赵匡胤在整个过程中一再自责以至于痛哭流涕,但"黄袍加身"更可能是他自编自导自演的一出闹剧。

6. Zhao Kuangyin became the first emperor, Taizu, of the Song Dynasty, which was to last for more than 300 years.

赵匡胤成了宋太祖,统治中国三百多年的宋朝也从此建立了。

## Wonderful Paragraph 精彩片段

### Paragraph 1

### E早年生涯
### arly Life

Emperor Taizu (927-976), born Zhao Kuangyin, was the founder of the Song Dynasty of China, reigning from 960 to 976. His family was of fairly modest origins and cannot be traced back with certainty further than the late Tang dynasty. Zhao Kuangyin had little interest in a Classical education and also joined the military eventually rising to be the commander of the Palace Army for the Second Zhou dynasty. It was this post that enabled him to rise to power. The last competent Second Zhou Emperor, Shizong (954-960) died leaving an infant boy on the throne. Zhao Kuangyin, as the commander of the Emperor's guard, allegedly reluctantly and only at theurging of his soldiers, took power in a coup detach.

### Paragraph 2

### A成就
### ccomplishments

In 960, Song Taizu reunited China after years of fragmentation and rebellion after the fall of the Tang dynasty in 907 and established the Song dynasty. He was remembered for, but not limited to, his reform of the examination system whereby entry to the bureaucracy favoured individuals who demonstrated academic ability rather than by birth. He also created political institutions that allowed a great deal of freedom of discussion and thought, which facilitated the growth of scientific advance, economic reforms as well as achievements in arts and literature. He is perhaps best known for weakening the military and sopreventing anyone else rising to power as he did.

## Paragraph 3

## Throne Transmission 继位

He reigned for 16 years and died in 976 at the age of 49. Unexpectedly he was succeeded by his younger brother even though he had four living sons. In the traditional historical accounts his mother, the Dowager Empress Du, warned him that just as he rose to power because Zhou Shizong had left an infant on the throne, someone else might usurp power if he did not name an adult as his heir. In folk memory Song Taizong is said to have murdered his brother andinvented his mother's advice as justification.

His temple name means "Grand Forefather".

## Paragraph 4

## Martial Arts 武术

Emperor Taizu created a Shaolin-based fighting style known as Emperor Taizu long fist. It is the core style of modern day Long Fist and is widely practiced all over the world.

## Cultural Links 文化链接

### 赵匡胤杯酒释兵权

在登基以后的几年里,赵匡胤平定了许多小国和反叛的节度使,对手除了强大的辽国,就剩了已是囊中之物的南唐和北汉,军中许多有实权的将领也开始骄傲跋扈起来。但赵匡胤也有了进一步的打算。

一天,散朝以后,赵匡胤把刚出征归来的石守信、王审琦、高怀德等几名执掌禁军的将领留下来,要与他们饮酒叙旧,酒过三巡,赵匡胤忽然沉默不语,长吁短叹起来,曾是他把兄弟的几位将领感到奇怪,暗想皇帝莫不是想起了初恋情人赵京娘?他们便问赵匡胤感叹的缘由,赵匡胤说自己从做了皇帝,就没睡过一天安稳觉,就怕有人反叛。众将领纷纷表自己的忠心,赵匡胤说,你们的忠心我相信,但有一天你们手下的人也给你们黄袍加身,你们恐怕也不得不反吧。几个将领吓得跪倒在地,求皇帝指条明路。赵匡胤说,大家年轻的时候出来投军,目的说白了就是为了高官厚禄封妻荫子,现在大家的年纪也大了,不如交出兵权,我多赏你们金银和良田,回去做个富翁颐养天年,咱们再结个亲家,君臣相互不猜疑这样多好!

第二天,各将领纷纷上书请求辞职,赵匡胤成功的亲自接管掌握了禁军,接着又用同样的手段,解除了节度使王彦超等人的兵权。

## Vocabulary 妙词连珠

| | |
|---|---|
| modest 谦虚的,谦让的,适度的 | demonstrate 示范,证明,论证 |
| infant 婴儿,幼儿 | transmission 播送,发射,传动,传送,传输,转播 |
| allegedly 依其申述 | |
| fragmentation 分裂,破碎 | usurp 篡夺,篡位,侵占 |
| bureaucracy 官僚,官僚作风,官僚机构 | justification 认为有理,认为正当,理由,辩护,释罪 |
| facilitate (不以人作主语的)使容易,使便利,推动,帮助,使容易,促进 | Emperor Taizu long fist 太祖长拳 |

# Unit 8  成吉思汗 Genghis Khan

## Key Sentences
流畅精句

1. He was the son of the chief of a Mongolian tribe and also the founder of the Mongolian State after he unified all the tribes when he was 45 years old. He was at his throne for 22 years and died at 66.
   他原为蒙古酋长之子,后统一蒙古,创立蒙古国,时年45岁。在位22年,终年66岁。

2. When Kublai Khan inherited his throne, he changed the title of his reign into the Yuan Dynasty and gave Genghis Khan the posthumous title Taizu of the Yuan Dynasty.
   忽必烈即位后,改国号为元,追谥成吉思汗为元太祖。

3. Genghis Khan was a man of great depth and bold strategy, and a master of the arts of war. He had obtained extraordinary great achievements.
   成吉思汗深沉有大略,用兵如神,奇勋伟绩甚众。

4. Since he spent all his life on horse-back, Genghis Khan knew well about his subjects. He also excelled at employing the fitted persons to the appropriate posts. He appointed officials according to their capabilites instead of to their origins. He was tolerant, dependable and intrepid.
   成吉思汗终生处于戎马生涯中,知人善任不问出身,不计前仇,量才录用,善于容众,讲求信义,英勇果断。

5. Genghis Khan was a figure of complicated characters.
   成吉思汗是一个复杂的历史人物。

6. On the one hand, he was superb and gifted. On the other he was also cruel and inhumane.

   他一方面是超人的、天才的，另一方面他又是残暴的、非人道的。

7. Illustrious and awesome as he was, he was called "a brute genius" for his cruelty and barbarism.

   这位世界征服者气势如虹，确有其野蛮、残忍的一面，是一位"天才的野蛮人"。

## Wonderful Paragraph
## 精彩片段

### Paragraph 1

## 成吉思汗 Genghis Khan

Genghis Khan (1162—1227), was a Mongol Khan and founder of the Mongol Empire, unifying independent Mongol tribes under his banner by 1206. One of the foremost leaders of world history, he is regarded with extreme respect by Mongols as a leader who eliminated centuries of dissension and brought political and economic stability in Eurasia, although with considerable loss of life and property to those that opposed him. His grandson and successor Kublai Khan established China's Yuan Dynasty (1271—1368) by re-establishing the invasion of Southern Song Dynasty. Khan's descendents continued to claim leadership over Mongolia until the 17th century, when the last Chingissids were over-ruled by the Manchu.

Genghis Khan's reputation was so powerful that many later leaders claimed to be descended from him: for example, Timur Lenk, Turkic conquerer and Babur, founder of India's Mughal Empire.

著名政治家
Famous Statesmen

Paragraph 2

# E 早年生涯
## arly Life

Genghis Khan was born by the name of Temuzin in 1162, the second son of Yesugay Ba'atur, a tribal chief of the Kiyad (singular: Kiyan). His mother was Hoelun of the Olkunut tribe. He was named after a defeated rival chief.

Temuzin's early life was a most difficult one. When he reached the marriageable age of 14, his father was murdered by the neighboring Tartars while returning home and Temuzin was inducted as the clan's chief. His clan abandoned him and his family, refusing to be led by a mere boy. For the next few years, he and his family lived the way of life of poor nomads, surviving primarily off rodents. In one instance he slew his half-brother over a dispute about sharing hunting spoils. In another, Temuzin was captured in a raid by his former tribe and held captive with a wooden collar around his neck. He later escaped with help from a sympathetic captor. His mother Hoelun taught him many lessons on how to survive in the harsh climate of Mongolia, especially the need for alliances with others, which would shape his understanding in his later years.

Uniting the tribes Temuzin began his slow ascent to power by allying himself with his father's friend Toghril, a local chief. He traded his coat for an army and joined the Keriat, a confederacy of Mongols led by Wang Khan. After successful campaigns against the Tartars (1202), Temuzin was adopted as Wang Khan's heir. This led to bitterness on the part of Senggum, Wang's former heir, who planned to assassinate Temuzin, after learning of Senggum's intentions, eventually defeated Senggum and his loyalists and succeeded to the title of Wang Khan. Temuzin eventually created a written code of laws for the Mongols called Yassa, and he demanded it to be followed very strictly in order to strengthen his organization and his power among his people.

Feeling the need to secure his borders from the south against the Jin

Dynasty and from the west against the Xi Xia, Genghis Khan organized his people to prepare for possible conflicts, especially with the Han poople. With his personal charisma and strong will, Genghis Khan finally managed to unite the tribes under a single system, a monumental feature for Mongols, who had a long history of internecine dispute and economic hardship.

In 1206 Temuzin had successfully united the formerly fragmented tribes of what is now Mongolia, and at a Kurultai (a council of Mongol chiefs) he was titled "Genghis Khan" or Universal Ruler (also "Ruler of all between the oceans").

## Cultural Links 文化链接

### 成吉思汗陵

坐落在伊克昭盟伊金霍洛旗境内。陵园依山傍水,环境优美,总占地面积55 544平方米,由三座镶嵌有彩色琉璃瓦的蒙古包殿堂建筑组成。主体建筑是仿元代城楼式的门庭和三个互相连通的蒙古包式大殿,分正殿、东西配殿、东西走廊、后殿六部分。

陵园正殿迎面是一尊高5米的成吉思汗汉白玉雕像,雕像背衬巨形地图,像前供有香炉,酥油灯长明不熄。后殿蒙古包式的黄色绸帐内,供奉着成吉思汗和夫人勃尔帖·兀真的灵柩。在其两侧的黄色绸帐里,安放着成吉思汗二夫人呼伦(忽兰)和三夫人伊绪(伊连)的灵柩以及成吉思汗两个胞弟别力古台和哈撒尔的灵柩。东殿内安放的是成吉思汗四子托雷及夫人的灵柩。西殿供奉的是象征成吉思汗九员大将的九支苏力定(一种长矛式的武器),还陈列着成吉思汗征战时用过的战刀和马鞭等物。东西走廊正面墙壁上绘有反映成吉思汗一生经历的重大事件的壁画。

每年农历的三月二十一日、五月十五日、九月十二日和十月初三日,成吉思汗的后裔达尔扈特蒙古人都要在此举行盛大的祭奠活动,场面宏大,十分壮观。这里还不定期地举办元代宫廷宴——诈马宴和鄂尔多斯婚礼表演。

# 著名政治家 Famous Statesmen

## Vocabulary 妙词连珠

Mongol 蒙古人
banner 旗帜，横幅，标语
eliminate 排除，消除除去
Eurasia 欧亚大陆
dissension 意见不同，纠纷，争执
descendents 下降者，下降物
over-rule 驳回，否决，支配，制服
marriageable 达到结婚年龄的，适宜结婚的
Tartar 鞑靼人，鞑靼语 塔塔尔人
induct 感应
mere 仅仅的，起码的，纯粹的
rodents 咬的，嚼的
sable 紫貂，黑貂，黑貂皮，丧服黑貂皮的，黑的，昏暗的
dowry 嫁妆，天资

conquest 征服战利品
ascent 上升，(地位，声望等的)提高，攀登，上坡路
ally 结盟，与……(在血统，性质等)有关联，同盟同盟国，支持者
assassinate 暗杀，行刺
monumental 纪念碑的，纪念物的，不朽的，非常的
internecine 互相残杀的，两败俱伤的，内部冲突的
emergent 紧急的，浮现的，突然出现的，自然发生的
charisma 超凡魅力，感召力，教皇般的指导力
fragmented 成碎片的，片断的

# Unit 9　朱元璋　Emperor Zhu Yuanzhang

## Key Sentences 流畅精句

1. Born into a poor family in Haozhou (northeast of present-day Fengyang, Anhui province), Zhu Yuanzhang lost his parents and elder brother in a plague in 1344.
   朱元璋(1328—1398)出生在濠州(今安徽凤阳东北),家境十分贫困。1344年,瘟疫夺去了朱元璋的父母和兄长。
2. The young boy took refuge in a nearby monastery.
   他只好到附近的寺庙当了和尚。
3. The hardships he endured during his wanderings tempered his strong will, which he relied on to take over the country.
   痛苦的生活无疑磨砺了他的意志,有利他日后成就帝王霸业。
4. The valiant and resourceful Zhu Yuanzhang soon became commander of the force.
   勇敢和谋略使朱元璋很快成为了这支义军的统帅。
5. Zhu Yuanzhang adopted the maxim: "building your walls high, accumulate grain extensively, and do not hasten to claim the throne," proposed by the old Confucian scholar Zhu Sheng.
   朱元璋采纳老儒朱升"高筑墙,广积粮,缓称王"的建议。
6. Keeping a low profile, he concentrated on developing his strength.
   低调谋求发展。
7. With victory following victory, he declared himself emperor in Nanjing in early 1368.
   1368年初,朱元璋在南京建立明王朝,自己登基做了明太祖。

## 著名政治家
## Famous Statesmen

## Wonderful Paragraph
### 精彩片段

**Paragraph 1**

# 洪武大帝
# The Hongwu Emperor

The Hongwu Emperor (1328—1398), personal name Zhu Yuanzhang, was the founder of the Ming Dynasty of China, and the first emperor of this dynasty from 1368 to 1398. His era name Hongwu means "Immensely Martial."

Among the Chinese populace there were strong feelings against the rule of "the foreigners" under the Mongols Yuan Dynasty which finally led to a peasant revolution, led by Hongwu, that pushed the Yuan dynasty back to the Mongolian steppes and established the Ming Dynasty in 1368. Hongwu, the founder of the Ming Dynasty, was one of the only two dynasty founders who emerged from the peasant class. The other one was Gaozu of Han. Mao Zedong and Deng Xiaoping are the two other peasant revolutionaries to have ruled the world's most populous nation.

**Paragraph 2**

# 早年生涯
# Early Life

Orphaned as a teenager, he entered a Buddhist monastery to avoid starvation. This is where he became literate, and at age 25 joined a rebel band, where his native ability soon brought him on top. Later, as a strong-willed rebel leader, he came in contact with the well-educated Confucian scholar gentry from whom he received an education in state affairs. He acquired training in the Red Turban Movement, which was a dissident religious sect combining cultural and religious traditions of Buddhism, Taoism, and others. No longer a Buddhist, he positioned himself as defender of Confucianism and neo-Confucian conventions and not as a popular rebel.

# 用英语说中国——古今名人
## Introduce China in English—Eminent Persons

Despite his humble origins, he emerged as a national leader against the collapsing Yuan Dynasty.

## Cultural Links 文化链接

### 一代帝范,节俭成风

朱元璋出身贫苦农家,不仅深深体谅农民生活的艰辛、物力的艰难,而且他还身体力行,带头倡导节俭。明朝建立后,按计划要在南京营建宫室。负责工程的人将图样送给他审定,他当即把雕琢考究的部分全去掉了。工程竣工后,他叫人在墙壁上画了许多怵目惊心的历史故事作装饰,让自己时刻不忘历史教训。有个官员想用好看的石头铺设宫殿地面,被他当场狠狠地教训了一顿。

朱元璋用的车舆器具服用等物,按惯例该用金饰的,但他下令以铜代替。主管这事的官员说,这用不了多少金子,朱元璋说,"朕富有四海,岂吝惜这点黄金。但是,所谓俭约,非身先之,何以率天下?而且奢侈的开始,都是由小到大的。"他睡的御床与中产人家的睡床没有多大区别,每天早膳,只有蔬菜就餐。

在朱元璋的影响下,宫中的后妃也十分注意节俭。他还命令太监在皇宫墙边种菜。为了让儿子们得到锻炼,他命令太监织造麻鞋、竹笠自用,规定诸王子出城稍远,要骑马十分之七,步行十分之三。

## Vocabulary 妙词连珠

| | |
|---|---|
| immensely 无限地,广大地,庞大地,非常 | monastery 修道院,僧侣 |
| martial 战争的,军事的,尚武的,威武的 | strong-willed 意志坚强的,固执己见的 |
| | gentry 贵族们 |
| orphan 孤儿,失去生母的幼小动物 | acquired 已获得的,已成习惯的,后天通过自己的努力得到的 |
| buddhism 佛教 | |

dissident 持不同政见者
sect 宗派，教派，教士会，流派，部分，段

humble 卑下的，微贱的，谦逊的，粗陋的；使……卑下，挫，贬抑
collapsing 毁坏，断裂

用英语说中国——古今名人
Introduce China in English—Eminent Persons

# Unit 10 康熙 Emperor Kangxi

## Key Sentences
流畅精句

1. He completely transformed a situation of internal unrest coupled with external turmoil in the early years of the dynasty, and steered it onto the road to prosperity.
   他彻底改变了清初内忧外患的局面,一手开创了后来的盛世。
2. In 1712 Emperor Kangxi declared that the court would "allow the people to recuperate and never add more levies."
   1712年,康熙慨然宣布:"滋生人丁,永不加赋。"
3. Kangxi did not become a wise emperor through mere chance. A child prodigy, he showed unusual sagacity when still young.
   康熙天资聪颖,自幼就表现出非凡的见识,加上后天的勤奋,成为一代明君绝非偶然。
4. A diligent learner throughout his life, he was not only well read in the Confucian classics, but also knowledgeable about many aspects of Western culture.
   他一生好学不倦,不仅深通儒家经典,对西方文化亦多所涉猎。
5. It would not be an exaggeration to call him a scholar of both Chinese and Western learning.
   以学贯中西誉之也不为过。
6. For more than half a century on the throne, he never slackened in his responsibilities.
   在执掌政权的漫长岁月中,他始终勤政不怠。

著名政治家
Famous Statesmen

## Wonderful Paragraph
## 精彩片段

### Paragraph 1

# 康熙大帝
# The Kangxi Emperor

The Kangxi Emperor ( Wade-Giles: Kang-hsi; 1654-1722 ) was the fourth Emperor of the Manchu Qing dynasty, and the second Qing emperor to rule over all of China, from 1661 to 1722. He is known as one of the greatest Chinese emperors in history. His reign of 61 years makes him the longest-reigning Emperor of China in history, though it should be noted that having ascended the throne aged eight, he did not exercise much, if any, control over the empire until later, that role being fulfilled by his four guardians and his grandmother the Dowager Empress Xiaozhuang.

Technically, the Kangxi Emperor inherited his father Shunzhi throne at the age of eight. His father died in his early twenties, and as Kangxi was not able to rule in his minority, the Shunzhi Emperor appointed Sonin, Suksaha, Ebilun, and Oboi as the Four Regents.

### Paragraph 2

# 执政初期
# The Beginning of the Reign

In a fierce power struggle, Oboi had Suksaha put to death, and seized absolute power as sole Regent. In 1669 the Emperor arrested Oboi with help from the Xiaozhuang Grand Dowager Empress and began to take control of the country himself.

In the spring of 1662, Kangxi ordered the Great Clearance in southern China, in order to fight the anti-Qing movement, begun by Ming Dynasty loyalists under the leadership of Zheng Chenggong ( also known as Koxinga ), to regain Beijing. This involved moving the entire population of the coastal regions of southern China inland.

He listed three major issues of concern, being the flood control of the Yellow River, the repairing of the Grand Canal and the Revolt of the Three Feudatories in South China. The Revolt of the Three Feudatories broke out in 1673 and Burni of the Chakhar Mongols also started a rebellion in 1675.

Kangxi crushed the rebellions and incorporated the Chakhar into the Eight Banners. After the surrender of the Zheng family, the Qing Dynasty annexed Taiwan in 1684. Soon afterwards, the coastal regions were ordered to be repopulated, and to encourage settlers, the Qing government gave a pecuniary incentive to each settling family.

In a diplomatic success, the Kangxi government helped mediate a truce in the long-running Trinh-Nguyen War in the year 1673. The war in Vietnam between these two powerful clans had been going on for 45 years with nothing to show for it. The peace treaty that was signed lasted for 101 years.

*Paragraph 3*

# R俄国与蒙古
# ussia and the Mongols

At the same time, the Emperor was faced with the Russian advance from the north. The Qing Dynasty and the Russian Empire fought along the Sahaliyan ula (Amur, or Heilongjiang) Valley region in 1650s, which ended with a Qing victory. The Russians invaded the northern frontier again in 1680s. After series of battles and negotiations, the two empires signed the Treaty of Nerchinsk in 1689 giving China the Heilongjiang valley and fixing a border.

In 1688 Galdan, the Zungar chief, invaded and occupied the Khalkha homeland. The Khalkha royal families and the first Jebtsundamba Khutughtu, sought help from the Qing Dynasty and, as a result, submitted to the Qing. In 1690, the Zungar and the Manchu Empire clashed at the battle of Ulaan Butun in Inner Mongolia, during which the Qing army was severely mauled by Galdan. In 1696, the Kangxi Emperor himself led the campaign against the Zungars. The Western section of the Qing army crushed Galdan's army at the Battle of Dsuunmod and Galdan died in the next year.

*Paragraph 4*

## C 文化贡献
## Cultural Achievements

The Kangxi Emperor ordered the compiling of the most complete dictionary of Chinese characters ever put together, The Kangxi Dictionary. He also invented a very useful and effective Chinese calendar.

The Kangxi Dictionary was a dictionary, compiled under an edict from the Qing Dynasty Emperor Kangxi of China in 1710.

The dictionary contains some 47 000 plus entries, with Chinese characters ordered under 214 Radical (Chinese character) with the pronunciation in traditional spelling, together with references to books, works and dictionaries which contain the entry character.

It also contained rime tables with characters ordered under rime classes, Tonal language, and initial syllable sounds.

## Cultural Links
### 文化链接

### 差点被当作"破烂"的康熙习字帖

康熙皇帝以写得一手好字而闻名天下，在旅顺博物馆里，收藏有玄烨跋兰亭序、跋曹娥碑、跋不自弃文，以及临王羲之、米芾、苏轼、董其昌等历代书法名家的墨迹22篇、302页，均为康熙皇帝26岁至43岁时的御笔，后被定为国家二级文物。

1991年，旅顺当地的一位居民将收藏的一些字画卖给了博物馆。第二天工作人员再次请这位居民来到馆里，问："您家里还有别的文物吗？"这位居民轻描淡写地说："再没什么好的了，剩下的都是破烂了。"刘广堂馆长坚持让其把这些"破烂"拿来，东西送来的时候很乱，但是刘广堂馆长用手一摸，那绢的手感特别好，细腻、均匀，颜色正，再看上面的字，墨迹绝非普

用英语说中国——古今名人
Introduce China in English—Eminent Persons

通人家,不仅颜色很深,而且黑中发亮,光泽度好,再仔细一看提款,竟然是康熙的字!

## Vocabulary 妙词连珠

| | |
|---|---|
| Manchu 满人;满族的 | sole 单独的,惟一的 |
| ascend 攀登,上升 | canal 运河,小道,导管,槽 |
| Dowager Empress 皇太后 | feudatory 臣属的,封地的 |
| regent 摄政者,董事;摄政的 | commendable 值得表扬的 |

# Unit 11  Guan Zhong 管仲

## Key Sentences
流畅精句

1. Duke Huan of the State of Qi was the first super-duke. Guan Zhong was the man who helped him build Qi into such a super-state.
   齐国的国王齐桓公是春秋时期第一个霸主,他的霸业主要是依靠大臣管仲的辅佐才得以完成。
2. Guan Zhong had been the aide to a rival prince before Duke Huan became duke of the state.
   管仲曾经帮齐国另一个王子跟齐桓公争王位。
3. He had almost killed Huan with an arrow during battle.
   还差一点把齐桓公射死。
4. Even so, Duke Huan did not hold a grudge against him, and appointed him Prime Minister due to his talent.
   但是齐桓公并不记仇,仍然根据他的才能任用他为齐国的宰相。
5. Guan Zhong implemented a number of reforms and soon turned Qi into a strong economic and military power.
   管仲对齐国的内政进行了一系列革新,齐国很快强盛起来,具备了成为霸主的经济和军事实力。
6. While Guan Zhong is a well-known historical figure, his friend Bao Shuya, who first recommended him to Duke Huan, is much less known.
   管仲是历史上众所周知的人物,而第一个把他推荐给齐桓公的他的朋友鲍叔牙,却没有他出名。

## Wonderful Paragraph
精彩片段

*Paragraph 1*

# Guan Zhong 管仲

Guan Zhong (died in 645 BC) was a politician in the Spring and Autumn Period. His given name was Yíwú (夷吾). Zhong was his courtesy name. Recommended by Bao Shuya, he was appointed Prime Minister by Duke Huan of Qi in 685 BC. Guan Zhong modernized the state of Qi by starting multiple reforms. Politically, he centralized power and divided the state into different villages, each carrying out a specific trade. Instead of relying on the traditional aristocracy for manpower, he applied levies to the village units directly. He also developed a better method for choosing talent to be governors. Under Guan Zhong, Qi shifted administrative responsibilities from hereditary aristocrats to professional bureaucrats.

Guan Zhong also introduced several important economic reforms. He created a uniform tax code. He also used state power to encourage the production of salt and iron; historians usually credit Guan Zhong for introducing state monopolies of salt and iron. During his term of office, the state of Qi became much stronger and Duke Huan of Qi gained hegemony among the states.

He is listed as the author of the Guan Zi encyclopedia, actually a much later (late Warring States) compilation of works from the scholars of the Jixia Academy.

## Cultural Links
文化链接

### 管仲和鲍叔牙

管仲年轻的时候,有一个经常来往的朋友叫鲍叔牙。鲍叔牙很了解管仲的贤能。后来鲍叔牙就向桓公推荐管仲。管仲被任用当了齐国的宰相后,齐国大治,齐桓公称霸诸国。

管仲说:"我当初不得志的时候,曾经与鲍叔牙合做买卖,分利润时,都是取大部分。鲍叔牙不认为我贪婪,而是知道我贫困。我曾经替鲍叔牙谋划事业,但是事业发展不顺利我也更加穷困,鲍叔牙不认为我愚蠢,而是知道我做事的外部条件不具备。我曾经数次当官又数次被国君驱逐,鲍叔牙不认为我无德无才,而是知道我是没遇到好的君主。我曾经三次在打仗时不积极参战,鲍叔牙不认为我胆小,而是知道我挂念老母亲。公子纠败了,召忽为公子死了,我却忍受囚禁的屈辱不自杀,鲍叔牙不认为我没有羞耻之心,而是知道我不在意小节,在意的是能否平定天下。生我的人是父母,真正了解我的人是鲍叔牙啊!"鲍叔牙推荐了管仲之后,把自己官职置于管仲之下来辅助他。

天下人称赞的不是管仲的贤能,而是称赞鲍叔牙能够举荐贤人!

## Vocabulary 妙词连珠

politician 政治家,政客
Duke Huan of Qi 齐桓公
modernize 使现代化
multiple 多样的,多重的
centralized 集中的,中央集权的
aristocracy 贵族,贵族政府,贵族统治
levy 征收,征税,征兵征收,征集,征用
administrative 管理的,行政的
responsibility 责任,职责
hereditary 世袭的,遗传的
aristocrat 贵族
bureaucrat 官僚主义者
monopoly 垄断,垄断者,专利权,专利事业
hegemony 霸权
encyclopedia 百科全书

# Unit 12　Shang Yang 商鞅

## Key Sentences 流畅精句

1. During the agitation for political reform in his time, Shang Yang's advocacy of reform was appreciated by the Qin State.
   在诸国实行变法改革的风潮中,商鞅的变法主张受到秦国的重视。
2. He accomplished reforms twice, which greatly enhanced the national economy and strengthened the military force of the state, thereby established the foundation of a powerful state.
   他两次变法,促进了经济发展,加强了军事力量,奠定了秦国富国强兵的基础。
3. Shang Yang demanded all his countrymen to learn and observe the law.
   商鞅要求天下民众都要知法、信法。
4. Shang Yang practised strict legalities and severe penal code and punished the aristocrats who committed violation of the laws.
   商鞅严法重刑,无情制裁违法乱制的贵族。
5. Shang Yang guided his countrymen to devote major efforts to developing agricultural economy and preparing for war.
   商鞅把民众引导到大力发展农业经济与常年备战的道路上来。
6. Shang Yang's political reform has been considered a turning point at which China historically advanced from partition to unity, from a slavery society to a centralized feudal empire.
   商鞅变法是中国历史由奴隶社会走向封建中央集权社会的转折点。

著名政治家
Famous Statesmen

## Wonderful Paragraph
## 精彩片段

### Paragraph 1

# S商鞅
# hang Yang

Shang Yang (Wade-Giles: Kung-sun Yang) (c. 390-338B.C.) was an important statesman of Qin in the Warring States Period of ancient China. With the support of Duke Xiao of Qin, Shang Yang enacted numerous reforms (in accordance with his legalist philosophy recorded in The Book of Lord Shang) in the state of Qin that changed Qin from a peripheral, backwards state into a militarily powerful and strongly centralized state, changing the administration by emphasizing meritocracy and devolving power from the nobility.

### Paragraph 2

# R商鞅变法
# eforms

Before Shang Yang's arrival in 361 BC, Qin was a backwards state. The vast majority of his reforms were taken from policies instituted elsewhere; however, Shang Yang's reforms were more thorough and extreme than those of other states. Under Shang Yang's tenure, Qin quickly caught up with and surpassed the reforms of other states.

After Duke Xiao of Qin, ascended to the Qin throne, Shang Yang left his lowly position in Wei to become the chief adviser in Qin, at Duke Xiao's behest. There his changes to the state's legal system propelled the Qin to prosperity. His policies built the foundation that enabled Qin to conquer all of China, uniting the country for the first time and ushering in the Qin dynasty.

He is credited by Han Feizi with the creation of two theories:
1. Ding Fa (fixing the standards)

2. Yi Min (treating the people as one)

*Paragraph 3*

## Legalist Approach
## 变法手段

Shang Yang believed in the rule of law and considered loyalty to the state to be above that of the family.

Shang Yang introduced two sets of changes to the Qin state. The first, in 356 BC, were as concludes:

1. Li Kui's Book of Law was implemented, with the important addition of a rule providing punishment equal to that of the perpetrator for those aware of a crime but failing to inform the government; codified reforms into enforceable laws.

2. Stripped the nobility of land right and assigned land to soldiers based upon military success. The army was also separated into twenty military ranks, based upon battlefield success.

3. As manpower was short in Qin, Shang Yang encouraged the cultivation of unsettled lands and wastelands, and favoured agriculture over commerce.

4. Shang Yang burnt Confucian books in an effort to curb the philosophy's influence.

Shang Yang introduced his second set of changes in 350 BC, which included a new, standardized system of land allocation and reforms to taxation.

*Paragraph 4*

## Domestic Policies
## 国内政策

Shang Yang introduced land reforms, privatized land, rewarded farmers who exceeded harvest quotas, enslaved farmers who failed to meet quotas, and used enslaved citizens as rewards for those who met government policies.

As manpower was short in Qin relative to the other states at the time, Shang Yang enacted policies to increase its manpower. As Qin peasants were recruited into the military, he encouraged active immigration of peasants from other states into Qin as a replacement workforce; this policy simultaneously increased the manpower of Qin and weakened the manpower of Qin's rivals. Shang Yang made laws forcing citizens to marry at a young age and passed tax laws to encourage raising multiple children. He also enacted policies to free convicts who worked in opening wastelands for agriculture.

Shang Yang abolished primogeniture and created a double tax on households that had more than one son living in the household, to break up large clans into nuclear families.

Shang Yang moved the capital to reduce the influence of nobles on the administration.

*Paragraph 5*

## D外交手段
## Diplomatic Intrigue

During Shang Yang's tenure, the state of Wei was a highly powerful neighboring state. During a battle during the 340 BC invasion of Wei, Shang Yang feigned interest in a peace treaty, met with the commander of the Wei army and captured him. Without their leader, the Wei army easily lost to the army of Qin and lost territory.

*Paragraph 6*

## S商鞅之死
## Shang Yang's Death

Deeply despised by the Qin nobility, Shang Yang could not survive Qin Xiaogong's death. The next ruler, King Huiwen, ordered the execution of

Shang Yang and his family, on grounds of rebellion; Shang had previously humiliated the new Duke "by causing him to be punished for an offense as though he were an ordinary citizen." Shang Yang went into hiding and tried to stay at a hotel. Ironically, the hotel owner refused because it was against Shang Yang's laws to admit a guest without proper identification. Shang Yang is said to have been executed by being fastened to four chariots and pulled apart. Despite his death, King Huiwen kept the reforms enacted by Shang Yang.

## Cultural Links 文化链接

### 商鞅的宿命

对于商鞅的悲惨命运的原因历史追问,史学家诸多点评,无非下面几点:一是改革方法过于霸道,借用秦孝公授予的绝对权力采取中间强行突破的方式,用斧头劈开一堵堵障碍墙,触动了许多权贵者的利益。在这过程中,为了树立威信,做事绝决,连秦国太子的两位师傅,因为偶然的小错,也要割鼻刺字,一点面子也不给,不给别人同时也不给自己留条后路。

改革的大靠山秦孝公死后,郁闷已久的太子即位,商鞅仍不知大祸已将临头。孰不知,太子的师傅在被割鼻之后,虽八年闭门不出,却每日派人注意着商鞅的一举一动,定时汇总分析,商鞅却自以为对秦国的变法有大功,大权独揽且行事张扬,仇家越结越多,自是死路一条。

## Vocabulary 妙词连珠

| | |
|---|---|
| enact 制定法律,颁布,扮演 | tenure (土地等的)使用和占有,(官职等的)保有,任期,(土地)使用期限 |
| peripheral 外围的 | |
| meritocracy 知识界精华 | |
| devolve 转移,传下 | behest [诗]命令,吩咐,要求 |
| propel 推进,驱使 | implement 贯彻,实现,执行 |

perpetrator 犯罪者,作恶者
codify 编成法典,使法律成文化
enforceable 可强行的,可强迫的,可实施的
quota 配额,限额
enslave 奴役,沉溺,束缚
recruit 征募新兵,复原
simultaneously 同时地
primogeniture 长子身份,长子继承权
tenure (土地等的)使用和占有,(官职等的)保有,任期,(土地)使用期限
feign 假装,装作,捏造
execution 实行,完成,执行,死刑,制作,(武器等的)破坏效果,杀伤力
humiliate 羞辱,使丢脸,耻辱

# Unit 13 Zhuge Liang 诸葛亮

## Key Sentences 流畅精句

1. Zhuge Liang was the epitome of loyalty and wisdom in the minds of the people.
   诸葛亮是人们心目中忠诚和智慧的化身。
2. Before he met Liu Bei, Zhuge Liang had been a recluse in Longzhong, where he read extensively and lived by farming.
   在遇见刘备之前,诸葛亮隐居在隆中(今湖北襄阳西),一面读书,一面种田。
3. Liu Bei heard about Zhuge Liang in AD 207, when he was still a subordinate of Liu Biao in Jingzhou.
   公元207年,寄居在荆州的刘备听说了诸葛亮的名声。
4. At this meeting, which was to be glorified by future generations, Zhuge Liang expounded on the current political situation in great detail. 在这次千古传诵的会面中,诸葛亮对天下形势进行了详尽透彻的分析。
5. The growth of the Three Kingdoms turned out to be just as Zhuge Liang had predicted.
   后来魏、蜀、吴三分天下的局面正如诸葛亮的预料。
6. The Kingdom of Shu came into being largely due to his personal efforts.
   而蜀国的这一分在很大程度上也是他个人努力的结果。
7. After Liu Bei died of illness in AD 223, Zhuge Liang continued to assist his son in running the kingdom.
   公元223年,刘备病逝,诸葛亮继续辅佐他的儿子治理蜀国。

著名政治家
Famous Statesmen

8. Comparable to his genius was his moral character.
   与他的才能交相辉映的是他高尚的个人品格。
9. Zhuge Liang did not realize his dream of reuniting China, even though he accomplished a great feat in organizing the Kingdom of Shu.
   虽然诸葛亮把蜀国管理得井井有条,但他终于没能实现统一中国的愿望。

## Wonderful Paragraph 精彩片段

### Paragraph 1

### N 名字 ames

Zhuge Liang (181—234) was one of the greatest strategists of post-Han China, as well as a statesman, an engineer and a scholar. Zhuge is an uncommon two-character compound Chinese family name

Name
- Simplified Chinese characters：诸葛亮
- Wade-Giles：Chuko Liang

Courtesy name
- Chinese characters：孔明
- Wade-Giles：K'ung-ming

Other names
- Crouching Dragon Xiansheng 卧龙先生 or The Crouching or Sleeping Dragon 卧龙
- Wade-Giles：Wo-lung Hsien-sheng

### Paragraph 2

### E 早年生涯 arly Life

Zhuge Liang was born in Yangdu County in Langya Commandry, at present-day Yishui County, Shandong Province. He was the second of three brothers and orphaned early; his mother died when he was nine, and his father when he was twelve. His uncle raised him and his siblings. When Cao Cao invaded Shandong in 195, his family was forced to flee south, and his uncle soon died of illness.

Although both his sisters married into important families with numerous connections in the area, for ten years he resided in Longzhong Commandry (in present-day Hubei province) with his elder brother Zhuge Jin in a simple peasant life—farming by day and studying by night. He got to know a group of friends among the intellectuals of the area. His reputation soon grew, and he was named the Crouching (or Sleeping) Dragon, wise among his peers in many areas. At the meantime, he married the daughter of another renowned scholar Huang Chenyan. His wife's name is rumored to be Huang Yueying. The Huang Family was also connected to several other well established clans in the region.

### Paragraph 3

## R一鸣惊人 ise to Prominence

The warlord Liu Bei harbored in the neighboring city Xiangyang under his distant relative and the governor of the Jing Region, Liu Biao. Legends recounted that Zhuge Liang joined Liu Bei only after Liu visited him in person three times. Zhuge Liang soon presented his famous Longzhong Plan before Liu, and he travelled in person to the Kingdom of Wu and formed an alliance with its ruler Sun Quan.

His elder brother, Zhuge Jin (诸葛瑾), served as a high official in the Kingdom of Wu.

In the Battle of Red Cliff of 208, the allied armies of Liu Bei and Sun Quan defeated Cao Cao, thus enabling Liu Bei to establish his own territories.

The union with Sun Quan broke down when Guan Yu retaliated on the

Kingdom of Wu in 219 after the surprise attack of Lü Meng. Guan Yu was defeated and decapitated. Liu Bei, infuriated with the execution of his long-time comrade, ignored all arguments of his well-meaning subjects and turned on the Kingdom of Wu, leading a huge army to seek revenge. He was also defeated in the ensuing Battle of Yiling and died in a lone fortress of "Baidi Cheng" (白帝城 "the White Emperor Fortress") after a hasty and humiliating retreat to his own borders. After the death of Liu Bei, Zhuge Liang became the prime minister under Liu Chan, Liu Bei's son, and renewed the alliance with Sun Quan.

### Paragraph 4

# 南征
## The Southern Expeditions

Before Zhuge Liang would embark on his Northern Expeditions he would facegreat opposition. He had to repel 5 armies of approximately 100 000 which marched against him after Yiling. These armies belonged to Wei and a new threat in the South, the Nanman people. Here are the armies that Zhuge Liang held off:
1) 100 000 troops from Wei marched to attack Yangping Pass
2) 100 000 troops under Meng Huo a Nanman army attacks Southern Shu
3) 100 000 troops from Wei attack Hanzhong
4) 100 000 troops of the Qiang tribe attack Xiping
5) 100 000 troops from Wu come after the battle of Yiling

All these invasions were countered however Zhuge Liang saw the attack in the South as a threat. Zhuge Liang felt that in order to march North he would first have to unify Shu completely. If he fought against the North while the Nanman people rebelled than the Nanman people would march further and perhaps even press into areas surrounding the capital. So rather than embarking on a Northern Campaign, Zhuge Liang sent a large force of 500 000 men to pacify the south first.

Ma Su (Ma Liang's brother) proposed the plan that Zhuge Liang should work toward getting the rebels to join him rather than killing all of them and he took this plan. Zhuge Liang defeated the rebel leader, Meng Huo, seven different times. During this campaign he got sick from the poison marshes in the area (according to the novel). Luckily he was healed to good health. Finally Meng Huo agreed to join Zhuge Liang and Zhuge Liang made Meng Huo king of the area again so he could govern it and the people would be happy. After this Zhuge Liang made his moves North.

*Paragraph 5*

## 北伐
## The Northern Expeditions

Zhuge Liang persuaded Jiang Wei, a general of Kingdom of Wei, to defect to the Kingdom of Shu. Jiang would be one of the important generals to continue to carry on Zhuge Liang's ideals and fight for the Kingdom of Shu after Zhuge Liang's untimely death in 234.

In his latter years, he launched invasion of the Kingdom of Wei six times, but all failed. On the seventh time, he died of overwork and illness in an army camp in Battle of Wuzhang Plain.

*Paragraph 6*

## 遗产
## Legacy

His name is synonymous with wisdom in Chinese language. He was believed to be the inventor of the landmine and a mysterious automatic transportation device described as a "wooden ox and floating horse" (木牛流马). He is credited with the invention of a repeating crossbow which is named after him, called Zhuge Nu. He is also credited for inventing the wheelbarrow. A kind of hot air balloon used for military signalling is named after him.

Some books rumored to be written by Zhuge Liang can be found today, for example the Sixteen Strategies of Zhuge Liang, and Mastering the Art of War are two that can be bought.

# 著名政治家 Famous Statesmen

## Cultural Links 文化链接

### 三顾茅庐

刘备屯住新野时,自知蹉跎半生之缘由是身边虽有关羽,张飞等猛将,而无出谋划策运筹帷幄之谋士,便礼贤下士,寻求良辅。在司马徽和徐庶的荐举下,刘备与关羽、张飞便来到襄阳隆中,拜访诸葛亮。

第一次来到茅庐时,亮已外出,三人返途中遇见亮好友崔州平;数日后,刘、关、张顶风冒雪,二顾茅庐。途中,遇亮好友石广元,孟公威。到达茅庐,只见亮弟诸葛均,方知亮已出游,备留下一笺,表达倾慕之意。返回时,在隆中山下小桥边遇见亮岳父黄承彦;过了一段时间,刘备与关羽、张飞三顾茅庐,适逢亮在家,但昼寝未醒。刘备吩咐关、张在门外等候,自己徐步而入,拱手立于阶下,直到亮醒后,方才相见。[三顾堂:建于清康熙五十八年(公元1719年),是刘备"三顾茅庐"、诸葛亮作《隆中对》的纪念堂。]

## Vocabulary 妙词连珠

sibling 兄弟,姐妹,同胞,同属
intellectual 智力的,有智力的,显示智力的
renowned 有名的,有声誉的
alliance 联盟,联合
retaliate 报复
decapitate 斩首
infuriate 狂怒的
ensue 跟着发生,继起
fortress 堡垒,要塞

hasty 匆忙的,草率的
humiliating 羞辱性的
embark 上船,上飞机,着手,从事,装于船上,登上
pacify 使平静,安慰,抚慰
marsh 湿地,沼泽,沼泽地
synonymous 同义的
landmine [军]地雷,投伞水雷
crossbow 石弓,弩
wheelbarrow 独轮手推车,手推车

# Unit 14  王安石  Wang Anshi

## Key Sentences
## 流畅精句

1. Wang Anshi was an initiative statesman in the Song Dynasty.
   王安石是宋朝富有革新精神的政治家。
2. Full of foresight and willpower, Wang Anshi proposed political reform when he was a young man.
   王安石有远见,有毅力,年轻时就提出了比较系统的变法主张。
3. In 1069, Song Shenzong, Emperor who was eager to find the way of governing the country, appointed Wang Anshi, vice prime minister, to carry out reform.
   1069年,求治心切的宋神宗任命王安石为参知政事,推行变法。
4. After he took office as the prime minister of the empire, he made a sum total of new laws issued, which enforced fundamentally the national financing and military consolidation of the country.
   他任宰相后,陆续颁布新法,新法内容分为理财和整军两大类。
5. The chief content and purpose of Wang Anshi's political reform lay in bringing about national prosperity and powerful military forces.
   王安石变法的主要内容和目的在于富国强兵。
6. His reform achieved remarkable success in the increase of national revenue, the construction of water conservancy works, and the improvement of combat effectiveness.
   他的新法在增加财政收入、兴修水利、提高军队战斗力方面都收到了显著成效。

著名政治家
Famous Statesmen

## Wonderful Paragraph
精彩片段

**Paragraph 1**

# W 王安石
**ang Anshi**

Wang anshi (1021—1086) was a Chinese economist, statesman and poet of the Song Dynasty (960—1279) who attempted some controversial, major socio-economic reforms. His courtesy name was Jiepu (介甫), and sobriquet Oldman Half-a-Mountain (半山老人).

At that time, the unprecedented development of large estates, whose owners managed to evade paying their share of taxes, resulted in an increasingly heavy burden of taxation falling on the peasantry. The drop in state revenues, a succession of budget deficits, and widespread inflation prompted the emperor to seek advice from Wang.

Wang believed that the state was responsible for providing its citizens the essentials for a decent living standard: "The state should take the entire management of commerce, industry, and agriculture into its own hands, with a view to succoring the working classes and preventing them from being ground into the dust by the rich."

Accordingly, under his direction the state initiated an agricultural loans measure to relieve the farming peasants of the burden of interest extracted from them by moneylenders, and to thereby prevent a consequent lack of capital from impeding agricultural development. To destroy speculation and break up the monopolies, he initiated a system of fixed commodity prices; and he appointed boards to regulate wages and plan pensions for the aged and unemployed. Wang Anshi also revamped the state examination system so that less emphasis was placed on literary style and memorization of the Chinese classic texts and more on practical knowledge, irking the Confucian scholar gentry and state bureaucracy. These reforms were known as the "new laws."

However, famous scholar-officials like Su Dongpo and Ouyang Xiu bitterly opposed these reforms on grounds of tradition. They believed Wang's reforms were against the moral fundamentals of the Two Emperors and would therefore prevent the Song from experiencing the prosperity and peace of the ancients. The tide tilted in favor of the conservatives due to renewed foreign conflict.

Modern observers have noted how remarkably close his theories were to modern concepts of the welfare state and planned economy.

In addition to his political achievements, Wang Anshi was a noted poet. He wrote poems in the Shi (poetry) form, modelled on those of Du Fu.

He was traditionally classed as one of the Eight Great Prose Masters of the Tang and Song Dynasty(唐宋八大家).

## Cultural Links
## 文化链接

### 王安石做双喜字肉

据说王安石年轻时赴京赶考,半路上遇见一个富户人家在用对诗的方法选女婿。这诗的上联是小姐自己出的,求对下联。上联写道:"天连碧树春滋雨,雨滋春树碧连天。"王安石略一思索,便吟出"地满红香花连凤,凤连花香红满地"。众人齐声称好,小姐闻知,也十分满意。于是,王安石与小姐约定科考后完婚。

凑巧的是,在科考场上考官收毕试卷后,主考官又另外出了一题:"地满红香花连凤,凤连花香红满地。"求对上联。王安石心中一喜,出口便道出:"天连碧树春滋雨,雨滋春树碧连天。"主考官闻言大喜,十分赞赏。

不久,王安石回去与小姐完婚,正在举行婚礼时,传来王安石高中状元的消息。真是喜上加喜,王安石高兴极了,新自下厨烹制"双喜字肉",这道菜不仅味道好,而且在制作上也别出心裁,每块肉上刻着的双喜字就更有意义。后来,人们就常常把它作为喜庆宴席上的一道菜,为的是增添更浓的喜庆气氛。

## Vocabulary 妙词连珠

controversial 争论的, 争议的
socioeconomic 社会经济学的
sobriquet 假名, 绰号
estate 状态, 不动产, 时期, 阶层, 财产
evade 规避, 逃避, 躲避
state revenue 财政收入
budget deficit 预算赤字
inflation 胀大, 夸张, 通货膨胀, (物价)暴涨
essential 本质的, 实质的, 基本的, 提炼的, 精华的
decent 正派的, 端庄的, 有分寸的, (服装)得体的, 大方的
succor 救援, 援助者, 救援人员
initiate 开始, 发动, 传授开始, 发起

extracted 萃取的
moneylender (尤指经营典当的)放债者
consequent 作为结果的, 随之发生的
impede 阻止
speculation 思索, 做投机买卖
monopoly 垄断, 垄断者, 专利权, 专利事业
revamp 修补
memorization 记住, 默记
irk 使厌倦, 使苦恼
bureaucracy 官僚, 官僚作风, 官僚机构
fundamental 基础的, 基本的
conservative 保守派

# Unit 15  Mao Zedong
毛泽东

## Key Sentences
流畅精句

1. He took up residence in Zhongnanhai, a compound next to the Forbidden City in Beijing.
   他居住在北京紫禁城附近的中南海。
2. Following the consolidation of power, Mao launched the First Five Year Plan (1953—1958).
   随着政权的巩固,毛泽东发起了1953年到1958年的第一个五年计划。
3. In 1969, Mao declared the Cultural Revolution to be over, although the official history marks the end of the Cultural Revolution in 1976.
   1969年,毛泽东表示要结束文化大革命,尽管历史上以1976年结束为准。
4. People regard Mao Zedong as a great revolutionary leader, although they also believe that he made serious mistakes later in his life.
   人们认为毛泽东是一位伟大的革命领袖,尽管也认为他在晚年犯了一些严重错误。
5. Mao's military writings continue to have a large amount of influence.
   毛泽东的军事著作仍旧产生着巨大的影响。
6. In the mid-1990s, Mao Zedong's picture began to appear on all new renminbi currency.
   20世纪90年代中期,毛泽东的头像开始在所有新发行的人民币上出现。

著名政治家
Famous Statesmen

## Wonderful Paragraph
## 精彩片段

**Paragraph 1**

# 毛泽东和他的早年生涯
# Mao Zedong and His Early Life

Mao Zedong (1893—1976) (also Mao Tse-Tung) was a Chinese Marxist military and political leader, who led the Chinese Communist Party (CCP) to victory against the Kuomintang (KMT) in the Chinese Civil War, leading to the establishment of the People's Republic of China on October 1, 1949 in Beijing.

The eldest child of a relatively prosperous peasant family, Mao was born on December 26, 1893 in a village called Shaoshan in Xiangtan County (湘潭县), Hunan province. During the 1911 Revolution, Mao served in a local regiment in Hunan. However, disliking military service, he returned to school in Changsha. Having graduated from the First Provincial Normal School of Hunan in 1918, Mao traveled with Professor Yang Changji, his high school teacher and future father-in-law, to Beijing during the May Fourth Movement in 1919. Professor Yang held a faculty position at Peking University. Because of Yang's recommendation, Mao worked as an assistant librarian at the University with Li Dazhao as curator. Over his stay in Beijing, he read as much as possible. He married Yang Kaihui, Professor Yang's daughter and also his fellow student.

Mao turned down an opportunity to study in France. Later, he claimed that it was because he firmly believed that China's problems could be studied and resolved only within China. As distinct from his contemporaries, Mao went the opposite direction, studying the peasant majority of China's population where he began his life as a professional revolutionist. On July 23, 1921, Mao, aged 27, attended the first session of the Congress of the Communist Party of China in Shanghai. Two years later, he was elected as one of the five commissars of the Central Committee of the Party during the third Congress session. In early 1927, Mao returned to Hunan where, in an urgent meeting held by the Communist Party, he made a report based on his investigations of the peasant uprisings in the wake of the Northern Expedition. This is considered the initial and decisive step towards the successful application of Mao's revolutionary theories.

> Paragraph 2

## 政治思想
## Political Ideas

Mao was introduced to Marxism in Beijing. The process of Mao becoming a Marxist was gradual. During the year 1920 in Hunan, Mao contributed a number of essays to newspapers advocating the autonomy of Hunan Province. He firmly believed that provincial autonomy was a prerequisite to local prosperity and that local prosperity would lead to a stronger and prosperous China.

In 1920, Mao also developed his theory of violent revolution. His theory was inspired by the Russian revolution and was likely influenced by the Chinese literary works: Outlaws of the Marsh and Romance of the Three Kingdoms. Mao sought to subvert the alliance of imperialism and feudalism in China. He thought the Nationalists to be both economically and politically vulnerable and thus that the revolution could not be steered by Nationalists. He concluded that violent revolution must be conducted by the proletariat under the supervision of a Communist party. Throughout the 1920s, Mao led several labor struggles based upon his studies of the propagation and organization of the contemporary labor movements. However, these struggles were successfully subdued by the government, and Mao fled from Changsha after he was labeled a radical activist. He pondered these failures and finally realized that 1) workers were unable to lead the revolution because they made up only a small portion of China's population and 2) unarmed labor struggles could not resolve the problems of imperial and feudal suppression.

Mao began to depend on Chinese peasants who later became staunch supporters of his theory of violent revolution. This dependence on the rural rather than the urban proletariat to instigate violent revolution distinguished Mao from his predecessors and contemporaries. Mao himself was from a peasant family, and thus he cultivated his reputation among the farmers and peasants and introduced them to Marxism.

*Paragraph 3*

## 中国的伟大领袖
## Leadership of China

The People's Republic of China was established on October 1 1949. It was the culmination of over two decades of civil and international war. From 1954 to 1959, Mao was the Chairman of the PRC. During this period, Mao was called Chairman Mao（毛主席）or the Great Leader Chairman Mao（伟大领袖毛主席）. In his speech declaring the foundation of the PRC, Mao announced: "The Chinese people have stood up!" Following the consolidation of power, Mao launched the First Five Year Plan (1953—1958). The plan aimed to end Chinese dependence upon agriculture in order to become a world power. The success of the First Five Year Plan was to encourage Mao to instigate the Second Five Year Plan, the Great Leap Forward, in 1958. Mao also launched a phase of rapid collectivization. The CCP introduced price controls as well as a Chinese character simplification aimed at increasing literacy. Land was taken from landlords and more wealthy peasants and given to poorer peasants. Large scale industrialization projects were also undertaken. Programs pursued during this time include the Hundred Flowers Campaign, in which Mao indicated his supposed willingness to consider different opinions about how China should be governed.

*Paragraph 4*

## 评价
## Evaluation

Many Chinese regard Mao Zedong as a great revolutionary leader, although they also believe that he made serious mistakes later in his life. According to Deng Xiaoping, Mao was "seventy-percent right and thirty-percent wrong", and his "contributions are primary and his mistakes secondary." The Great Leap Forward and the Cultural Revolution were also considered to be major disasters in his policy by his critics and even many of his supporters. Mao has also been blamed for not encouraging birth control and for creating a demographic bump, which later Chinese leaders responded to with the one child policy.

Supporters of Mao credit him with advancing the social and economic development of Chinese society. They point out that before 1949, for instance, the illiteracy rate in Mainland China was 80 percent, and life expectancy was a meager 35 years. At his death, illiteracy had declined to less than seven percent, and average life expectancy had increased to more than 70 years (alternative statistics also quote improvements, though not nearly as dramatic). In addition to these increases, the total population of China increased 57% to 700 million, from the constant 400 million mark during the span between the Opium War and the Chinese Civil War. Supporters also state that, under Mao's regime, China ended its "Century of Humiliation" from Western imperialism and regained its status as a major world power. They also state their belief that Mao also industrialized China to a considerable extent and ensured China's sovereignty during his rule. They also argue that the Maoist era improved women's rights by abolishing prostitution. Indeed, Mao once famously remarked that "Women hold up half the heavens".

There is more consensus on Mao's role as a military strategist and tactician during the Chinese Civil War and the Korean War. The ideology of Maoism has influenced many communists around the world, including Third World revolutionary movements such as Cambodia's Khmer Rouge, The Communist Party of Peru, and the revolutionary movement in Nepal.

## 著名政治家 Famous Statesmen

### Cultural Links 文化链接

## 吉斯——毛泽东的专车

1949年12月16日,毛泽东率中国代表团访前苏联期间,毛泽东一直乘坐"吉斯115"。回国时,斯大林就把这辆车和一辆"吉斯110"赠送给了毛泽东。此后,这两辆坐驾就一直伴随着他。

"吉斯110"通身黑色,在前苏联也只限于高级领导人使用,并不作为商品出售。该车是防弹保险车,车窗玻璃厚10余厘米,借助一套液压系统才能升降;车门关上后,还有一根很粗的链子锁;车身自重6吨,轮胎外带是双层结构,底盘装有厚厚的钢板;车厢内还有一道可升降的厚玻璃,能与前面司机的座位隔开,既防弹,又保密。

据说毛泽东坐车很特别,他从来不坐别人的车,却极愿意别人来挤坐他的车,有时实在没人来坐毛泽东的车,他甚至会把开道车和尾随车里的警卫人员拉来,挤在自己的车里,简直是把自己的座驾当作"面的"使用。他的"吉斯115"车经常会挤满了人。周恩来、陈毅、贺龙等领导同志都深知毛泽东的这个癖好,只要有机会,就会去搭乘毛泽东的车。

1992年,军事博物馆筹办纪念建军65周年展览,发现了有关"吉斯110"的线索。工作人员赶到杭州,经国务院有关部门与浙江省公安厅联系,同意把这辆车赠送给军事博物馆。这就是军事博物馆中展出的这辆"吉斯110"老式轿车的来历。

### Vocabulary 妙词连珠

| | |
|---|---|
| Kuomintang 国民党 | faculty 才能,本领,能力,全体教员,(大学的)系,科,(授予的)权力 |
| relatively 相关地 | |
| prosperous 繁荣的 | |
| regiment 团,大群 | curator 馆长,监护人 |
| session 会议,开庭 | initial 最初的,词首的,初始的 |
| commissar 代表,政委 | decisive 决定性的 |

gradual 逐渐的,逐步的,渐进的
autonomy 自治
prerequisite 先决条件;首要必备的
sought seek 的过去式和过去分词
subvert 推翻,暗中破坏,搅乱
imperialism 帝国主义,帝制
feudalism 灭亡
vulnerable 易受攻击的,易受……的攻击
proletariat (古罗马社会中的)最下层阶级,工人阶级,尤指无产阶级
supervision 监督,管理
propagate 繁殖,传播,宣传
subdue 征服
label 标签,签条,商标,标志
radical 根本的,基本的,激进的
ponder 沉思,考虑
suppression 镇压,抑制
staunch 坚定的
proletariat (古罗马社会中的)最下层阶级,工人阶级,尤指无产阶级

instigate 鼓动
predecessor 前辈,前任,(被取代的)原有事物
culmination 顶点
consolidation 巩固,合并
the Great Leap Forward 大跃进
phase 阶段,状态,相,相位
collectivization simplification 集体化
controversy 论争,辩论,论战
Cultural Revolution 文化大革命
expectancy 期待,期望
illiteracy 文盲
quote 引用,引证,提供,提出,报(价)
extent 广度,宽度,长度,范围,程度,区域,[律]＜英＞扣押,＜美＞临时所有令令
sovereignty 君主,主权,主权国家
prostitution 卖淫,堕落,滥用,糟蹋
consensus 一致同意,多数人的意见,舆论
tactician 战术家,策士

# Unit 16 周恩来 Zhou Enlai

## Key Sentences 流畅精句

1. Enlai was an orphan at the age of ten.
   周恩来十岁时成了一名孤儿。
2. His goal was to become a teacher so that he could have influence on the youth of China. But in early May 1919, dejected and without completing his education, he left Japan.
   他的理想是成为一名教师进而影响中国的青年人。但是在1919年五月初,他怀着沮丧的心情没有完成学业就离开了日本。
3. Zhou first came to national prominence as an activist during the May Fourth Movement.
   周恩来在五四运动期间作为一名活跃分子而家喻户晓。
4. In 1949, with the establishment of the People's Republic of China, Zhou assumed the role of Prime Minister and Minister of Foreign Affairs.
   1949年新中国成立后,周恩来出任中华人民共和国总理和外交部长。
5. Zhou's first major domestic focus after becoming premier was China's economy, at an ill stage after decades of war.
   周恩来担任总理后第一个关注的是经历数十年战乱后的中国经济。
6. During the Qingming Festival in April 1976, there is an incident popularly known as the Tiananmen Incident.
   1976年4月的清明节期间,发生了众所周知的天安门事件。

# 用英语说中国——古今名人
## Introduce China in English—Eminent Persons

## Wonderful Paragraph
### 精彩片段

**Paragraph 1**

## 周恩来的早年生涯及教育背景
## Zhou Enlai's Early Years and Education

Zhou Enlai (Wade-Giles: Chou En-lai) (March 5, 1898-January 8, 1976), a prominent Communist Party of China leader, was Premier of the People's Republic of China from 1949 until his death.

Zhou Enlai was born in Huai An, Jiangsu Province. His family, although of the educated scholar class, was not well off. Zhou Enlai was the eldest son and eldest grandson of the Zhou family. Enlai was an orphan at the age of ten. At the age of twelve Enlai was enrolled in the Tong Guan model school that taught "new learning", where Enlai learned about freedom, democracy and the American and French revolutions.

In 1913, at the age of fifteen, Enlai graduated from Tong Guan and in September of that year he was enrolled in the Nankai school, located in Tianjin. Throughout the period of his schooling China was in great turmoil. Enlai could see that China was being ruined by foreign intervention. He shared in the wrath, the protest, and the indignation at the plight of China.

The next step in Enlai's education was to attend university in Tokyo. His goal was to become a teacher so that he could have influence on the youth of China. But in early May 1919, dejected and without completing his education, he left Japan. Enlai arrived in Tianjin on May 9th, in time to take part in the momentous May Fourth Movement of 1919.

**Paragraph 2**

## 革命活动
## Revolutionary Activities

Zhou first came to national prominence as an activist during the May Fourth Movement. He had enrolled as a student in the literature department of Nankai University, which enabled him to visit the campus, but he never attended classes. He became one of the organizers of the Tianjin Students Union, whose avowed aim was "to struggle against the warlords and against imperialism, and to save China from extinction." Enlai became the editor of the student union's newspaper, Tianjin Student. In September, he founded the Awareness Society with twelve men and eight women. Fifteen year old Deng Yingchao, Enlai's future wife, was one of the founding female members. Zhou was instrumental in the merger between the all male Tianjin Students Union and the all female Women's Patriotic Association.

In January 1920, the police raided the printing press and arrested several members of the Awareness Society. Enlai led a group of students to protest the arrests, and was himself arrested along with 28 others. After the trial in July, they were found guilty of a minor offence and released. An attempt was made by the Comintern to induct Zhou into the Communist Party of China, but although he was studying Marxism he remained uncommitted. Instead of being selected to go to Moscow for training, he was chosen to go to France as a student organizer. Deng Yingchao was left in charge of the Awareness Society in his absence.

**Paragraph 3**

## 旅欧岁月
## The European Years

On November 7, 1920, Zhou Enlai and 196 other Chinese students sailed from Shanghai for Marseilles, France. At Marseilles they were met by a member of the Sino-French Education Committee and boarded a train to Paris. Almost as soon as he arrived Zhou became embroiled in a wrangle between the students and the education authorities running the "work and study" program. Zhou traveled to Britain in January; he applied for and was accepted as a student at Edinburgh University. But the university term didn't start until October so he returned to France, moving in with Liu Tsingyang and Zhang Shenfu, who were setting up a Communist cell. Zhou joined the group and was entrusted with political and organizational work.

There were 2 000 Chinese students in France, some 200 each in Belgium and England and between 300 and 400 in Germany. For the next four years Zhou was the chief recruiter, organizer and coordinator of activities of the Socialist Youth League.

**Paragraph 4**

## The First United Front

In January, 1924, Sun Yat-sen had officially proclaimed an alliance between the Kuomintang and the Communists, and a plan for a military expedition to unify China and destroy the warlords. In October, shortly after he arrived back from Europe, Zhou Enlai was appointed director of the political department at the Whampoa Military Academy in Guangzhou.

Zhou soon realized the Kuomintang was riddled with intrigue. The powerful right wing of the Kuomintang was bitterly opposed to the Communist alliance. Zhou was convinced that the CCP, in order to survive must have an army of its own. He and his friend Nie Rongzhen set about to organize a nucleus of officer cadets who were CCP members and who would follow the principles of Marx.

On August 8 1925, he and Deng Yingchao were finally married. The couple remained childless, but adopted many orphaned children of "revolutionary martyrs".

After Sun's death the Kuomintang was run by a triumvirate composed of Chiang Kai-shek. In 1926, a state of emergency was declared and curfews were imposed. Zhou had just returned from Shantou and was also detained for 48 hours. On his release he confronted Chiang and accused him of undermining the United Front but failed. Chiang then dismissed all the CCP officers from the First Army. Zhou Enlai was relieved of all his duties associated with the First United front, effectively giving complete control of the United Front to Chiang Kai-shek.

著名政治家
Famous Statesmen

*Paragraph 5*

# 总理之职位与任期
# Premiership

In 1949, with the establishment of the People's Republic of China, Zhou assumed the role of Prime Minister and Minister of Foreign Affairs. In June 1953, he made the five declarations for peace. He headed the Communist Chinese delegation to the Geneva Conference and to the Bandung Conference (1955). In 1958, the post of Minister of Foreign Affairs was passed to Chen Yi but Zhou remained Prime Minister until his death in 1976.

Known as an able diplomat, Zhou was largely responsible for the re-establishment of contacts with the West in the early 1970s. He welcomed US President Richard Nixon to China in February 1972, and signed the Shanghai Communiqué.

Discovering he had cancer, he began to pass many of his responsibilities onto Deng Xiaoping. During the late stages of the Cultural Revolution, Zhou was the target of the Gang of Four's political campaigns.

Many Chinese youths view him as their political idol. Some scholars even believe that Zhou's influences on Chinese youths are even greater than the most famous Chinese leader, Mao. However, There is no doubt that he was fundamentally a believer in the Communist ideal on which modern China was founded.

*Paragraph 6*

# 逝世及各界反应
# Death and Reactions

Zhou was hospitalized in 1974 for bladder cancer, but continued to conduct work from the hospital, with Deng Xiaoping as the First Deputy Premier, handling most of the important State Council matters. Zhou died on the morning of January 8 1976, months before Mao Zedong. Zhou's death brought messages of condolences from many non-aligned states that he affected during his tenure as an effective diplomat and negotiator on the world stage, and many states saw Zhou's death as a terrible loss.

Since his death, a memorial hall has been dedicated to him and his beloved wife in Tianjin, named Tianjin Zhou Enlai Deng Yingchao Memorial Hall, and the issue of national stamps commemorating the 1 year anniversary of his death in 1977, and again in 1998 commemorating his 100th birthday.

## Cultural Links 文化链接

### "我要中国料子"

进北京后,周总理第一次做衣服,选中了"红都"服装店。工作人员介绍:"这是闻名全国的高级服装店。"

周总理笑容满面:"我就是慕名而来的。"

面对工作人员介绍的英国呢料、澳大利亚毛料等各色的外国布料,周总理摇摇头,说:"我要中国料子,无论毛料布料都要国产的。"

这次他做了一套青色粗呢毛料中山服、一套蓝卡其布夹衣和一套灰色平纹布中山装。这几件衣服一直穿到1963年,始终光滑整洁、挺挺括括。

衣服穿了10年仍然挺挺括括,其中当然有奥妙。周总理有两只袖套,办公时必定套在胳膊上,这样就保护臂肘不会磨损得太快。然而,他一天工作长达十七八个小时,天长日久仍不免磨损磨破,于是,便送去"红都"请裁缝织补,一般人是看不出来的。

## Vocabulary 妙词连珠

prominent 卓越的,显著的,突出的
democracy 民主政治,民主主义
prominence 突出,显著,突出物
avow 承认

imperialism 帝国主义,帝制
extinction 消失,消灭,废止
instrumental 仪器的,器械的
merger 合并,归并

# 著名政治家 Famous Statesmen

patriotic 爱国的,有爱国心的
raid 袭击,搜捕
embroil 使卷入,牵连,使纠缠
recruiter 征兵人员,招聘人员
coordinator 协调者,同等的人或物
alliance 联盟,联合
intrigue 阴谋,诡计;密谋,私通
triumvirate 三人执政,三头政治,三头统治

impose 征税,强加,以……欺骗
detain 拘留,留住,阻止
accuse 控告,谴责,非难
undermine 破坏
Gang of Four 四人帮
idol 偶像,崇拜物,幻象
bladder 膀胱,气泡,球胆
condolence 哀悼,吊唁
anniversary 周年纪念

# 3 民族英雄
## National Heroes

## Unit 1  苏武 Su Wu

### Key Sentences
### 流畅精句

1. Su Wu pulled out his dagger and attempted suicide.
   苏武当即欲引刀自杀。
2. The Hun king, out of appreciation of his loyalty, became even more earnest in persuading.
   匈奴王非常欣赏他的气节,更加想让他归顺匈奴。
3. But the badly wounded Su Wu was resolute, despite all manner of Hun threats and temptations.
   然而无论他们如何威逼利诱,身负重伤的苏武始终没有半点动摇。
4. The Hun king eventually sent him into exile to the North Sea (present-day Lake Baikal in eastern Siberia) to herd sheep. He told Su Wu that he was to stay there until the rams produced milk.
   匈奴王没有办法,只好叫他到北海(今西伯利亚贝加尔湖)去放羊,并说等公羊产奶了才放他回去。
5. Su Wu lived off seeds buried by wild rats and always kept his envoy's staff on hand.
   苏武靠挖野鼠所藏的草籽为食,始终拿着表明汉使身份的节杖。

6. When he finally returned to Chang'an in 81 BC, Su Wu, who had left the capital in the prime of his youth, was already an old man with white hair.
   公元前81年,苏武回到了长安,壮年出使的他这时已是白发苍苍。
7. Su Wu has since been celebrated as an exemplar of national loyalty. Temples built in his memory could be found everywhere in the country as late as the Tang Dynasty.
   苏武作为忠于祖国的典型得到了后人永远的崇敬,直到唐代中国各地都还有纪念他的庙宇。

## Wonderful Paragraph
### 精彩片段

**Paragraph 1**

## Mission to Xiongnu
### 出使匈奴

Su Wu (140—60 BC) was a diplomat and statesman during China's Han Dynasty, well-known in Chinese history for his faithfulness to his mission and his empire.

In 100 BC, there was a short-lived détente between long-term adversaries Han and Xiongnu. One year earlier, in 101 BC, there had been a new chanyu who came into power in Xiongnu—Chanyu Qiedihou (且鞮侯), who had expressed interest in peace with Han and who, as a goodwill gesture, had allowed some Han diplomats who had been detained by Xiongnu to return to Han, along with gifts from the chanyu.

In response, in 100 BC, Emperor Wu commissioned Su, then the deputy commander of the imperial guards, to serve as an ambassador to Xiongnu. His deputy was fellow deputy commander Zhang Sheng (张胜), and the third in command was Chang Hui (常惠). However, once they arrived at the Xiongnu chanyu's headquarters, Chanyu Qiedihou was far more arrogant than expected, which angered Zhang. In response, Zhang plotted with two Xiongnu officials, the Prince of Gou and Yu Chang (虞常), to assassinate Chanyu Qiedihou's half-Chinese advisor Wei Lü (卫律) and kidnap the chanyu's mother.

The Prince of Gou and Yu Chang carried out their plot while the chanyu was away on a hunt, but someone alerted the chanyu, who quickly returned and killed the Prince of Gou in battle and captured Yu. Yu admitted to plotting with Zhang. Zhang, alarmed, informed Su, who had been unaware of Zhang's plot. Aware that the chanyu was planning on forcing him to surrender to Xiongnu, Su tried to preserve his dignity by committing suicide with his sword. Chanyu Qiedihou, impressed with Su's heroism, sent messengers to care for Su's recovery, while putting Zhang and Chang under arrest.

*Paragraph 2*

## 流放期间
## Life in Exile

Unable to force Su to surrender, Chanyu Qiedihou decided to try to torture him by starvation, and so put him in a cellar without food and drink. However, for several days, Su survived by consuming wool from his coat and the snow that fell into the cellar. The chanyu was further surprised and thought that the gods were protecting him. The chanyu then exiled him to Lake Baikal and ordered him to tend a flock of rams—telling him that he would be allowed to go home when the rams would produce milk.

During exile, Su often lacked food, as the food supplies coming from the Xiongnu headquarters were not arriving steadily. He often had to resort to eating grass roots and wild rodents. Regardless of the difficulties, however, Su always held onto the imperial staff, and he used it as the shepherd's rod—that the decorative hairs on the staff eventually all fell off.

Twice, during exile, the chanyu sent Li Ling, who had surrendered to Xiongnu after being defeated on the battlefield in 99 BC, to visit Su. The first time, Li informed Su that his two brothers had both been accused of crimes and committed suicide; that his mother had died; and that his wife had remarried. He tried to convince Su to surrender, but Su refused. On the second occasion, Li informed him of Emperor Wu's passing, and Su was so despondent that in mourning that he vomited blood.

*Paragraph 3*

## 重返汉朝
## Return to Han

In 81 BC, Han was again in a détente with Xiongnu, when Han ambassadors inquired of Su's fate. The Xiongnu government claimed that Su had long died. However, Su's old assistant Zhang (Zhang became surrendered) secretly informed the ambassadors of Su's exile, and the ambassadors, under Zhang's suggestion, told then—Chanyu Huyandi that Emperor Zhao had killed a migratory bird while hunting, and that a letter from Su seeking help was found on the bird's foot. Surprised, Chanyu Huyandi admitted that Su was in fact still alive, and recalled him and allowed him to go home. In all, he was in exile for 19 years.

Once Su returned to Han, he was given the position of Director of Colonization (典属国), a high-ranking official post. He remained in that post at least until the early years of Emperor Xuan's reign—late 70s BC.

*Paragraph 4*

## 对中国历史的影响
## Impact on Chinese History

Su was often regarded as the epitome of faithful service in light of great odds and trials. His story was often invoked when acts of great faith or courage were performed by officials. His story, as undetailed as it was in actual history, often became subjects of drama, poetry, and songs throughout Chinese history.

用英语说中国——古今名人
# Introduce China in English—Eminent Persons

## Cultural Links 文化链接

## 李陵与苏武

史载,苏武刚被扣后,匈奴单于曾派汉人李陵去劝降,被苏武断然拒绝。等苏武苦熬19年胜利归汉时,李陵又很羡慕,曾置酒相送,可见李陵的苦闷心情。

在司马迁笔下,除了投降一事外,李陵可以说是个完美的人。司马迁说自己与李陵同在宫中为官,相互间关系一般,志趣也不同,更没有酒桌上的交情。但观其人,讲孝道、守信义,为国家不计生死。正因为李陵不是那种"坏透了"的叛徒,因此,他虽然背负千古骂名,但作为异族人,他生活在匈奴一直到死,他心里的苦楚也就成了后代一些文人的着墨点。于是,他们杜撰了诗文,托名李陵,抒发思国怀乡之情,因此,李陵也博得后世不少人的同情。作为一个悲剧人物,李陵的一生同样值得人们了解。

## Vocabulary 妙词连珠

| | |
|---|---|
| adversary 敌手,对手 | rodent 咬的,嚼的,[动物]啮齿目的,侵蚀性的 |
| chanyu 单于 | |
| detain 拘留,留住 | accuse 控告,谴责,非难 |
| deputy 代理人,代表 | despondent 沮丧的 |
| ambassador 大使 | mourn 哀悼,忧伤,服丧 |
| arrogant 傲慢的,自大的 | vomit 呕吐,呕吐物,催吐剂 |
| plot 小块土地,地区图,图,秘密计划(特指阴谋),(小说的)情节,结构 | migratory 迁移的,流浪的 |
| | odd 奇数的,单数的,单只的,不成对的,临时的,不固定的,带零头,余的 |
| torture 折磨,痛苦,拷问,拷打 | |
| cellar 地窖,地下室,窖,藏酒量 | trial 试验,考验,审讯,审判 |
| exile 放逐,充军,流放,流犯,被放逐者 | invoke 调用 |

# Unit 2  Yang Ye
### 杨业

## Key Sentences
### 流畅精句

1. Yang Ye had made great military contributions to Northern Han, Known as "the Znvincible Yang".
   杨业在北汉时就屡立战功,被称为"杨无敌"。
2. From then on Liao troops would beat a hasty retreat at the mere sight of Yang's banner.
   自此之后,辽军看见杨业的旗帜就仓皇退走。
3. Yang Ye's troops were killed, including his son Yang Yanyu. Yang Ye himself was badly wounded and captured.
   最后,杨业的部队全军覆没,儿子杨延玉战死,他自己也重伤被俘。
4. Yang Ye died in hunger strike on the way to Liao.
   在被押往辽国的路上,杨业绝食而死。
5. Out of their respect for the heroic spirit of Yang Ye, the people of the Liao Dynasty built a temple for him at the place where he died.
   杨业的英雄气概甚至赢得了敌人的尊敬,辽国人民在他死的地方建立了祭祀他的庙宇。
6. His son Yang Yanzhao and grandson Yang wenguang carried on his cause.
   他的儿子杨延昭、孙子杨文广继承他的事业。
7. The heroic deeds of the three generations of the Yang family evolved into stories that have come down to the present day.
   杨业祖孙三代抗辽的事迹被人们敷演成"杨家将"故事,至今在中国民间广为流传。

# Introduce China in English—Eminent Persons

## Wonderful Paragraph
### 精彩片段

**Paragraph 1**

## 杨家将
## Yangjia Jiang

Yangjia Jiang (杨家将; lit. Generals of the Yang Clan) is a series of novels and plays which detail the exploits of the Yang military family over four generations of peace and turmoil during the Song Dynasty. Set during the later years of the Northern Song empire, the stories recount the unflinching loyalty of the Yang family heirs.

**Paragraph 2**

## 历史缘由
## Historical Basis

The History of the Song Dynasty (《宋史》) provides limited detail of the historical Yang family. It is clear, however, that there existed a Northern Han general by the name of Yang Ye (Yang Jiye). Prior to becoming a commissioner of the military, he was known for his tactical prowess and unmatched gallantry on the battlefield. When the Northern Han was engulfed by the Song armies, Yang Ye was conscripted by Emperor Taizong of Song, and was charged with the defense of the Northern borders against the Khitans. He had previously won an engagement against the Khitans during the Yan Men Campaign, and as a result, the Khitan armies now trembled at the mere sight of the capable general. However, higher court officials became envious of his stature and soon began their plot against him.

In the year 986 (Third Year of the Yongxi Reign of the Taizong Emperor), Song armies underwent a massive expedition to the Northern frontier. Yang Ye was the vice-commander under Pan Mei, and together, they secured the four regions of Yun, Ying, Huan, and Shuo. Meanwhile, the forces led by Cao Bin, another Song general, were routed, and both Yang Ye and Pan Mei were forced to evacuate the peoples of the four regions. As Yang Ye escorted the populace to safer locales, he and his men were ambushed by a sizable Khitan force. Knowing full well that the chance of victory was slim, Pan Mei nevertheless ordered Yang Ye to initiate the counter-offensive, and the battle raged on until at last they were driven into Chen Jia Gu. Although Pan Mei had promised reinforcements there, Yang Ye and his men instead came across a deserted valley, and within days he and his soldiers (including his son Yang Yanyu) were completed wiped out. Yang Ye himself was captured by the Khitans and died three days later of hunger strike.

## Cultural Links 文化链接

### 杨家将的民族精神影响后人

杨家将一代接一代地为保卫祖国恪尽职守的事迹不断走入传说、故事、戏曲舞台和影视剧创作。北宋著名文学家欧阳修,称赞杨业、杨延昭"父子皆名将,其智勇号称无敌,至今天下之士至于里儿野竖,皆能道之。"宋元之际,民间艺人把杨家将的故事编成戏曲,搬上舞台。到了明代,民间文学家又把他们的故事编成《杨家将演义》、《杨家将传》,用小说评书的形式在社会民间广泛传播。这些传说和故事,把杨家将英勇战斗、牺牲的过程,叙述得十分详细和感人。他们还把宋代功臣潘美描绘成大奸臣做陪衬,使杨家将的英雄形象和崇高家风更加高大和完美。七郎八虎闯幽州、血战金沙滩、穆桂英挂帅、杨门女将、十二寡妇征西、佘太君百岁挂帅、杨排风……一个个栩栩如生的爱国者形象,在世间广为流传,家喻户晓,尽人皆知,以至分不清哪些是史实,哪些是演义和传说。

# 用英语说中国——古今名人
## Introduce China in English—Eminent Persons

## Vocabulary 妙词连珠

turmoil 骚动,混乱
recount 叙述
prior 优先的,在前的;预先
tactical 战术的
prowess 威力
gallantry 勇敢
engulf 卷入,吞没,狼吞虎咽
conscript 被征入伍的士兵;征募
Khitan 契丹
engagement 约会,婚约,诺言,交战,接站,雇拥,[机]接合
tremble 战栗,颤抖
envious 嫉妒的,羡慕的
stature 身高,身材,(精神,道德等的)高度
locale 现场,场所

massive 厚重的,大块的,魁伟的,结实的
expedition 远征,探险队,迅速,派遣
evacuate 疏散,撤出,排泄
escort 护卫(队),护送,陪同(人员),护卫队
ambush 埋伏,伏兵
sizable 相当大的,大小相当的
initiate 开始,发动,传授
reinforcement 增援,加强,加固,援军
deserted 荒芜的,荒废的,为人所弃的
unflinching loyalty 尽忠报国
commissioner 政府中部门长官

# Unit 3  Yue Fei 岳飞

## Key Sentences 流畅精句

1. Yue Fei was a patriotic military commander of the southern Song Dynasty and a national hero in resisting the invading Jin people.
   岳飞是南宋时期著名军事家,也是一位抗金英雄。
2. As a young man, he was diligent and adept in wushu skills.
   他年轻的时候勤奋好学,精习武术。
3. Therefore, Yue Fei's mother lighted joss sticks and candles in front of the sacred ancestral temple, wishing to tattoo the characters "serving the motherland with selfless loyalty" on the back of Yue Fei.
   于是,岳母在神圣家庙之前焚香点烛,要在岳飞背上刺下"精忠报国"。
4. This story has become a classic piece of teaching material for the later generations to eulogize patriotism.
   这个故事已成为后世爱国主义的经典教材。
5. During the Second World War, the evocation of this ancient hero encouraged hundreds of thousands of Chinese troops and civilians in their fight against Japaness invaders.
   在第二次世界大战期间,作为民族英雄的岳飞是鼓舞千千万万军民抗日的斗志。
6. Born into a peasant family, Yue Fei joined the army as an ordinary soldier. By rendering meritorious service, he gradually rose to be the most important general of his time.
   岳飞出身农家,靠军功从一名普通的士兵逐步成长为当时最重要的将领。

## Wonderful Paragraph 精彩片段

### Paragraph 1

# B 出生及早年生涯
# irth and Early Life

He was born into a poor tenant farmer's family. His family village, Yue Village, was located in Tangyin County, Anyang Prefecture, Henan Province.

As a child, Yue Fei learned military strategy from reading Sun Tzu's "Art of War"（孙子兵法）every night before he went to bed. This knowledge would help him later in life as a Song general.

### Paragraph 2

# M 练兵之道
# artial Training

His first martial teacher was a then-famous spear and sword master from the same county named Chen Guang（陈广）. He began teaching Yue Fei spearplay when the boy was 11 years old. However, the book E Wang Shi（鄂王事）, by Sun Qiu（孙遘）, states Chen Guang was hired by Yue Fei's maternal grandfather, Yao Daweng（姚大翁）, when the boy reached the Conferring Hat period of his life. His second martial teacher was the archer Zhou Tong, who taught Yue Fei archery.

Becoming proficient in warfare at an early age, Yue Fei narrowly escaped execution after killing Cai Gui（蔡桂）, the "Prince of Liang", in the martial arts tournament of the Imperial Military Exams.

### Paragraph 3

# M 战功卓越
# ilitary Record

Yue Fei did not join the army until 1122, but he quickly rose through the ranks to become a general in only six years. As a valiant and tactically astute general, Yue Fei led many successful campaigns against the forces of the Jin Dynasty. Taking advantage of the difficulties which his opponents' cavalry experienced in the hilly terrain of Southern China, he was able to score victories although his troops were frequently outnumbered. His forces succeeded in regaining territory south of the Yangtze and Huai Rivers. He was also known for his strict discipline of his legions, forbidding them to pillage, even when facing the harshest of conditions. In all, Yue Fei participated in 126 battles and won them all.

**Paragraph 4**

## M武术artial Arts

Yue Fei created his own fighting form with a spear, famously known as Yuejia qiang(岳家枪), and all soldiers trained in it.

Several other martial arts have been attributed to Yue Fei, including Yuejia quan (Yue Family Boxing), Wuji quan (Emptiness Boxing), Ying Jow Pai (Eagle Claw), Xingyi quan (Form-Will Boxing), Fanzi quan (Tumbling Boxing), and Chuojiao quan (Feet-Poking Boxing), among others.

**Paragraph 5**

## P诗篇oetry

He was a role model for followers of Confucian ideals and moral values, as well as being an accomplished martial artist and poet.

At the age of 30, Yue Fei wrote his most famous poem, Manjiang Hong(满江红). This poem reflects the raw hatred he felt towards the Jin, as well as the sorrow he felt when his efforts to recoup northern lands lost to the Jin were halted by Southern Song officials of the "Peace Faction".

## Paragraph 6

## D 岳飞之死
eath

In 1126, several years before Yue Fei became a general, the militant Jurchen of the Jin Dynasty invaded the north of the country forcing the Song out of their capital Kaifeng and capturing the emperor of the time Emperor Qinzong who was sent into captivity in Manchuria. This marked the end of the Northern Song, and the beginning of the Southern Song Dynasty under Emperor Gaozong.

Yue Fei fought a long campaign against the invading Jurchen in an effort to retake the north of the country. Just when he was threatening to attack and retake Kaifeng, corrupt officials advised Emperor Gaozong to recall Yue Fei to the capital and sue for peace with the Jurchen. Fearing that a defeat at Kaifeng may cause the Jurchen to release Qinzong, threatening his claim to the throne, the emperor followed their advice. Yue Fei was ordered to return twelve times in the form of twelve gold plaques. Knowing that a success at Kaifeng could lead to internal strife Yue Fei submitted to the orders of his emperor and returned to the capital where he was imprisoned and where the traitor Qin Hui (秦桧) would eventually arrange for him to be executed on false charges.

## Paragraph 7

## K 秦桧跪像
neeling Iron Statues

Qin Hui could not find a reason to execute the captured Yue Fei and was about to release him. However, Qin Hui's wife, Lady Wang (王氏), made the suggestion that since the emperor held absolute power, Qin Hui having the authority of the emperor, needed no reason to execute Yue Fei. He and his adopted-son, Yue Yun (岳云) (1119-1142), were sentenced to death and executed on charges that were not proven but instead "could be true" (莫须有). The phrase has entered the Chinese language as an expression to refer to fabricated charges. For their part in Yue Fei's death, iron statues of Qin Hui, Lady Wang, and two of Qin Hui's subordinates, Moqi Xie (万俟卨) and Zhang Jun (张浚), were made to kneel before Yue Fei's tomb (located by Hangzhou's West Lake). For centuries, these statues have been cursed, spat and urinated upon by young and old.

## Cultural Links 文化链接

### 岳王庙前的联中绝唱

西子湖畔的岳王庙前,树立着这样一副动人心魄的对联,在意境上堪称一绝:

上联:青山有幸埋忠骨;

下联:白铁无辜铸佞臣。

据记载,南宋为岳飞建庙时,并无此联,是后世一位祭奠者,松江县一女子徐氏,触景生情,一挥而就的,流传至今。

该联对仗工整,落笔不在形——不去刻画秦桧一党跪像的丑态;而在意——以周围情景行文,宛若天然之笔,意境与人们的心境融为一体。难怪清朝文坛巨匠纪晓岚看到后,赞不绝口。后来他也构思出一联:

上联:报国精忠,三字狱冤千古白;

下联:仰天长啸,一曲词唱满江红。

## Vocabulary 妙词连珠

| | |
|---|---|
| tenant 承租人,房客,租客 | proficient 精通 |
| spearplay 枪术 | execution 实行,完成,执行,死刑,制作(武器等的)破坏效果,杀伤力 |
| maternal 母亲的,似母亲的,母性的 | |
| Conferring Hat 及冠(古代15岁—20岁称为及冠) | tournament 比赛,锦标赛,联赛 |
| archery 箭术 | valiant 勇敢的,英勇的 |

tactically 战术的
astute 机敏的,狡猾的
cavalry 骑兵
terrain 地形
pillage 掠夺
harsh 粗糙的,荒芜的,苛刻的,刺耳的,刺目的
hatred 憎恨,乱意,仇恨
halt 停止,暂停,中断
militant 好战的,积极从事或支持使用武力的

corrupt 腐败的,贪污的,被破坏的,混浊的,(语法)误用的
plague 瘟疫,麻烦,苦恼,灾祸
strife 斗争,冲突,竞争
fabricated 制作,构成,捏造,伪造,虚构
subordinate 次要的,从属的,下级的
urinate 小便,撒尿

民族英雄
National Heroes

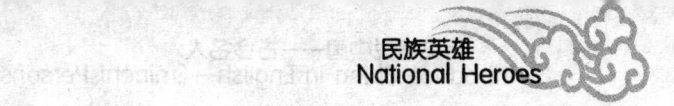

# Unit 4  文天祥 Wen Tianxiang

## Key Sentences 流畅精句

1. Wen Tianxiang, a loyal minister appeared at the time when the Southern Song Dynasty was collapsing.
   文天祥是南宋灭亡之际涌现出的一位忠臣烈士。
2. In the 15th year of Zhiyuan Reign of the Yuan Dynasty (1278 A.D.), Wen Tianxiang was captured in upoling.
   至元十五年(公元 1278 年),文天祥在广东五坡岭不幸被俘。
3. When passing through Lingdingyang, a place outside the mouth of the Zhujiang River, Wen Tianxiang composed the widely-read poem with mixed feelings.
   路过珠江口外的零丁洋时,文天祥百感交集,挥笔写下了传颂千古的(《过零丁洋》)诗。
4. The Yuan Dynasty could conquer the Song Dynasty that had lasted for 300 years and built great empire, but it could not conquer Wen Tianxiang's loyalty to the Song Dynasty.
   元朝可以征服一个历时 300 年的宋王朝,也能建立一个空前绝后的大帝国,却征服不了文天祥对宋朝的忠贞。
5. For over a thousand years, Wen Tianxiang's great spirit has inspired generations of Chinese people to fight unyieldingly for their own country.
   千百年来,文天祥的浩然正气,鼓舞着一代代志士仁人为国家、为民族,进行着不屈的斗争。

6. In January 1283, Wen Tianxiang died a heroic death at the Chaishi execution ground in Dadu.
1283年1月，文天祥在大都柴市刑场英勇就义。

## Wonderful Paragraph
精彩片段

**Paragraph 1**

# Wen Tianxiang
文天祥

Wen Tianxiang (Wade-Giles: Wen Tien-hsiang, 1236 —1283), also Man Tin Cheung, Duke of Xingguo, "The Song Dynasty's Top Ranking Scholar and Prime Minister, the West River's Filial Son and Loyal Subject."

Wen Tianxiang is considered one of the most famous symbols of loyalty and patriotism in China. His writings on righteousness are still widely taught in schools today.

Wen was born in 1236 in Luling (Ji'an), Jiangxi Province during the Song Dynasty. In 1256 he was the top scholar in the imperial examinations and eventually achieved the rank of Prime Minister.

In 1278, Wen was captured by the invading Yuan armies of Kublai Khan, "offered" a Yuan post, and ordered to convince the remaining Song forces to surrender. Wen refused both and suffered for 4 years in a military prison before his execution in 1283. During this time he wrote the famous classics "Song of Righteousness" (正气歌), and "Passing Lingdingyang" (过零丁洋).

**Paragraph 2**

# Wen Tianxiang Monuments
文天祥纪念堂

**Jiangxi**

Wen Tianxiang's hometown in Ji'an, Jiangxi honors the famous national hero with a mausoleum. Exhibitions of paintings, calligraphy, and even army uniforms supposedly left by Wen are displayed in the Wen Family Ancestral Temple in Futian. The Wen Tianxiang Mausoleum is located in Wohushan.

**Beijing**

The Memorial to Prime Minister Wen Tianxiang was built in 1376 during the reign of the Ming Emperor Hongwu. The location of Wen's execution is thought to be near the entrance to Fuxue Alley in the East City District of Beijing and a memorial has been established on the northern side of the entrance to South Fuxue Alley near Beixinqiao.

"The Song Dynasty's Top Ranking Scholar and Prime Minister, the West River's Filial Son and Loyal Subject," is carved into the columns of the memorial's main hall.

**Hong Kong**

The San Tin village in the New Territories of Hong Kong, have many surnamed "Wen" ("Man" in Cantonese). The "Wen" villagers trace their ancestry to Wen Tianxiang via Wen Tianshui (Man Tin-Sui), also a famous Song Dynasty general and the cousin of Wen Tianxiang.

A Wen Tianxiang Memorial Park and "Wen" ancestral hall and residences (Tai Fu Tai) in San Tin is a popular historical attraction in Hong Kong.

## Cultural Links
文化链接

## 留取丹心照汗青

文天祥死后留下了大量诗文,其中如《过零丁洋》中的"人生自古谁无死,留取丹心照汗青";狱中所作的《正气歌》以及死后从其衣带中发现的"衣带诏"(孔曰"成仁",孟曰"取义",惟其义尽,所以仁至,读圣贤书,所学何事?而今而后,庶几无愧)都已成为光照日月、气壮山河的绝唱,成为民族精神财富的宝贵部分。文天祥也因此成为永垂不朽的民族英雄。

# 用英语说中国——古今名人
## Introduce China in English—Eminent Persons

### Vocabulary
### 妙词连珠

| | |
|---|---|
| righteousness 正当, 正义, 正直 | mausoleum 陵墓 |
| assertion 主张, 断言, 声明 | ancestral 祖先的, 祖传的 |
| lineage 血统, 世系 | column 圆柱, 柱状物, 专栏, 纵队 |
| dialect 方言, 语调 | memorial 纪念物, 纪念馆, 纪念仪式, 请愿书 |
| monument 纪念碑 | |

# Unit 5　戚继光　Qi Jiguang

## Key Sentences　流畅精句

1. In the Ming Dynasty, many frustrated Japanese warriors and pirates organized themselves into groups and made harassment at the coastal areas in southeast China.
   明朝时,日本许多失意的武士和浪人组成海盗集团,骚扰中国东南沿海一带。

2. During Jiajing years, the frontier defense was weak and the Wokou grew increasingly rampant.
   嘉靖年间,明朝边备废弛,倭寇日趋猖獗。

3. Qi Jiguang was transferred to the eastern part of Zhejiang Province to guard against Japanese aggressors.
   戚继光被调到浙东防倭。

4. He recruited a group of miners and peasants at Jinhua, gave them hard training and formed a new army named General Qi's Army.
   他招募一批矿工、农民,在金华严格训练,组成一支新军,号称"戚家军"。

5. General Qi's Army had strict discipline and were brave in battle, so they won the support of the people.
   "戚家军"纪律严明,作战勇敢,深得人民拥护。

6. Qi Jiguang created a battle foundation called the mandarin duck foundation in which long weapons and short weapons were used cooperatively.
   戚继光研究出一种长短兵器互相配合的阵法,叫做"鸳鸯阵"。

7. General Qi's Army fought nine battles against them and won a complete victory.

戚家军与倭寇展开激战，九战九捷，大获全胜。

## Wonderful Paragraph
## 精彩片段

**Paragraph 1**

# 早年生涯
# Early Life

Qi Jiguang (1528—1588) was a Chinese military general and national hero during the Ming Dynasty. He was best remembered for his courage and leadership in the fight against Japanese pirates along the east coast of China, as well as his reinforcement work on the Great Wall of China.

Qi Jiguang was born in the town of Luqiao (鲁桥) in Shandong province to a family with a long military tradition. His forefather served as a military leader under Zhu Yuanzhang and died in battle.

Qi Jiguang's father, Qi Jingtong (戚景通), was an honest and upright man. He cultivated in his son a yearning for knowledge as well as a firm set of morals. When his father died, Qi Jiguang took over the acommandership of Dengzhou Garrison at the age of seventeen. Besides building up naval defense at the garrison, he also had to lead his troops to help in the defense of Jizhou (苏州), against East Mongolian raiders during spring time from 1548 to 1552.

At twenty-two, Qi Jiguang headed for Beijing to take part in the martial arts section of the imperial examination. During this time, East Mongolian troops led by Altan Khan broke through the northern defense and laid siege on Beijing. Candidates participating in the martial arts exam were also mobilized to defend the capital. Qi Jiguang displayed extraordinary valor and military ingenuity during the battle, which eventually saw the defeat of the invaders.

民族英雄
National Heroes

**Paragraph 2**

# 抗倭之战
# Battles Against Japanese Pirates

In the fall of 1555, Qi Jiguang was sent to Zhejiang, where the Japanese pirates colluded with their Chinese counterparts and expanded their forces. Together with two other renowned generals of his time, Yu Dayou and Tan Lun(谭纶), Qi Jiguang led the Ming soldiers to a decisive victory at Cengang (岑港) in 1558. Henceafter, his troops continued to deal fatal blows to the pirates at Taozhu (桃渚), Haimen Garrison (海门卫) and Taizhou(台州).

With the situation in Zhejiang under control, Qi Jiguang began to concentrate on training a disciplined and effective army. He drafted mainly miners and farmers from the county of Yiwu because he believed these people to be honest and hardworking.

The first trial for Qi Jiguang's new army came in 1559. After a month-long battle with Japanese pirates in the Taizhou Prefecture, with the pirates suffering over five thousand casualties, Qi Jiguang's army established a name for itself among both the people of Zhejiang and its enemies.

Partly as a result of Qi Jiguang's military success in Zhejiang, pirate activities surged in the province of Fujian. More than ten thousand pirates had established strongholds along the coast from Fu'an (福安) in the north to Zhangzhou in the south. In July 1562, Qi Jiguang led six thousand elite troops south into Fujian. Within two months, his army eradicated three major lairs of Japanese pirates at Hengyu, Niutian (牛田) and Lindun (林墩).

However, his own army also suffered significant losses to fighting and diseases. Seeing the pirate infestation in Fujian subdued, Qi Jiguang then returned to Zhejiang to regroup his force. The Japanese pirates took the opportunity to invade Fujian again, this time succeeding in conquering Xinghua (兴化) (present day Putian). In April 1563, Qi Jiguang led ten thousand troops into Fujian and regained Xinghua. Over the next year, a series of victories by Qi Jiguang's army finally saw the pirate problem in Fujian fully resolved.

A final major battle against Japanese pirates was fought on the island of Nan'ao（南澳）, which lies near the boundary between the provinces of Fujian and Guangdong, in September 1565. There Qi Jiguang joined arms with his old comrade Yu Dayou again to defeat the remnant of the combined Japanese and Chinese pirate force.

> Paragraph 3

## Y 北成边关 ears on the Northern Frontier

With the pirate situation along the coast under control, Qi Jiguang was called to Beijing in late 1567 to take charge of training troops for the imperial guards. In the next year, he was given command of the troops in Jizhou to defend against the Mongols. Qi Jiguang soon began the repair work on the segment of the Great Wall between Shanhai Pass（山海关）and Juyong Pass（居庸关）. Meanwhile, he also directed the construction of watchtowers along the wall. After two years of hard work, more than a thousand watchtowers were completed, giving the defensive capability in the north a great boost.

> Paragraph 4

## A 成就 chievements

Qi Jiguang was mostly credited with cleaning the Southeast China coast off Wokou Raid. Althought he isn't the only general that contributed to the effort, many historians regarded as the one that contribued the most. It is also in his lifetime, did the historians called the end of Wokou era.

**Wodao**

Qi Jiguang equipped his militia with the Japanese katana, which the Chinese called Wodao. The Wodao will continued as the main weapon used by Chinese soldiers in the Ming era.

## Books by Qi Jiguang

Not only was Qi Jiguang a brilliant general, he also left behind his invaluable practical experience in the form of two books on military strategy—Ji Xiao Xin Shu and Record of Military Training. He also wrote a great number of poems and proses, which he compiled into the Collection of Zhizhi Hall (止止堂集), named after his study hall during his office in Jizhou.

Qi Jiguang also conducted a month-long military exercise involving more than 100 000 troops in winter 1572. From the experience of the maneuver he wrote Records of Military Training, which became an invaluable reference for military leaders after him. Over the sixteen years when Qi Jiguang was in Jizhou, not a single Mongolian raider crossed to the south of the Great Wall.

In early 1583, Qi Jiguang was relieved of his duty on the northern frontier and assigned an idle post in Guangdong. His already ill health worsened in the next two years, forcing him to retire to his hometown. He finally died in 1588, days before the Lunar New Year.

## Guang Bing

According to legends, a kind of hard pancake called guang bing (光饼) which is still widely consumed in Fujian province today was named after Qi Jiguang. When Qi Jiguang led his troops into Fujian in 1562, the Japanese pirates, fearing his name, engaged mainly in guerrilla-style battles. To enable Qi Jiguang's troops to march for days in pursuit of the enemy, the people of Fujian baked for them many disc-shaped cakes roughly the size of a palm. In the center of these cakes holes were made so that they could be strung together to be conveniently carried along. Later, to commemorate Qi Jiguang's victory against the pirate raiders, the cakes were named guang bing.

用英语说中国——古今名人
Introduce China in English—Eminent Persons

## Cultural Links 文化链接

### 威名远播的戚家军

公元1557年,为对付入侵浙江沿海的倭寇,明嘉靖帝命时任山东登州卫都指挥佥事的戚继光,调任浙江都司充参将,负责抗倭斗争。戚继光到达浙江后,第一件事就是着手训练一支新军。

1559年,他亲自到金华、义乌等地招募3 000新兵,他严格选兵,并严格教育,教导士兵"正心术,立志向"、"以保民为职"。要求遵守纪律,服从节制;严格训练,只练实用的搏击技巧,教以击刺法。将这支队伍训练成纪律严明,能征善战的"戚家军"。

在战斗中,戚家军先以火器、弓箭作掩护,敌人进入百步之内发火器,进入六十步内发弓箭,敌人再进,便用"鸳鸯阵"冲杀。"鸳鸯阵"是一种戚继光独创的和倭寇进行短距离肉搏的战斗组合。此阵运用灵活机动,正好抑制住了倭寇优势的发挥。戚继光率领"戚家军",经过"鸳鸯阵"法的演练后,在与倭寇的作战中,每战皆捷。

## Vocabulary 妙词连珠

reinforcement 增援,加强,加固,援军
upright 垂直的,竖式的,正直的
garrison 卫戍部队,驻军,卫戍地,要塞
siege 包围,围城,长期努力,不断袭击,围攻击
mobilize 动员
valor 英勇,勇猛
pirate 海盗,盗印者,盗版者,侵犯专利权者

collude 串通,勾结,共谋
henceafter 自此以后,今后
casualty 伤亡
elite <法>[集合名词]精华,精锐,中坚分子
eradicate 根除
lair 窝
subdued 屈服的,被抑制的,柔和的,减弱的
remnant 残余,剩作,零料,残迹
segment 段,节,片断

# National Heroes 民族英雄

infestation(害虫,盗贼等)群袭,出没,横行
militia 民兵
prose 散文
maneuver 机动
worsen (使)变得更坏,恶化,损害
commemorate 纪念

# Unit 6　Shi Kefa
## 史可法

## Key Sentences
## 流畅精句

1. Firmly determined to restore the Ming Dynasty, Shi Kefa became a thorn in the side of the other officials in the court.
   一心恢复明朝的大臣史可法在朝廷上遭到排挤。
2. As a commander, Shi Kefa had the support and respect of his subordinates as he shared all hardships with soldiers.
   作为将领,一向与士卒同甘苦的史可法深得士兵的拥戴。
3. While a prisoner, Shi Kefa refused to surrender despite the repeated attempts at persuasion by the Qing troops, and he was eventually killed.
   入狱后,清军百计劝降,史可法始终不屈,最终慷慨就义。
4. The Qing troops soaked Yangzhou in blood, killing hundreds of thousands of its citizens and turning it into a ghost city.
   清军在扬州进行了报复性屠杀,数十万居民被害,富庶的扬州因此变成了一座空城。
5. After his death, Shi Kefa became a rallying cry for anti-Qing campaigns.
   虽死犹生的史可法成为抗清的一面旗帜。
6. The Ming power in Nanjing collapsed soon after the death of Shi Kefa, but people in other parts of the country carried on the anti-Qing struggle for many years.
   南京的明朝政权在史可法死后随后覆亡,但各地人民反抗清朝的斗争仍然此起彼伏。

民族英雄
National Heroes

## Wonderful Paragraph
精彩片段

### Paragraph 1

# Shi Kefa
## 史可法

Shi Kefa (1601—1650) was a Ming general, who in the last days of the Ming dynasty gave his life resisting the advancing Qing armies. The victorious Qing subsequently raised a memorial to him in recognition of his courage.

Shi Kefa was 44 years old when he was put in charge of the doomed city of Yangzhou. At the time, the Ming Empire was already beginning to collapse and the Ming soldiers had lost their will to fight. However, Shi Kefa was still able to convince his men that a defense of the city was possible. The Manchurians under Prince Dodo (多铎) tried to lay siege to the walls of Yangchow repeatedly, but with little success. Shi Kefa had trained his men to use European rifles (designed by the Jesuits), and dealt heavy blows on the Manchurians. It was said that the casualties were so high that the corpses of the fallen Manchu army reached the height of the city's wall. In fact, this was supposedly how the Manchurians finally breached the wall of the city, by climbing over the dead corpses of their comrades. As the Manchurians scaled the city wall, the weakened Ming troops, low on morale, made no effort to fight or run. Shi Kefa, much saddened by the weakness of his countrymen, ordered his officers to behead him. However, they could not bring themselves to kill such a hero. He was soon captured by the Manchurians and brought to trial before the Manchu commander, Prince Dodo.

Prince Dodo, much impressed by Shi Kefa's loyalty as a general and his brilliant strategies fending off the Manchurians with a doomed army, stated "You have done your duty, general; now I will glady grant you a post." (前以书谒请,而先生不从。今忠义既成,当畀重任,为我收拾江

南。)However, Shi Kefa refused to abandon the great Ming dynasty, wishing rather to commit suicide and vanish along with it. Dodo continued trying to persuade Shi Kefa to join his side for several weeks, but was not successful. Thus, Shi Kefa was granted his wish to die along with his beloved dynasty.

The Shi Kefa Memorial, a temple devoted to the memory of the local hero, is located in Yangzhou.

## Cultural Links
### 文化链接

## 史可法与扬州十日

扬州是江南顽强抵抗清军的第一座城,也是清军入关以来首次遇到的军民一体的坚强抵抗。为了对扬州人民进行报复,于是多铎下令,烧杀抢掠持续十天。历史上把这件惨案称作"扬州十日"。

大屠杀之后,史可法的养子史德威进城寻找史可法的遗体。由于当时天气较热,尸体已经腐烂,无法辨认。史德威只好把史可法生前穿过的袍子和用过的笏板,埋葬在扬州城外的梅花岭上。这就是到现在还保存的史可法"衣冠墓"。乾隆四十一年(1776年)正月追谥"忠正"。因此牌坊上题额为"史忠正公墓"。

## Vocabulary
### 妙词连珠

| | |
|---|---|
| subsequently 后来,随后 | siege 包围,围城,长期努力,不断袭击,围攻 |
| recognition 赞誉,承认,重视野,公认,赏识,识别 | casualty 伤亡 |
| doomed 命定的 | breach 违背,破坏,破裂,裂口 |
| manchurian 中国东北人 | sadden 悲哀 |

# Unit 7 郑成功 Zheng Chenggong

## Key Sentences
流畅精句

1. After attempting in vain to dissuade his father, Zheng Chenggong raised the banner of "disobeying my father for the sake of my country."
   苦劝父亲未果,于是郑成功举起"背父救国"的大旗。
2. Taiwan had been Chinese territory from ancient times.
   台湾自古就是中国领土。
3. The Dutch invaded the island in 1624 and subsequently turned it into their colony. They built Taiwan city (present-day Anping) the same year and Chiqian city (present-day Tainan) the following year.
   1624年,荷兰人侵入台湾,开始了在台湾的殖民统治。他们修筑了台湾城(在今台湾安平),次年又修筑了赤嵌城(在今台湾台南)。
4. Zheng Chenggong's army landed in Taiwan at the end of the 4th month of 1661.
   1661年4月底,郑成功的部队在台湾登陆。
5. On the 1st day of the 2nd month of 1662, the desperate Dutch were forced to sign a treaty of surrender. Taiwan was returned to the motherland.
   1662年2月1日,面临绝境的荷兰人被迫签字投降,台湾重新回到了祖国的怀抱。
6. Zheng Chenggong died not long after he retook Taiwan, in his prime at 39.
   郑成功在收复台湾之后不久即因病去世,年仅39岁。

# Wonderful Paragraph
精彩片段

### Paragraph 1

## 国姓爷及其童年
## Koxinga and His Childhood

Koxinga（国姓爷）is the popular name of Zheng Chenggong（Wade-Giles）Cheng Ch'eng-kung; Cheng Kung）(1624-1662), who was a List of famous military commanders at the end of the Ming Dynasty. He was a prominent leader of the anti-Qing movement opposing the Manchu Qing Dynasty, and a Han Chinese general who seized Taiwan from Netherlands colonial rule in 1661.

Koxinga was born to Zheng Zhilong（郑芝龙）, a Chinese merchant and pirate in 1624. He was raised there until seven and moved to Quanzhou, in the Fujian province of China. He studied at Nanjing Taixue (The Imperial Central College in Ming dynasty of China) when he was young. He is still known in Japan by his birth name as Tei Seikō, or by his popular name as Kokusen'ya.

### Paragraph 2

## 明朝忠良
## Loyalty to the Ming Empire

Beijing fell in 1644 to rebels led by Li Zicheng, and the last emperor Chongzhen of China hanged himself on a tree at modern-day Jingshan Park in Beijing. Aided by Wu Sangui, Manchurian armies knocked off the rebels with ease and took the city. In the district below the Chang Jiang, there were many anti-Qing people of principle and ambition who wanted to restore descendants of the Ming Dynasty to the Imperial throne. One of these descendants, Prince Tang, was aided to gain power in Fuzhou by Huang Daozhou and Zheng Zhilong, Koxinga's father. When the Qing captured Prince Tang, Koxinga was in Zhangzhou raising soldiers and supplies. He heard the news that his father was preparing to surrender to the Qing court and hurried to Quanzhou to persuade him against this plan, but his father refused to listen and turned himself in.

## Paragraph 3

### 母亲之死
### Death of His Mother

Not long afterwards the Qing army captured Quanzhou, and Koxinga's mother either committed suicide out of loyalty to the Ming Dynasty or was raped and killed by Qing troops. When Koxinga heard this news he led an army to attack Quanzhou, forcing the Qing troops back. After giving his mother a proper burial Koxinga proceeded to assemble a group of comrades with the same goal who together swore an allegiance to the Ming in defiance of the Qing.

## Paragraph 4

### 与清抗争
### Fighting the Qing

He sent forces to attack the Qing forces in the area of Fujian and Guangdong. While defending Zhangzhou and Quanzhou, he once fought all the way to the walls of the city of Nanjing. But in the end, his forces were no match for the Qing. The Qing court sent a huge army to attack him and many of Koxinga's generals had died in battle, which left him no option but retreat.

## Paragraph 5

### 登陆台湾
### Taiwanese Landing

In 1661, Koxinga led his troops to a landing at Lu'ermen to attack Taiwan. By the end of the year, he had chased out the Dutch, who had controlled Taiwan for 38 years. Koxinga had devoted himself to making Taiwan into an effective base for anti-Qing sympathizers who wanted to restore the

Ming Dynasty to power.

At the age of 39, Koxinga died of malaria. His son, Zheng Jing, succeeded as the King of Taiwan.

### Paragraph 6

## Legacy

There is a temple dedicated to Koxinga and his mother in Tainan County, Taiwan.

He has been considered a national hero by Chinese nationalists both in China because he was a Ming loyalist and an anti-Manchu leader and for his role in expelling the Dutch from Taiwan which Chinese nationalists portray as establishing Chinese rule over the island.

## Cultural Links
文化链接

### 郑成功执法如山

有一次,郑家军的"虎骑亲军"中将领董源欲侮辱一民女,民女不从,董源竟把她抛入江中,活活淹死。民女的父亲告到郑成功的叔父郑鸿达帐前,反被他毒打一顿赶了出去。后来,他听说国姓爷亲到石井督师,特来告状。

事情败漏,董源只好如实招供。他自以为堂姐是郑成功的夫人董氏,国姓爷定会手下留情。谁知郑成功听后怒不可遏:"人命关天,岂能轻赦?宗亲犯法,更难宽容。董源辱杀民女,罪应斩首,以儆效尤;鸿达袒亲违法,罚银30两,以为鉴戒!"郑成功喝令把董源押出去斩首,同时又责令叔父郑鸿达拿出30两银子交给老伯,作其安家度日费用。郑成功握着老伯的手,抱歉地说:"本藩属下军纪不严,有失众望,愧对乡亲!"

老伯忙说:"叩谢国姓爷为民申冤的深恩厚德,只是这日后……"

郑成功站在石台上,威严地对在场的将士们说:"日后,无论是谁,但凡违军法、害黎民,本藩尚方宝剑定然不饶。"说到这里,抽出腰间那柄熠熠闪

光的宝剑,向着巨石猛然劈下,厉声大喝:"斩其头如劈此石!"只听"啪"的一声巨响,巨石被劈成两半。至今,"海上视师"石上,还留着这个裂痕。

## Vocabulary 妙词连珠

| | |
|---|---|
| merchant 商人,批发商,贸易商,店主 | assemble 集合,聚集,装配 |
| aid 帮助,援助,帮助者,有帮助的事物 | swore swear 的过去式 |
| | allegiance 忠贞,效忠 |
| restore 恢复,使回复,归还,交还,修复,重建 | defiance 挑战,蔑视,挑衅 |
| | malaria 疟疾,瘴气 |
| proceed 进行,继续下去,发生 | mandarin 官话,普通话 |

# Unit 8  林则徐 Lin Zexu

## Key Sentences
## 流畅精句

1. In December 1838, Emperor Daoguang appointed Lin Zexu imperial envoy commanding the Guangdong navy to ban on opim-smoking and opium trade in Guangzhou.
   1838年12月,道光皇帝任命林则徐为钦差大臣,节制广东水师,驰往广州查禁鸦片。
2. With the assistance of the patriotic officials and the people of Guangzhou, Lin Zexu issued an order that merchants from Britain, the US and other countries hand over all their opium and stop smuggling opium any longer.
   在广州爱国官员、人民群众的协助下,林则徐严令英美等国商人悉数缴出鸦片,并具结保证,永不夹带鸦片入境。
3. The foreign merchants were forced to surrender 19 000 boxes of opium plus 2 119 sackes, 2 376 254 jin (1 188 127 kilograms) in all.
   外国商人被迫交出鸦片19 000多箱又2 119袋,共2 376 254斤。
4. From June 3 to 25, 1839, Lin Zexu headed officers and civilians to destroy all the surrendered opium before the public in Humen.
   1839年6月3日至25日,林则徐率领沿海官民,在虎门海滩将收缴的鸦片全部当众销毁。
5. The just feat gave the Chinese people great encouragement.
   此次正义壮举大长了中国人的民族志气。

民族英雄
National Heroes

## Wonderful Paragraph
精彩片段

**Paragraph 1**

# Lin Zexu
林则徐

Lin Zexu (1785—1850) was a Chinese scholar and official during the Qing dynasty. He is most famous for his active fight against opium smuggling in Guangzhou, which is usually considered to be the primary catalyst for the First Opium War 1839—1842.

Lin was born in Fuzhou, in the Fujian province. In 1811 he received the Jinshi degree, the highest title in the imperial examinations, and the same year he was appointed to the prestigious Hanlin Academy. He rose rapidly through various grades of provincial service, and became Governor-General of Hunan and Hubei in 1837.

A formidable bureaucrat known for his thoroughness and integrity, Lin was sent to Guangdong to halt the importation of opium by the British prior to the First Opium War (1838). He confiscated more than 20 000 chests of opium already at the port and supervised their destruction. He later blockaded the port from European ships. Lin also wrote a letter to Queen Victoria of Britain warning her that China was adopting a stricter policy towards everyone, Chinese or foreign, who brought opium into China. This letter expressed a desire that Victoria would act "in accordance with decent feeling" and support his efforts. The letter was however never delivered to the queen but was published in The Times. Open hostilities between China and Britain started in 1839.

Lin's failure to secure a decisive victory against the British led to his replacement by Qishan in September 1840. As punishment for his failures, he was demoted and sent to exile in Ili in Xinjiang. However, the Chinese government still considered Lin to be an official of rare virtue, and sent him off to take care of difficult situations. He died in 1850 while on the way to

Guangxi, where the government was sending him to help put down the Taiping Rebellion.

## Cultural Links
## 文化链接

### 林则徐研制戒毒药品

　　林则徐担任湖广总督时,除了严禁鸦片、收缴烟具外,还研究、配制了戒鸦片的药品,同时又慷慨捐出自己薪金制出"戒瘾丸"两千多份,免费发送给一般吸烟的贫民。当时湖北省内,除了官制断瘾丸外,凡是省城各地药铺均有戒烟药出售。

　　林则徐研制的戒烟药有四种,分别为"忌酸丸"、"补正丸"、"四物饮"、"瓜汁饮"。其中"瓜汁饮"最为简易。其制法是:南瓜正在开花时,连花、叶、根、藤一起拔起,用水洗净,放入石臼中捣烂,取汁常服,半个月后,烟瘾即可去掉。这种单方在民间流行后,效果良好。

　　此外,林则徐还邀请一些名医用中药配成"断瘾丸",责令吸食者服用,起到了一定的戒毒作用。有人将"断瘾丸"的配方编成歌诀:"林公断瘾桔红参,米壳覆花炒枣仁。明党半夏炮姜炭,茯苓杞子益智仁。"

## Vocabulary
## 妙词连珠

| | |
|---|---|
| opium 鸦片 | confiscat 没收,充公,查抄,征用 |
| catalyst 催化剂 | destruction blockade 阻塞封锁 |
| prestigious 享有声望的,声望很高的 | demote 使降级,使降职 |
| formidable 强大的,令人敬畏的 | exile 放逐,充军,流放,流犯,被放逐者;放逐,流放 |
| bureaucrat 官僚主义者 | patriot 爱国者 |
| integrity 正直,诚实,完整,完全 | crate 板条箱,柳条箱 |
| halt 停止,暂停,中断;使停止 | commemorat 纪念 |

# 民族英雄
# National Heroes

# Unit 9  孙中山 Sun Yat-sen

## Key Sentences
## 流畅精句

1. In the autumn of 1894, Sun Yat-sen founded the first Chinese bourgeois revolutionary organization, the Reviving China Society (Xing Zhong Hui). The Chiense bourgeois revolutionary group came into being.
   1894年秋，孙中山建立了中国资产阶级第一个革命团体——兴中会，中国资产阶级革命派初步形成。

2. The next year, Sun Yat-sen set the headquarters of the Reviving China Society in Hong Kong.
   次年，孙中山在香港成立兴中会总部。

3. In August 1905, Sun Yat-sen, Huang Xing and the others united the revolutionary organiztions all over the country and founded the Chinese Revolutionary League in Japan, with its headquarters located in Tokyo. Sun Yat-sen was elected head of the league.
   1905年8月，孙中山、黄兴等人将全国的革命团体组织起来，在日本成立了中国同盟会，选举孙中山为同盟会总理，设总部于东京。

4. The Chinese Revoltiounary League took Sun Yat-sen's proposals as its revolutionary objectives—"Drive out invaders, restore China, found a republic and equalize land ownership."
   同盟会以孙中山提出的"驱除鞑虏，恢复中华，建立民国，平均地权"为革命宗旨。

5. On the night of October 10, 1911, inspired by the Literature Society and the Joint Progress Society, the first shot of the revolution was fired in Wuchang.

1911年10月10日晚,在文学社、共进会的组织发动下,武昌城内打响了辛亥革命的第一枪。

6. On December 19, he was elected provisional president by overwhelming majority at the meeting held in Nanjing by delegates from different provinces.

12月19日,在各省代表于南京举行的临时大总统选举中,孙中山以绝对多数当选。

7. On New Year's Day of 1912, Sun Yat-sen assumed office in Nanjing and declared the founding of the provisional government of the Republic of China.

1912年元旦,孙中山在南京就职,宣布中华民国临时政府成立。

8. The Chinese Revolution of 1911 was a great democratic revolutionary movement, which overthrew the rule of the Qing Dynasty and terminated the autocratic monarchy system that had lasted for over 2 000 years.

辛亥革命推翻了清王朝的统治,结束了2 000多年的君主专制制度,是一场伟大的民主革命运动。

## Wonderful Paragraph 精彩片段

**Paragraph 1**

# F"国父"
# ather of the Nation

Sun Yat-sen(孙逸仙)(November 12, 1866—March 12, 1925)was a Chinese revolutionary and political leader who is often referred to as the "father of modern China". Sun played an instrumental and leadership role in the eventual overthrow of the Qing Dynasty in 1911. He was the first provisional president when the Republic of China was founded in 1912. He later co-founded the Kuomintang(KMT)where he served as its first leader.

Sun was a uniting figure in post-imperial China, and remains unique among 20th-century Chinese politicians for being widely revered in both mainland China and Taiwan. On both sides of the Straits he is frequently seen as the father to republican China. In Taiwan, he is known by the title officially given to him, Father of the Nation (国父), as in his posthumous name Father of the Nation, Mr Sun Yat-sen. On the mainland, Sun is also seen as a Chinese nationalist, the "Forerunner of the Revolution" (革命先行者) and "the Father of Modern China". Although Sun is considered one of the greatest leaders of modern China, his political life was one of constant struggle and frequent exile. After the success of the revolution, he quickly fell out of power in the newly-founded Republic of China, and led successive revolutionary governments as a challenge to the warlords who controlled much of the nation. Unfortunately, Sun did not live to see his party bring about consolidation of power over the country. His party, which formed a fragile alliance with the communists, split into two factions after his death. Sun's chief legacy resides in his developing a political philosophy known as the Three Principles of the People (nationalism, civil liberties, and the people's livelihood), which still heavily influences Chinese government today.

## Paragraph 2

## 名字 Names

Like many other Chinese historical figures, Sun Yat-sen used several names throughout his life, and he is known under several of these names, which can be quite confusing for the Westerner. Names, which are not taken lightly in China, are central to Chinese culture. This reverence goes as far back as Confucius and his insistence on using correct names. In addition to the names and aliases listed below, Sun also used many other aliases while he was a revolutionary in exile. According to one study, he used as many as thirty different names.

The "real" name of Sun Yat-sen (the concept of real or original name is not as clear-cut in China as it is in the Western world, as will become obvious below), the name inscribed in the genealogical records of his family, is Sun Deming (孙德明). This "register name" is the name under which his extended relatives of the Sun family would have known him; and it was a name that was used on formal occasions, such as when he got married.

In 1883, Sun was baptized as a Christian, and he started his studies in Hong Kong. On that occasion, he chose himself a pseudonym: Rixin (日新). Later, his professor of Chinese literature changed this pseudonym into Yixian (逸仙). Unlike in Standard Mandarin, pronunciation of both pseudonyms are similar to Yat-sen in the local Cantonese. This was the name that he used in his frequent contacts with Westerners which became his most often used name in the West. However, in the Chinese world, almost nobody uses the Mandarin version Sun Yixian, nor the Cantonese version Sun Yat-sen.

In 1897, Sun arrived in Japan. Desiring to remain hidden from Japanese authorities, he renamed himself Nakayama Shō (中山樵). After his return to China in 1911, the alias Nakayama was transliterated into Zhongshan. Today, the overwhelming majority of Chinese people know Sun under the name Sun Zhongshan. Often it is shortened to Zhongshan only (as is usually done for Chinese names to show respect), and inside China one can find many instances of Zhongshan Avenue, Zhongshan Park, etc.

Another "official" name is Sun Wen (孙文), the "school name" used by Sun Yat-sen when attending school. This is the way he signed his name, especially after the establishment of the Republic of China in 1912. All official documents executed after this date were signed Sun Wen.

## Cultural Links
文化链接

### 孙中山妙联入官府

清朝光绪年间,孙中山留学归来,途经武昌总督府,想见湖广总督张之洞,他递上"学者孙文求见之洞兄"的名片。门卫随即将名片呈上,张之洞一瞧很不高兴,问门卫来者何人？门卫回答是一儒生。张总督令人拿来纸笔写了一行字,叫门卫交给孙中山。孙中山一看,纸上写着:"持三字帖,见一品官,儒生妄敢称兄弟",这分明是一副对联的上联。孙中山微微一笑,对出了下联,又请门卫呈送给张之洞,张之洞看见上书:"行千里路,读万卷书,布衣亦可傲王侯",不觉暗暗吃惊,"呀,儒生不可小视!"于是,急命门卫大开中门,亲自迎接这位才华横溢的孙中山。

## Vocabulary 妙词连珠

instrumental 仪器的,器械的,乐器的
overthrow 推翻,打倒,扔得过远的球
provisional 临时的
KMT 国民党
nationalist 国家主义者,民族主义者
consolidation 巩固,合并
fragile 易碎的,脆的
Three Principles of the People 三民主义
nationalism 民族

civil liberties 民权
the people's livelihood 民生
reverence 尊敬,敬重,敬礼,尊严,威望,尊敬的……阁下
alias 别名,化名
inscribe 记下
genealogical 宗谱的,系谱的,家系的
baptize 给人施洗礼(作为入基督教的标志),洗炼,命名(作为洗礼仪式的一部分)
pseudonym 假名,笔名
transliterate 音译

# 4 著名科学家
## *Famous Scientists*

## Unit 1 蔡伦 Cai Lun

### Key Sentences 流畅精句

1. According to historical records, Cai Lun in the Eastern Han Dynasty was the first person who, using such materials as bark, hards, rugs and old fishnet, made what was to be termed as paper.
   据史书记载,东汉人蔡伦最先发明了以树皮、麻头、破布、旧鱼网等为原料制作的纸。
2. In the Tang Dynasty, the papermaking industry reached its climax.
   到唐代,造纸业达到鼎盛。
3. The popularity of China's papermaking began in the 4th century.
   中国造纸术的外传,是从4世纪开始的。
4. By the middle of the 19th century, China's manual papermaking had been popularized throughout the world, laying asolid foundation in the development of mechanical papermaking.
   至19世纪中叶,中国的手工造纸术已传遍全球,它们为机械造纸术的产生与发展奠定了基础。

著名科学家
Famous Scientists

## Wonderful Paragraph
### 精彩片段

**Paragraph 1**

# Cai Lun 蔡伦

Cai Lun (Wade-Giles: Ts'ai Lun) (c. 50—121), courtesy name Jingzhong (敬仲), was a Chinese eunuch, who is conventionally regarded as the inventor of paper, in forms recognizable in modern times as paper (as opposed to Egyptian papyrus).

He was born in Guiyang during the Eastern Han Dynasty, and became a paperwork secretary (中常侍) of Emperor He. For papermaking, he tried materials like bark, hemp, silk, and even fishing net, but his exact formula has been lost to history. The emperor was pleased with the invention and granted Cai an aristocratic title and great wealth. Later, he became involved in intrigue, as a supporter of Empress Dou. He was involved in the death of her romantic rival, Consort Song. Afterwards, he became an associate of Empress Deng Sui. In 121, after Consort Song's grandson Emperor An assumed power after Empress Deng's death, Cai was ordered to report to prison. Before he was to report, he committed suicide by drinking poison after taking a bath and dressing in fine robes.

While paper is widely used worldwide today, the creator of this extremely important invention is little-known outside East Asia. After Cai invented paper in 105, it immediately became widely used in China. In 751, some Chinese paper makers were captured by Arabs after Tang troops were annihilated in the Battle of Talas River. The techniques of papermaking then spread to the West.

Cai's contribution is considered one of the most important inventions in history, since it enabled China to develop its civilization much faster than with earlier writing materials (primarily bamboo), and it did the same with Europe when it was introduced in the 12th century or the 13th century.

# 用英语说中国——古今名人
# Introduce China in English—Eminent Persons

## Cultural Links 文化链接

### 蔡侯纸

蔡伦从小就到皇宫里去当太监,后被提升为中常侍。他还做过管理宫廷用品的官——尚方令,监督工匠为皇室制造宝剑和其他各种器械,因而经常和工匠们接触。劳动人民的精湛技术和创造精神,给了他很大的影响。

当时,蔡伦看到大家写字很不方便,竹简和木简太笨重,丝帛太贵,丝绵纸不可能大量生产,都有缺点。于是,他总结了前人造纸的经验,带领工匠们用树皮麻头、破布和破鱼网等原料来造纸。他们先把树皮、麻头、破布和破鱼网等东西剪碎或切断,放在水里浸渍相当时间,再捣烂成浆状物,还可能经过蒸煮,然后在席子上摊成薄片,放在太阳底下晒干,这样就变成纸了。

用这种方法造出来的纸,体轻质薄,很适合写字,受到了人们的欢迎。东汉元兴元年(公元 105 年),蔡伦把这个重大的成就报告了汉和帝,汉和帝赞扬了他一番。从此,全国各地都开始用这样的方法造纸,时有"蔡侯纸"之称。

## Vocabulary 妙词连珠

| | |
|---|---|
| eunuch 太监,宦官 | aristocratic 贵族的 |
| papyrus 纸草,草制成之纸 | robe 礼服,制服 |
| bark 树皮 | annihilate 消灭,歼灭 |
| hemp 大麻,纤维 | intrigue 阴谋,诡计 |

# Unit 2  Zhang Heng
张衡

## Key Sentences
流畅精句

1. Zhang Heng was an astronomer in the East Han Dynasty, founder of the ancient Celestial Theory about the structure of the universe.
   张衡是东汉天文学家,中国古代宇宙结构理论"浑天说"的创始人。

2. He makes a record of 2 500 planets visible in central China and the first star chart of the country.
   他记录了中原地区能看到的2 500颗恒星,并且画出了中国第一张完备的星图。

3. Regarding the formation of the lunar eclipses, he makes the correct interpretation that the moon itself does not give light but reflects the light from the sun.
   他正确解释了月食成因:月亮本身不发光,受到太阳的照射才反射出光来。

4. Besides, he invents the world's first automatic astronomical apparatus—a water-powered celestial globe and makes the seismographs for detecting directions of the earthquake and observing meteorological phenomena.
   他还创造了世界上第一架自动的天文仪器——流水转动的浑天仪,创造了测定地震方向的地动仪和观测气象的候风仪。

## Wonderful Paragraph

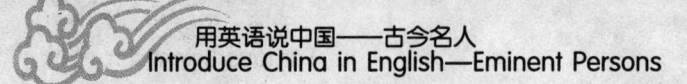

### Paragraph 1

# Zhang Heng
# 张衡

Zhang Heng (78—139), also spelled as Chang Heng, was an astronomy, mathematics, inventor, artist and literary scholar in the Eastern Han Dynasty of China.

Born in what is now Nanyang County, Henan Province, he was an accomplished writer at age 12. At age 16, he left home to pursue his study in the capital cities. He spent at least 10 years of his youth in literature studies and writing. He published several well recognized literary writings.

He switched to astronomy after age 30. He became a government official at age 38. He took on several positions since then (包括郎中，太史令，尚书). When he was a government minister, he cleaned up some corruption in the local government.

In the year 123 he corrected the Chinese calendar to bring it into line with the seasons.

In 132, Zhang invented the first seismograph for measuring earthquakes.

He theorized that the universe was like an egg with the stars on the shell and the earth as the yolk.

Zhang Heng was the first person in China to construct a rotating celestial globe. He also invented the odometer.

In one of his publications Ling Xian (《灵宪》a summary of astronomical theories at the time), he approximated pi as 730/232 (or approx 3.1466). In one of his formulae for spherical volume calculation, he also used pi as square root of 10 (or approx 3.162).

## Cultural Links 文化链接

### 蛤蟆戏龙的故事

公元132年，张衡制造出了中国乃至世界上第一个能预报地震的仪器，取名"地动仪"。

这架"地动仪"是用青铜铸造而成的，形状像一个圆圆的大酒坛，直径近一米，中心有一根粗的铜柱子，外围有八根细的铜杆子，四周浇铸着八条龙，八条龙头分别连着里面的八根铜杆子，龙头微微向上，对着东、南、西、北、东北、东南、西北、西南八个方向。每条龙的嘴里含着一个小铜球，每个龙头的下面，蹲着一只铜蛤蟆，它们都抬着头，张大嘴巴，随时都可以接住龙嘴里吐出来的小铜球。哈蟆和龙头的样子非常有趣，好像在互相戏耍。人们就用"哈蟆戏龙"来形容"地动仪"的外貌。按照张衡的设计，如果哪个方向发生了地震，"地动仪"的铜杆就会朝哪个方向倾斜，然后带动龙头，使那个方向的龙嘴张开，小铜球就会从龙嘴里吐出来，掉到蛤蟆嘴里，发出"当"的一声，向人们报告那个方向发生了地震，以便政府做好抢救和善后工作。

公元133年，洛阳发生地震，张衡的"地动仪"准确地测到了。此后四年里，洛阳地区又先后发生三次地震，张衡的"地动仪"都测到了，没有一次失误。就连138年2月距洛阳遥远的甘肃发生地震也预测到了。这时候，人们才真正相信张衡的"地动仪"不仅是"蛤蟆戏龙"，而是真正有用的科学仪器。从此以后，中国开始了用仪器远距离观测和记录地震的历史。

## Vocabulary 妙词连珠

| | |
|---|---|
| seismograph 地震仪，测震仪 | celestial globe [天]星象仪，天球仪 |
| earthquake 地震 | odometer 里程表 |
| yolk 蛋黄 | approx 大约，大概 |

# Unit 3　Hua Tuo 华佗

## Key Sentences
### 流畅精句

1. Hua Tuo led a simple life, away from fame and fortune.
   华佗淡于名利，不慕富贵。
2. He would rather become a traveling physician for ordinary people, who in turn held him in great reverence.
   他宁愿做民间医生，深受人民爱戴。
3. Hua Tuo was an expert in several medical fields, such as internal medicine, surgery, gynecology, pediatrics and acupuncture.
   华佗精通很多医学领域，如内、外、妇、儿、针灸各科。
4. He was the first person to perform surgery with the aid of anesthesia (by applying Ma Fei San, a herbal anesthetic he invented), some 1 600 years before Europeans did.
   华佗创用麻沸散，是用药物麻醉进行外科手术的先驱者，西医用麻醉药至少比华佗晚 1 600 年。
5. His expertise in surgical operation earned him the title of Father of Chinese Surgery.
   他精于外科手术，是外科学的鼻祖。
6. Unfortunately, almost all of his medical works, such as Hua Tuo Fang (Hua Tuo's prescriptions), Hua Tuo Nei Shi (Hua Tuo on Internal Medicine) and Zhen Zhongs' Jiu Ci Jing (The Methods of Using Acupuncture and Moxibustion), were lost.
   华佗一生的著作有《华佗方》、《华佗内事》、《枕中灸刺经》等，可惜均已散失。

## Famous Scientists

### Wonderful Paragraph
精彩片段

**Paragraph 1**

# H华佗
## ua Tuo

Hua Tuo is a famous physician of the Han Dynasty who is so widely respected that his name and image adorn numerous products (e. g., as a brand name for acupuncture needles and for medicated plasters) and a set of frequently used acupuncture points. He is known for the early qi gong exercise set known as the frolics of the five animals, in which one imitates the actions of tigers, deer, bears, apes, and birds; these practices were later incorporated into various health promoting martial arts practices, such as taijiquan. His name is always mentioned in relation to surgery, as he was considered the first surgeon of China, and one of the last famous surgeons of ancient China.

**Paragraph 2**

# H华佗生平
## ua Tuo's Life

Hua Tuo was born around 141 A. D., in Qiao of Peiguo (today called Bo) county, in what is now Anhui Province, one of the four major herb distribution centers of modern China. He lived for about 100 years, having died around 207 A. D. He was an older contemporary of China's famous herbalist Zhang Zhongjing, who died around 220 A. D. In the Chronicles of the Later Han Dynasty, it is said that: "Knowing well the way to keep one in good health, Hua Tuo still appeared in the prime of his life when he was almost 100, and so was regarded as immortal." It is said that Cao Cao, ruler of the state of Wei, had Hua Tuo put to death for reasons that are unclear. According to the Records of the Wei Dynasty (Wei Zhi), Cao Cao had Hua

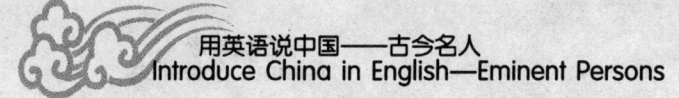

Tuo killed in 208 A. D. at age 97.

According to the limited existing reports of his life, it is said that Hua Tuo studied and mastered various classics, especially those related to medical and health measures, but also astronomy, geography, literature, history, and agriculture, when he was young. He was stimulated to pursue a career in medicine after seeing so many people die of epidemics, famines, and injuries from wars (Zhang Zhongjing also mentioned the epidemics as leading him to undertake medicine as a career). He studied tirelessly while practicing medicine, and became expert in several fields, including acupuncture, gynecology, pediatrics, and surgery. For the latter, he invented various herbal anesthetics. One, known as numbing powder (Mafei San), was taken with alcohol before surgery. His ancient prescriptions are lost, but the ingredients are thought to include cannabis and datura, which had been recorded later, during the Song Dynasty, as an anesthetic.

### Paragraph 3

## 遗产 Legacy

Legends of Hua Tuo's work are mentioned in historical novels, such as Romance of the Three Kingdoms and Taiping's Comprehensive Anthology of Stories. It was a tradition in the past that when a patient had recovered due to the efforts of a competent physician, the family would present a congratulatory board to the doctor inscribed with the words: A Second Hua Tuo.

Two specific cases of abdominal operations were relayed in Hua Tuo's official biography:

- A patient who went to Hua Tuo was told: "Your disease has been chronic, and you should receive an abdominal operation, but even that could lengthen your life by not more than ten years." The patient, being in great pain, consented to the surgery and was cured immediately, but he died exactly ten years later.

• A patient who suffered from abdominal pain for more than 10 days and had depilation of his beard and eyebrows asked Hua Tuo for treatment. The doctor diagnosed him as having a deterioration in the abdomen, asked him to drink the anesthesia, then explored his abdomen and removed the deteriorated part, sutured and plastered the abdomen, and administered some herbs. The patient recovered after 100 days.

There is also the story of general Guan Yu, whose arm was pierced by a poisoned arrow during a battle; General Guan calmly sat playing a board game as he allowed Hua Tuo to clean his flesh down to the bone to remove necrosis, with no anesthetic. This event is a popular historical subject in Chinese art.

**Paragraph 4**

## 神医华佗
## Miracle Working Doctor

Hua Tuo has been called the "miracle working doctor" (also translated as divine physician; shenyi) because of his emphasis on using a small number of acupuncture points or small number of herbs in a prescription to attain good results. Being an accomplished Taoist and following its principles, he did not seek fame or fortune, though much praise was heaped upon him. He served as a physician in what are now Jiangsu and Shandong Provinces adjacent to his home Province of Anhui, and turned down offers for government service.

It is said that Hua Tuo wrote several books, but none of them has been handed down, so his teachings remain largely unknown. One story is that while in prison awaiting his death, Hua Tuo handed over his works, collectively referred to as the Book of the Black Bag, to the prison ward and asked him to help save people's lives with his medical books, but the warden dared not accept it, and Hua Tuo burned it. It is thought that some of

Hua Tuo's teachings have been preserved within other books that came out in subsequent centuries, such as the Pulse Classic, Prescriptions Worth a Thousand Gold, and Medical Secrets of an Official.

Despite Hua Tuo's reputation in the field, the loss of his works resulted in the first monographs on surgery being erroneously attributed to others. There were many short documents produced during the time from the end of the Han Dynasty through the 5th century, of which one survives, called Liu Junzi's Mysterious Remedies. Like the other documents of this time, it mainly focused on lancing of carbuncles and cleaning out deep ulcers, as well as some other superficial surgeries, not the abdominal surgery that Hua Tuo is said to have done.

## Cultural Links
## 文化链接

### 外科鼻祖

　　一天清晨，霞光曦微。有两个人用车推着一个病人到华佗诊所来看病。病人腹部疼得厉害，面色苍白，两腿弯曲并精神委靡不振。华佗给病人摸了脉搏，而后轻轻地解开病人的衣服，用手按按肚子，病人突然怪叫了一声。他又仔细地望了望病人的神色，对病者的家里人说："生的是肠痈（阑尾炎），要立即开刀！"于是把病人抬上手术台。华佗让病人用酒送服"麻沸散"。过了不一会儿，病人失去知觉。又让徒弟给病人腹部涂药消毒。手术的准备工作完成了，华佗用消过毒的刀子将病人腹部剖开，他把手伸入腹腔，割去阑尾，再用药制的桑皮纸线缝好刀口，敷上特制的消炎药膏。做完手术，华佗告诉病人家属："过七、八天刀口就会长好，一个月后就可参加劳动。"

## Vocabulary 妙词连珠

acupuncture 针刺疗法
medicated plaster 药膏
the frolics of the five animals 五禽戏
ape 猿
martial arts 武术
contemporary 同时代的人
herbalist 草药医生
epidemic 传染的,流行性 时疫,流行病
gynecology 妇科医学
pediatrics 小儿科
anesthetic 麻醉剂,麻药 麻醉的
numbing 使麻木的,使失去感觉的
cannabis 大麻
congratulatory 庆祝的,祝贺的
depilation 脱毛
suture 缝合,缝合处,缝合用的线 缝合
acute appendicitis 急性阑尾炎
intestinal 肠的,肠内的,(疾病)侵袭肠的
ointment 药膏
necrosis 坏疽,骨疽
unscathed 没有受伤的,未受伤

用英语说中国——古今名人
Introduce China in English—Eminent Persons

# Unit 4  祖冲之 Zu Chongzhi

## Key Sentences
流畅精句

1. He did not take for granted the established theories of previous scholars and was skeptical to their specious academic conclusions.
   他主张决不"虚推古人",批判地接受前代的学术遗产,敢于怀疑古人错误陈旧的结论。

2. After careful observations, he compiled an updated one called the "Daming Calendar" the best at his time. In the entire history of China, Zu Chongzshi became the first to take into consideration in calendar calculations the differences between the tropical and sidereal years.
   经过实际观测,他编制了新历法大明历,在中国历法史上第一次考虑了岁差影响,是当时最好的历法。

3. As a mathematician, Zu Chongzi's most remarkable achievement was the calculation of pi.
   作为数学家,祖冲之的卓越贡献就是对圆周率的推算。

4. The "precise value" he worked out is a number between 3.1415926 and 3.1415927.
   他计算出圆周率是介于3.1415926和3.1415927之间。

5. In the Tang Dynasty, the mathematical work Zhui Shu (or Method of Interpolation) compiled by Zu (now lost) was a required textbook at the Academy of Mathematics, in which students were obliged to read it for four years, the longest time any textbook was required to work on. This book was later circulated to Japan and Korea.
   他的数学专著《缀术》在唐代曾作为国子监算学馆的必读书,学习期限4年,是时限最长的一种,后来还流传至日本和朝鲜。

6. He was also the inventor of a "tilted container" used to bail water and a long distance boat believed to have the capacity of traveling over 50 kilometers a day.

他还制造过一种千里船,并在江上试航,日行百余里。

## Wonderful Paragraph
精彩片段

**Paragraph 1**

# Zu Chongzhi
祖冲之

Born 429, Jiankang (modern Nanjing, Jiangsu Province), died 500, Zu Chongzhis was Chinese astronomer, mathematician, and engineer who created the Daming calendar and found several close approximations forp.

Like his grandfather and father, Zu Chongzhi was a state functionary. About 462 he submitted a memorandum to the throne that criticized the current calendar, the Yuanjia (created by He Chengtian [370-447]), and proposed a new calendar system that would provide a more precise number of lunations per year and take into consideration the precession of the equinoxes. His calendar, the Daming calendar, was finally adopted in 510 through the efforts of his son, Zu Gengzhi.

Li Chunfeng (602—670) called Zu Chongzhi the best mathematician ever and gave him credit for three approximations of $\pi$: 22/7, 355/113, and the interval $3.1415926 < \pi < 3.1415927$; the third result remained the best in the world until improved by the Arab mathematician al-Kashi (flourished c. 1400). Zu also worked on the mathematical theory of music and metrology, and he constructed several devices, such as a semilegendary "south-pointing carriage" (most likely a mechanical device that kept a pointer in a fixed position); the carriage was topped by a symbolic figure that, once properly aligned, would always point to the south.

用英语说中国——古今名人
# Introduce China in English—Eminent Persons

## Cultural Links 文化链接

## 祖冲之

祖冲之在数学上的杰出成就,是关于圆周率的计算。秦汉以前,人们以"径一周三"作为圆周率,这就是"古率"。后来发现古率误差太大,圆周率应是"圆径一而周三有余",不过究竟余多少,意见不一。直到三国时期,刘徽提出了计算圆周率的科学方法——"割圆术",用圆内接正多边形的周长来逼近圆周长。刘徽计算到圆内接96边形,求得 π = 3.14,并指出,内接正多边形的边数越多,所求得的 π 值越精确。祖冲之在前人成就的基础上,经过刻苦钻研,反复演算,求出 π 在 3.1415926 与 3.1415927 之间。并得出了 π 分数形式的近似值,取 22/7 为约率,取 355/133 为密率,其中 355/133 取六位小数是 3.141929,它是分子分母在 1000 以内最接近 π 值的分数。祖冲之究竟用什么方法得出这一结果,现在无从考查。若设想他按刘徽的"割圆术"方法去求的话,就要计算到圆内接 16 384 边形,这需要花费多少时间和付出多么巨大的劳动啊!由此可见他在治学上的顽强毅力和聪明才智是令人钦佩的。祖冲之计算得出的密率,外国数学家获得同样结果,已是一千多年以后的事了。为了纪念祖冲之的杰出贡献,有些外国数学史家建议把 π = 叫做"祖率"。

## Vocabulary 妙词连珠

| | |
|---|---|
| astronomer 天文学家 | metrology 度量衡学,度量衡 |
| mathematician 数学家 | semilegendary 半传奇的 |
| approximation 接近,走近,[数]近似值 | symbolic 象征的,符号的 |
| | semilegendary 半传奇的,近乎传奇的 |
| functionary 职员,官员,负责人员 | |
| lunation 阴历月 | align 排列 |
| precession 运动 | south-pointing carriage 指南车 |
| equinox 昼夜平分点,春分或秋分 | |

# Unit 5　Shen Kuo
## 沈括

## Key Sentences
### 流畅精句

1. Shen Kuo was a scientist in the North Song Dynasty.
   沈括是北宋时的科学家。
2. His immortal masterpiece *Meng Xi Bi Tan*, in which the word "shiyou"(petroleum) was used for the first time in the literature of Chinese history, was his remarkable contribution to science.
   他的不朽名著《梦溪笔谈》，为自然科学作出了卓越贡献。书中最早使用了"石油"这个名称。
3. He advocated that the solar calendar with thrity-one or thirty days a month and "lichun" as the beginning of the year be used to replace the lunar calendar.
   他提出彻底废止阴历而改用阳历的主张，以十二气历定月份，立春为岁首，大月31天、小月30天。
4. In mathematics, his important achievement is "Xijishu" and "Huiyuanshu".
   在数学方面，他主要的成就是"隙积术"和"会圆术"。
5. In physics, he makes such experiments as concave mirror imagery and sound resonance.
   物理学方面做过凹面镜成像实验和声音共振实验。
6. And in geography and geology, he builds up the cubic model of the topography of the North Liao state and compiles the atlas of the North Song Dynasty.
   在地理、地质学方面他以流水侵袭作用解释奇异地貌成因，以化石推测水陆变迁情况，制成辽北立体地形模型，编制成北宋疆域地图集。

# Introduce China in English—Eminent Persons

7. He also keeps records of the significant achievement of science in his time such as the early-time compass device, the discovery of the magnetic declination of the earth, the type printing, steel smelting and copper smelting.

   他还记述了当时一些重大科技成就，如早期指南针装置、地球磁偏角的发现、活字印刷术、炼钢和炼铜法等。

8. In addition, he makes intensive study of herbs nd medicine, on which his works include Lingyuan Fang and Liang Fang.

   另外，他还精研药用植物与医学，著有《灵苑方》和《良方》。

## Wonderful Paragraph 精彩片段

### Paragraph 1

## Shen Kuo 沈括

Shen Kuo (1031—1091) was a Chinese scientist, polymath, general, diplomat, and financial officer who was the inventor of compasses for navigation.

In the book *Meng Xi Bi Tan* (Dream Pool Essays) (1088) he wrote about mineralogy, erosion, sedimentation and uplift, mathematics, astronomy, and metereology. The literal translation of *Meng Xi Bi Tan* is Brush talks from Dream Brook. The name derives from his property on the outskirts of Jiangsu (Zhenjiang), a place of great beauty which he named "Dream Brook" and where he lived in isolation for the last seven years of his life.

Kuo discovered that compasses do not point true north but to the magnetic north pole. This was a decisive step to make them useful for navigation.

He formulated a hypothesis for the process of land formation; based on his observation of fossil shells in a geological stratum in a mountain hundreds of miles from the ocean, he inferred that the land was formed by erosion of the mountains and by deposition of silt. Shen Kuo was not only a geologist; his memoirs list "regularities underlying phenomena" in magnetism, astronomy, and engineering. He also wrote about Yi Xing (672-717), a Buddhist monk and his calculation of possible positions on a go board, but without a sign for zero he had difficulties expressing the number.

## Cultural Links 文化链接

### 文武双全的沈括

沈括文武双全,不仅在科学上取得了辉煌的成绩,而且为保卫北宋的疆土也作出过重要贡献。北宋时期,阶级矛盾和民族矛盾都十分尖锐。辽和西夏贵族统治者经常侵扰中原地区,掳掠人口牲畜,给社会经济带来很大破坏。沈括坚定地站在主战派一边,在熙宁七年(公元 1074 年)担任河北西路察访使和军器监长官期间,他攻读兵书,精心研究城防、阵法、兵车、兵器、战略战术等军事问题,编成《修城法式条约》和《边州阵法》等军事著作,把一些先进的科学技术成功地应用在军事科学上。同时,沈括对弓弩甲胄和刀枪等武器的制造也都作过深入研究,为提高兵器和装备的质量作出了一定贡献。

## Vocabulary 妙词连珠

| | |
|---|---|
| polymath 博学者 | stratum [地] 地层 |
| compasses 罗盘 | silt 淤泥,残渣,煤粉,泥沙;(使) |
| erosion 腐蚀,侵蚀 | 淤塞,充塞 |
| mineralogy 矿物学 | memoir 论文集 |
| sedimentation 沉淀,沉降 | underlying 在下面的,根本的,潜 |
| hypothesis 假设 | 在的 |

用英语说中国——古今名人
Introduce China in English—Eminent Persons

# Unit 6 李时珍 Li Shizhen

## Key Sentences
流畅精句

1. Li Shizhen was a pharmacist in the Ming Dynasty.
   李时珍是明朝医学家。
2. Li Shizhen wrote the world-famous monumental masterpiece "Bencaogangmu" (Compendium of Materia Medica).
   李时珍写成了举世闻名的中医药著作《本草纲目》。
3. His classifications of plants and animals were based on rather scientific approaches at that time.
   他对植物和动物的分类是采用了当时比较科学的方法。
4. Denouncing sharply the absurd practice of taking "magic pills" for longevity, he treated on curative effect of herbs in clinical practice and made new solutions such as Semen Hydnocarpi to cure leprosy and Rhizoma Smilacis glabrae to cure syphilis.
   他痛斥了服食所谓"仙丹"以求长生不老的荒谬行为。在疗效方面重视临床实践,如对大风子治麻风、土茯苓治梅毒等有新的结论。
5. He also made corrections to the mistakes in the ancient medicinal works in terms of names, catalogues and origin of the medicinal herbs.
   他还纠正了古代本草书中某些药名、品种、产地等方面的错误。
6. He held that human thinking process took place in the brain rather than in the heart.
   他指出人的思维不在心而在脑。

## Wonderful Paragraph
精彩片段

### Paragraph 1

# Li Shizhen
李时珍

    Li Shizhen (1518—1593) of Chaizhou in Hubei province, is considered to have been China's greatest naturalist. He was very interested in the proper classification of the components of nature. His major contribution to medicine was the forty year project of sifting through the vast array of herbal lore and writing down the information that was, in his view, a reliable reflection of reality. His book, the "Bencao Gang Mu; 1596", has been used as a pharmacopoeia, but it was also treatise on botany, zoology, mineralogy and metallurgy. The book was reprinted frequently and five of the original edition still exist. "Ben Cao Gang Mu" contains 1892 different herbs, and is divided into 6 sections, 52 scrolls and 60 different categories. Li Shizhen was a great scientist; he risked his life numerous time as he researched the life and habitat of Chai snakes, who at the time were considered a precious medicine. He then also published the "Chai Snake Compilation".

## Cultural Links
文化链接

### 药渣辨真假

    传说明代名医李时珍,一天外出采药,看到一个村庄田园荒芜,无人下地劳动,原来这个村的人都得了"流感"。在一个茅草屋里,他看见一位老人正在床上呻吟,急忙取出药来,让老人喝下,停了一会,老人出了一身汗,症状减轻了许多。李时珍询问了一下情况,才知道村里先后来过几个走江湖的郎中,给他们开过药,还说什么"吃上一副药,包管你药到病除"。可是吃了十来副了,仍不见效。李时珍便找来煎过的药渣,仔细一看,大部分是假药。假药怎能治好病呢?老百姓上当受骗了,他们对庸医痛恨不已。李时珍看药渣的事,传遍了附近的村庄,人们纷纷把江湖郎中配制的草药和带来的药渣叫李时珍鉴别,因为人太多,看不过来,只好让大家把药渣倒在村前的路口上,一个个摊开放好,逐个查看,拣出真药,扔掉假药、劣药,并教大家如何识别伪劣中草药,防止再上当受骗。从此以后,病人就把煎服过的药渣倒在路口处,盼望过路的良医识别真假,于是这个风俗就盛行起来。

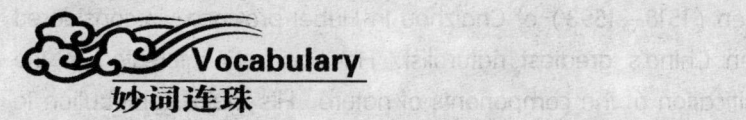

## Vocabulary 妙词连珠

| | |
|---|---|
| lore 学问,知识 | absurd 荒谬的,可笑的 |
| pharmacopoeia 药典 | leprocy 像麻风的 |
| botany 植物学 | syphilis [医] 梅毒 |
| metallurgy 冶金,冶金术 | catalogue 目录 |
| component 成分 | sift 详审 |
| pharmacist 配药者,药剂师 | array 排列,编队,军队,衣服,大批 |
| monumental 纪念碑的,纪念物的,不朽的,非常的 | herbal 草药的 |
| | reliable 可靠的,可信赖的 |
| compendium 纲要,概略 | treatise 论文,论述 |
| classification 分类,分级 | zoology 动物学,生态 |
| approach 接近,逼近,走进,方法,步骤,途径,通路 | mineraalogy [矿] 矿相学 |
| | compilation 编辑 |
| denounce 公开指责,公然抨击,谴责 | |

# Unit 7　Xu Guangqi　徐光启

## Key Sentences 流畅精句

1. Xu Guangqi was the first one who introduced European natural science to China and translated geometry into Chiense (six volumes of Geometry Original).
   他是把欧洲自然科学介绍到中国的第一人,最早翻译了几何学著作《几何原本》。

2. He introduced the European clock and the telescope invented by Galileo, with which he drew up a map called "All planets in the Celestial Sphere".
   他引进了欧洲的时钟和伽利略发明的望远镜,绘制了一幅《全天球恒星图》。

3. He took charge of the revision of the calendar and translated and edited Chongzhen Almanac by means of Tycho system.
   他还主持历法的修订,采用第谷体系编译《崇祯历书》。

4. His most influential work on science and technology was the immense book entitled Complete Treatise on Agriculture, consisting of 12 phyla, 60 volumes, and altogether over 700 000 words.
   他的最大成就是著有农业科学巨著《农政全书》,此书分为12门,60卷,70余万字。

5. Xu Guangqi held that agriculture was the foundation to make the country rich and military strength was fundamental to make the country powerful.
   徐光启以农业为富国之本,以正兵为强之本,重视军事科学技术的研究。

# 用英语说中国——古今名人
## Introduce China in English—Eminent Persons

6. He was concerned about the manufacture of arms, especially that of firearms. He was the first in China to put forward the theory of applying artillery in warfare.
   他关心武器制造,尤其是火器制造,堪称中国军事技术史上提出火炮在战争中应用理论的第一人。

## Wonderful Paragraph
### 精彩片段

### Paragraph 1

# X 徐光启
## u Guangqi

Xu Guangqi (1562—1633) was a Chinese agricultural scientist and mathematician born in Shanghai.

He received the equivalent of his bachelor's degree at 19, but did not receive higher degrees until his thirties. He lived in a period when Chinese mathematics had gone into decline. The earlier efforts at algebra had been almost forgotten. Xu blamed some of the failures on a decline interest in practical science in China and became something of a critic of Chinese society.

He was a colleague and coauthor of Matteo Ricci. This influence led to his being baptized Catholic in 1604. In 1607 Xu Guangqi and Matteo Ricci translated the first parts of Euclid's Elements into Chinese. His conversion to Roman Catholicism led him to change his name to Paul Xu. After this his criticism of Chinese intellectual life became harsher and he came to deem China to be inferior to the West, specifically in mathematics. He also believed that adopting Western military armaments would save them from the Manchu, but this idea failed after the Manchu themselves learned to make European cannons. His descendants remained staunchly Catholic into the nineteenth century.

His tomb still exists in Shanghai in Guangqi Park just a short walk from the Xujiahui Cathedral in the Xujiahui area on Nandan Road（南丹路）.

## Cultural Links 文化链接

### 徐光启与利玛窦

1600年，一个偶然的机会，徐光启看到利玛窦绘制的《坤舆万国全图》，他惊呆了：地球是圆的，这是一个他所未知的广袤世界，于是写下了《题万国二圜图序》一文。为此，他在南京访问了利玛窦，这是徐光启一生中最大的转折，也是他开始学习、接受并向国人介绍西方科学的起点。此后，他与利玛窦合作翻译《几何原本》。在我国最早的美术机构——土山湾画馆，就有徐光启、利玛窦等人水彩肖像画。《坤舆万国全图》现藏于南京博物院，而土山湾画馆当时画的徐光启、利玛窦等人物画像，现存于美国旧金山大学"利玛窦中西文化历史研究所"。

## Vocabulary 妙词连珠

| | |
|---|---|
| polymath 博学者 | stratum ［地］地层 |
| compasses 罗盘 | silt 淤泥，残渣，煤粉，泥沙；（使）淤塞，充塞 |
| erosion 腐蚀，侵蚀 | |
| mineralogy 矿物学 | memoir 论文集 |
| sedimentation 沉淀，沉降 | underlying 在下面的，根本的，潜在的 |
| hypothesis 假设 | |

# Unit 8  Tsien Hsue-shen
钱学森

## Key Sentences
流畅精句

1. In 1945 Tsien Hsue-shen married Jiang Ying, the daughter of Jiang Baili.
   1945年,钱学森与蒋百里的女儿蒋英结婚。
2. Around CalTech, the dangerous and explosive nature of their work earned them the nickname, the "Suicide Squad."
   在加利福尼亚理工学院,他们所从事的工作的危险易爆性质为他们赢得了"自杀小组"的绰号。
3. Tsien Hsue-shen found himself unable to pursue his career and within two weeks announced plans to return to China.
   钱学森发现他自己不能再继续他的工作,两周后他提出回国的计划。
4. After Tsien's announcement the U.S. government wavered between deporting him and refusing to allow his departure due to his knowledge.
   在钱学森声明后,他的学识使美国政府就是否把他驱逐出境还是拒绝他的离境请求而犹豫不决。
5. During his incarceration Tsien received support from his colleagues at Caltech including Cal Tech President Lee DuBridge who flew to Washington to argue Tsien's case.
   在钱学森被软禁期间他得到了来自加利福尼亚理工学院他的同事的支持,包括院长 Lee DuBridge 也曾飞往华盛顿亲自协商他的问题。

6. Most of Tsien's research works became the foundation for the Tsien Library at Xi'an Jiaotong University with rest of them went to the Institute of Mechanics.

钱学森的绝大部分研究著作成为西安交通大学钱学森图书馆的奠基之作,少部分送往机械研究院。

## Wonderful Paragraph
精彩片段

### Paragraph 1

# T钱学森
sien Hsue-shen

Tsien Hsue-shen (born December 11, 1911) is a scientist who was a major figure in the missile and space programs of both the United States and People's Republic of China (PRC).

Tsien was a co-founder of the Jet Propulsion Laboratory at the California Institute of Technology, and became the "Father of Chinese Rocketry" (or "King of Rocketry") when he returned to China after being accused of being a communist by the United States government during the red scare of the 1950s the same way Wu Ningkun was accused of being an American spy in mainland China.

Asteroid 3763 Qianxuesen was named after him.

### Paragraph 2

# E早年生涯及教育背景
arly Life and Education

Tsien Hsue-shen was born in the eastern Chinese city of Hangzhou. He left Hangzhou at the age of three when his father obtained a post in the Ministry of Education. He graduated from Chiao Tung University (currently Shanghai Jiaotong University) in 1934 and in August of 1935 Tsien Hsue-shen left China on a Boxer Rebellion Scholarship to study at the Massachusetts Institute of Technology.

In 1936 Tsien Hsue-shen went to the California Institute of Technology to commence graduate studies on the referral of Theodore von Karman. Tsien obtained his doctorate in 1939 and would remain at CalTech for 20 years, ultimately becoming the Goddard Professor and establishing a reputation as one of the leading rocket scientists in the United States.

## Paragraph 3

## 旅美期间
## In the United States

In 1943, Tsien and two others in the CalTech rocketry group drafted the first document to use the name Jet Propulsion Laboratory; it was a proposal to the Army to develop missiles in response to Germany's V-2 rocket. This led to the Private A, which flew in 1944; and later the Corporal, the WAC Corporal, etc.

After World War II he served in the United States Army as a Lieutenant Colonel. Tsien Hsue-shen was sent by the Army to Germany and was part of the team that examined captured German V-2 rockets.

Soon after Tsien applied for U.S. citizenship in 1950, allegations were made that he was a communist and his security clearance was revoked. Tsien Hsue-shen became the subject of five years of secret diplomacy and negotiation between the United States and PRC. During this time he lived under virtual house arrest. Tsien found himself in conflict with the U.S. Immigration and Naturalization Service including an arrest for carrying secret documents which ultimately turned out to be simple logarithmic tables. During his incarceration Tsien received support from his colleagues at Caltech including Caltech President Lee DuBridge who flew to Washington to argue Tsien's case.

## 著名科学家
## Famous Scientists

### Paragraph 4

# R回到中国
# eturn to China

In 1955 Tsien was released and deported from the United States as a part of post-Korean war negotiations to free American prisoners of war held by China. He went to work as head of the Chinese missile program immediately upon his arrival in China. Tsien deliberately left his research papers behind when he left the United States. Tsien joined the Communist Party of China in 1958.

Tsien established the Institute of Mechanics and began to retrain Chinese engineers in the techniques he had learned in the United States and retool the infrastructure of the Chinese program. Within a year Tsien submitted a proposal to establish a ballistic missile program. This proposal was accepted and Tsien was named the first director of the program in late 1956. By 1958 Tsien had finalized the plans of the Dongfeng missile which was first successfully launched in 1964 just prior to China's first successful nuclear weapon's test. Tsien's program was also responsible for the development of the widespread Silkworm missile.

Tsien retired in 1991 and has maintained a low public profile in Beijing.

China launched its manned space program in 1992 and used Tsien's research as the basis for the Long March rocket which successfully launched the Shenzhou V mission in October of 2003. The elderly Tsien was able to watch China's first manned space mission on television from his hospital bed.

## Cultural Links
## 文化链接

### 钱学森的风度

对于年轻人的大胆创议,只要是科学的,钱学森积极支持。有一次,在基地做导弹的全程试验,开始时发现,这次试验可能达不到预定的射程。这时一位叫王永志的年轻人,向钱学森提出了一个大胆的设想:泄掉一部分推进剂,这和一般的思路刚好相反。但王永进坚持说,他经过计算,认为泄掉一部分推进剂,可以减轻导弹的起飞重量,反而能增加射程,达到设计要求。钱学森听后认为这位年轻人说得有道理,于是他在现场大胆决定:按王永志的意见办。结果这次试验达到了预期的目的。

## Vocabulary 妙词连珠

| | |
|---|---|
| asteroid 小行星 | revoke 撤回,废除,宣告无效 |
| referral 提名,推举,被推举的人 | deport 举止,驱逐 |
| doctorate 博士头衔 | logarithmic 对数的 |

# 5 文化名人
*Eminent Literati*

## Unit 1 Qu Yuan
屈原

### Key Sentences
流畅精句

1. Qu Yuan was the first great poet, and one of the greatest poets in Chinese history.
   屈原是中国历史上第一位伟大诗人,也是最伟大的诗人之一。
2. His poetry and his noble spirit are a treasure of the Chinese nation.
   他的诗作和高贵人格是中华民族的宝贵财富。
3. The status that chuci has enjoyed in the history of Chinese literature may be largely attributed to the existence of Qu Yuan, while sao style, another name for chuci, came from none other than his representative masterpiece poem, "Li Sao".
   楚辞在中国文学史上的地位主要是因为屈原的存在,而楚辞的别称"骚体"也正是来源于他的代表作《离骚》。
4. As a statesman, he cherished great hopes that his country would one day become stronger, and toward this goal he strove unremittingly throughout his life.
   作为一个政治家,他毕生梦想着祖国的强大并为此不懈奋斗。

5. As the most important chuci poet, his poems are filled with beautiful rhetoric, ever so sublime and romantic.

   作为最重要的楚辞作家,他的诗作修辞华美,气魄宏大,浪漫得无以复加。

6. His phenomenal literary achievements make him a great master of Chinese romantic oetry, but his noble personality wins him more respect from later scholars.

   文学上的卓越成就使屈原成了中国浪漫主义诗歌的宗师,但后代文人对他的景仰更多是因为他的高尚人格。

7. Qu Yuan drowned himself in the Miluo River on the fifth day of the fifth lunar month, in utter despair over the fate of his motherland.

   农历五月五日,对祖国前途终于绝望的屈原在汨罗江投江自尽。

## Wonderful Paragraph 精彩片段

### Paragraph 1

### 简介 Biography

Qu Yuan (340-278B.C.?) was a Chinese patriotic poet from southern Chu during the Warring States Period. His works are mostly found in an anthology of poetry known as Chu Ci. His death is commemorated on Duan Wu Festival (端午节), commonly known as the Dragon Boat Festival.

Qu Yuan was a minister in the government of the state of Chu, descended of nobility and a champion of political loyalty and truth eager to maintain the Chu state's sovereignty. Qu Yuan advocated a policy of alliance with the other kingdoms of the period against the hegemonic state of Qin, which threatened to dominate them all. The Chu king, however, fell under the influence of other corrupt, jealous ministers who slandered Qu Yuan, and banished his most loyal counselor. It is said that Qu Yuan returned first to his family's home town. In his exile, he spent much of this time collecting legends and rearranging folk odes while travelling the countryside, producing some of the greatest poetry in Chinese literature while expressing his fervent love for his state and his deepest concern for its future.

In 278 BC, learning of the capture of his country's capital, Ying, by General Bai Qi of the state of Qin, Qu Yuan is said to have written the lengthy poem of lamentation called "Lament for Ying" and later to have waded into the Miluo river in today's Hunan Province holding a great rock in order to commit ritual suicide as a form of protest against the corruption of the era.

*Paragraph 2*

## Reputation 荣誉

Qu Yuan is generally recognized as the first great Chinese poet with record. He initiated the style of Sao, which is named after his work Li Sao, in which he abandoned the classic four-character verses used in poems of Shi Jing and adopted verses with varying lengths, which gives the poem more rhythm and latitude in expression. Qu Yuan is also regarded as one of the most prominent figures of Romanticism in Chinese literature, and his masterpieces influenced some of the greatest Romanticist poets in Tang Dynasty such as Li Bai and Du Fu.

Other than his literary influence, Qu Yuan is also held as the earliest patriotic poet in China history. His political idealism and unbendable patriotism have served as the model for Chinese intellectuals until today.

*Paragraph 3*

## Works 著作

Scholars have debated the authenticity of several of Qu Yuan's works since the Western Han dynasty (202 BCE — 9). The most authoritative historical record, Sima Qian's Records of the Grand Historian (Shi Ji) mentions five of Qu Yuan's works: Li Sao, Tian Wen, Zhao Hun, Ai Ying ("Lament for Ying"), Huai Sha. According to Wang Yi of the Eastern Han dynasty, a total of 25 works can be attributed to Qu Yuan: Li Sao, Jiu Ge (consisting of 11 pieces), Tian Wen, Jiu Zhang (consisting of 9 pieces), Yuan You, Pu Ju, Yu Fu. Wang Yi chose to attribute Zhao Hun to another poet Song Yu; most modern scholars, however, consider Zhao Hun to be Qu Yuan's original work, whereas Yuan You, Pu Ju, and Yu Fu are believed to have been composed by others.

## Cultural Links 文化链接

### 端午节与屈原

屈原,是春秋时期楚怀王的大臣。他倡导举贤授能,富国强兵,力主联齐抗秦,遭谗去职,被赶出都城,流放到沅、湘流域。他在流放中,写下了忧国忧民的《离骚》、《天问》、《九歌》等不朽诗篇(因而,端午节也称诗人节)。公元前278年,秦军攻破楚国京都。屈原不忍舍弃自己的祖国,于五月五日抱石投汨罗江自尽。

传说屈原死后,楚国百姓纷纷涌到汨罗江边去凭吊屈原。渔夫们划起船只,在江上来回打捞他的真身。有位渔夫拿出为屈原准备的饭团、鸡蛋等食物丢进江里,说是让鱼龙虾蟹吃饱了,就不会去咬屈大夫的身体了。人们见后纷纷仿效。一位老医师则拿来一坛雄黄酒倒进江里,说是要药晕蛟龙水兽,以免伤害屈大夫。后来为怕饭团为蛟龙所食,人们想出用楝树叶包饭,外缠彩丝,发展成粽子。

以后,在每年的五月初五,就有了龙舟竞渡、吃粽子、喝雄黄酒的风俗;以此来纪念爱国诗人屈原。

文化名人
Eminent Literati

## Vocabulary 妙词连珠

patriotic 爱国的，有爱国心的
sovereignty 君主，主权，主权国家
hegemonic 支配的，霸权的
slander 诽谤
counselor 顾问，法律顾问
fervent 炽热的

latitude 纬度，范围，（用复数）地区，行动或言论的自由（范围）
romanticism 浪漫精神，浪漫主义
debate 争论，辩论
verse 韵文，诗，诗节，诗句，诗篇

# Unit 2  Zhang Qian
张骞

## Key Sentences
流畅精句

1. Zhang Qian was a famous explorer and imperial diplomat during the period referred to as the Western Han Dynasty.
   张骞是西汉时期著名的探险家、外交家。
2. In 139 B.C. Zhang Qian was dispatched by Emperor Wu to the Western Regions (Xiyu) to seek a military alliance with the Greater Yuezhi (modern Tajikistan), with the intent to execute a cooperative attack against the Xiongnu tribes.
   公元前139年,汉武帝希望与大月氏相约联合夹攻匈奴,派张骞西去联络。
3. It took Zhan Qian 13 years to reach the Gui River where the people of the Greater Yuezhi lived.
   张骞历时13载抵达月氏所居的妫水一带。
4. On route he was captured twice by the Xiongnu and detained for over ten years. During his detention he married a Xiongnu woman and with her had a son, but his loyalty to the Han emperor never wavered.
   其中一次西行中,他曾两次被匈奴扣留长达10多年,还娶妻生子,但他一直"持汉节不失"。
5. Zhang Qian documented the cultures and lifestyles of the peoples of the Western Regions, and for the firsttime, the Chinese emperor was informed about India, the Middle East and even some European countries.

出使使张骞充分了解西域各地的山川景物与风土人情,第一次给中国皇帝带回了关于印度、中东以至欧洲诸国的消息。
6. In 123 B. C. , Zhang Qian followed General Wei Qing in a major military raid against the Xiongnu.
公元前123年,张骞随大将军卫青出征匈奴。
7. His guidance led to a number of victories, which succeeded in ending the harassment by the Xiongnu of the Han Dynasty. Zhang Qian was therefore conferred the title of Marquis of Bowang.
在他的引导下,平息了多年来北方匈奴对汉王朝的骚扰,张骞因此被封为博望侯。

## Wonderful Paragraph 精彩片段

### Paragraph 1

## Zhang Qian 张骞

Zhang Qian(?-114B. C.) was a Chinese explorer and imperial envoy in the 2nd century BCE, during the time of the Han Dynasty. He was the first official diplomat to bring back reliable information about Central Asia to the Chinese imperial court, then under Emperor Wu of Han, and played an important pioneering role in the Chinese colonisation and conquest of the region now known as Xinjiang. Zhang Qian's accounts of his explorations of Central Asia are detailed in the early Han historical chronicles ("史记", or "Records of the Great Historian"), compiled by Sima Qian in the 1st century BCE.

### Paragraph 2

## First Embassy to the West 出使西域

Zhang Qian was born in Chenggu county(成固), Hanzhong commandery（汉中）in western China. He entered the capital Chang'an between 140 BCE and 134 BCE as a Gentleman（郎）, serving Emperor Wu of Han. At the time the Xiongnu tribes controlled modern Inner Mongolia and dominated much of modern Western Regions.

The Han court despatched Zhang Qian to the Western Regions in 138 BC with a delegation of over one hundred members, including a surrendered Xiongnu guide. The objective of Zhang Qian's first mission was to seek a military alliance with the Greater Yuezhi（大月氏）, in modern Tajikistan. On route he was captured by the Xiongnu and detained for ten years. There he married a Xiongnu wife and gained the trust of the Xiongnu leader.

When Zhang finally made it to Yuezhi lands, he found that they were too settled to want war against the Xiongnu. He spent about one year in Yuezhi and Bactrian territory, documenting their cultures, lifestyles and economy, before returning to China.

*Paragraph 3*

## R 返回中土
## Return to China

On his return trip Zhang Qian was again captured by the Xiongnu, who again spared his life because they valued his sense of duty and composure in the face of death. Two years later the Xiongnu leader died and in the midst of chaos Zhang Qian escaped.

Zhang Qian returned in 125 BCE with detailed news for the Emperor, which showed that sophisticated civilizations existed to the West, with which China could advantageously develop relations. The Shiji relates that "the emperor learned of the Dayuan, Daxia, Anxi, and the others, all great states rich in unusual products whose people cultivated the land and made their living in much the same way as the Chinese. All these states, he was told, were military weak and prized Han goods and wealth".

His second expedition was more organised, a trade mission to the Wu-sun people in 119 BCE. This was a success and led to trade between

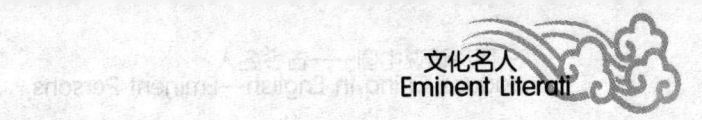

China and Persia.

Following Zhang Qian's embassy and report, commercial relations between China and Central Asia flourished, as many Chinese missions were sent throughout the 1st century BCE: "The largest of these embassiest forcing states numbered several hundred persons, while even the smaller parties included over 100 members... In the course of one year anywhere from five to six to over ten parties would be sent out."

## Cultural Links 文化链接

### 为什么叫"丝绸之路"

早年，人们对这条东西往来的通路没有给予一个统一的固定名称。1877年，德国地理学家李希霍芬（F. von Richthofen）在他所写的《中国》一书中，首次把汉代中国和中亚南部、西部以及印度之间的丝绸贸易为主的交通路线，称作"丝绸之路"（Silk Road）。其后，德国历史学家赫尔曼（A. Herrmann）在1910年出版的《中国和叙利亚之间的古代丝绸之路》一书中，根据新发现的文物考古资料，进一步把丝绸之路延伸到地中海西岸和小亚细亚，确定了丝绸之路的基本内涵，即它是中国古代经由中亚通往南亚、西亚以及欧洲、北非的陆上贸易交往的通道，因为大量的中国丝和丝织品经由此路西传，故此称作"丝绸之路"，简称"丝路"。

## Vocabulary 妙词连珠

| | |
|---|---|
| envoy 外交使节，特使 | composure 镇静，沉着 |
| chronicle 编年史 | sophisticate 久经世故的人，老油条，精于……之道的人 |
| embassy 大使及其随员，大使的派遣，大使馆 | advantageously 有利地，方便地 |
| despatch 派遣 | flourished 繁茂的，繁荣的，欣欣向荣的 |
| delegation 代表团，授权，委托 | |
| alliance 联盟，联合 | |

用英语说中国——古今名人
Introduce China in English—Eminent Persons

# Unit 3  Sima Qian
司马迁

## Key Sentences
流畅精句

1. His father Sima Tan served as Taishiling. Sima Qian later succeeded his father's work and started compiling Shiji (or Records of the Historian).
   父亲司马谈曾任太史令,司马迁继任太史令后,开始了《史记》的写作。

2. Shiji is an overview of Chinese history covering events from Huang Di to Emperor Wudi in the Han Dynasty, consisting of 130 chapters with more than 520 000 Chinese characters.
   《史记》上起黄帝,下迄太初,全书130章,共52万多字。

3. For Sima Qian, to compile such a book was to "investigate the interrelationship between the human and the universe, to generalize the rules of historical evolution and to formulate a unique historical view".
   司马迁写《史记》,目的是为了"究天人之际,通古今之变,成一家之言"。

4. In presenting historical facts, Sima Qian infused emotional descriptions, expressing his intense love and hate.
   在客观史事的叙述中司马迁倾注了浓厚的抒情因素,表现出鲜明的爱憎感情。

5. Shiji is not only a masterpiece about history; it is also a great literary work. Lu Xun regarded this book as "the first and last great work ever written by a historian; it is Qu Yuan's Li Sao without rhyme."
   《史记》是一部伟大的历史著作,又是一部伟大的文学著作,被鲁迅称赞为"史家之绝唱,无韵之离骚"。

文化名人
Eminent Literati

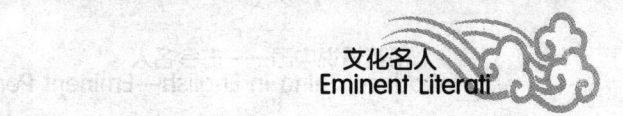

6. Sima Qian was a cultural giant in the Chinese history of historical studies, literature and philosophy.
   司马迁是集史学家、文学家、思想家于一身的文化巨人。

## Wonderful Paragraph
精彩片段

**Paragraph 1**

### 司马迁早年生涯及教育背景
### Sima Qian's Early Life and Education

Sima Qian (145—c. 90B. C.) was a Prefect of the Grand Scribes (太史令) of the Han Dynasty. He is regarded as the father of Chinese historiography because of his highly praised work, Shiji, an overview of the history of China covering more than two thousand years from the Yellow Emperor (黄帝) to Emperor Wu of Han dynasty. His work laid the foundation for later Chinese historiography.

Sima Qian was born and grew up in Longmen, near present-day Hancheng. He was raised in a family of historiographers. Under the influence of his father, at the age of ten, Sima Qian was already well versed in old writings. At the age of twenty, with the support of his father, Sima Qian started a journey throughout the country, collecting useful first-hand historical records for his main work, Shiji. The purpose of his journey was to verify the ancient rumors and legends and to visit ancient monuments, including the renowned graves of the ancient sage kings Yu and Shun. After his travels, he was chosen to be the Palace Attendant (郎中) in the government, whose duties were to inspect different parts of the country with Emperor Wu. In 110BC, at the age of thirty five, sina Qian was sent westward on a military expedition against some "barbarian" tribes. From 109 BC, Sima Qian started to compile Shiji and inherited his father's inspiration. In 99 BC, Sima Qian got involved in the Li Ling (李陵) Affair. Li Guangli (李广利) and Li Ling, two military officers, were ordered to lead a campaign against the

Xiongnu (匈奴) in the north. Having been defeated and taken as captives, Emperor Wu attributed the defeat to Li Ling.

Emperor Wu thought Sima Qian's defence of Li Ling was an attack on Emperor Wu's brother-in-law who was fighting against Xiongnu without much success. Subsequently, he was sentenced to death. At that time, execution could be replaced either by money or mutilation (i. e. castration). Since Sima Qian did not have enough money to atone his fault, he chose the latter and was then thrown into prison.

In 96 BC, Sima Qian was released from prison. The three-year ordeal in prison did not frighten Sima Qian away. On the contrary, it became a driving force compelling him to succeed his family's legacy of recounting history. So he continued to write Shiji, which was finally finished in 91 BC.

*Paragraph 2*

## 史学家 Historian

Although the style and form of Chinese historical writings varied through the ages, Sima Qian's Shiji has since dictated the proceeding quality and style. Not only is this due to the fact that the Chinese historical form was codified in the second dynastic history by Ban Gu's (班固) Han Shu (汉书), but historians regard Sima Qian's work as their model, which stands as the "official format" of the history of China.

In writing Shiji, Sima Qian initiated a new writing style by presenting history in a series of biographies. His work extends over 130 chapters-not in historical sequence, but was divided into particular subjects, including annals, chronicles, treatises-on music, ceremonies, calendars, religion, economics, and extended biographies. Before Sima Qian, histories were written as dynastic history; his idea of a general history affected later historiographers like Zhengqiao (郑樵) in writing Tongshi (通史) and Sima Guang (司马光) in writing Zizhi Tongjian (资治通鉴). Sima Qian even affected the writing style of histories in other places, as seen in The History of Korea, which was written as a general history.

文化名人
Eminent Literati

**Paragraph 3**

# 文学形象的塑造
## Literary Figure

Sima Qian's Shiji is respected as a model of biographical literature with high literary value.

**Skillful depiction**: its artistry was mainly reflected in the skillful portrayal of many distinctive characters which were based on true historical information. Sima Qian was also good at illustrating the response of the character by placing him in a sharp confrontation and letting his words and deeds speak for him. The use of conversations in his writing also makes the descriptions more vibrant and realistic.

**Innovative approach**: Sima Qian also initiated a new approach in writing history. The language used in Shiji was informal, humorous and full of variations. This was an innovative way of writing at that time and thus it has always been esteemed as the highest achievement of classical Chinese writing.

**Concise language**: Sima Qian formed his own simple, concise, fluent, and easy-to-read style. He made his own comments while recounting the historical events. In writing the biographies in Shiji, he avoided making general descriptions. Instead, he tried to catch the essence of the events and portrayed the characters concretely and thus the characters in Shiji gave the readers vivid images with strong artistic appeal.

**Influence on literature**: Sima Qian's writings were influential to Chinese writing, which become a role model for various types of prose within the neo-classical movement of the Tang-Song (唐宋) period. The great use of characterisation and plotting also influenced fictional writing, including the classical short stories of the middle and late medieval period (Tang-Ming), as well as the vernacular novel of the late imperial period. Shiji still stands as a "textbook" for the studies of classical Chinese worldwide.

**Other literary works**: apart from Shiji, Sima Qian had written eight rhapsodies, which are compiled in Ban Gu's Hanshu. Sima Qian expressed his suffering during the Li Ling Affair and his perseverance in writing Shiji in these rhapsodies.

## Cultural Links
## 文化链接

### 《报任安书》

《报任安书》是司马迁任中书令时写给他的朋友任安的一封信,见于《汉书·司马迁传》及《文选》卷四十一。任安,字少卿,西汉荥阳人。年轻时比较贫困,后来做了大将军卫青的舍人,由于卫青的荐举,当了郎中,后迁为益州刺史。征和二年(前91)朝中发生巫蛊案,江充乘机诬陷戾太子(刘据),戾太子发兵诛杀江充等,与丞相(刘屈氂)军大战于长安,当时任安担任北军使者护军(监理京城禁卫军北军的官),乱中接受戾太子要他发兵的命令,但按兵未动。戾太子事件平定后,汉武帝认为任安"坐观成败","怀诈,有不忠之心",论罪腰斩。任安入狱后曾写信给司马迁,希望他"尽推贤进士之义",搭救自己。直到任安临刑前,司马迁才写了这封著名的回信。在这封信中,司马迁以无比愤激的心情,叙述自己蒙受的耻辱,倾吐他内心的痛苦和不满,说明自己"隐忍苟活"的原因,表达"就极刑而无愠色"、坚持完成《史记》的决心,同时也反映了他的文学观和生死观。所以,这封信是一篇研究《史记》和司马迁的生活、思想的重要文章。

## Vocabulary
## 妙词连珠

| | |
|---|---|
| historiography 编史,历史之编纂 | chronicle 编年史 |
| verse 韵文,诗,诗节,诗句,诗篇 | treatise 论文,论述 |
| verify 检验,校验,查证,核实 | depiction 描写,叙述 |
| barbarian 粗鲁无礼的人,野蛮人 | confrontation 面对,面对面,对质 |
| execution 实行,完成,执行,死刑,制作 | vibrant 振动 |
| ordeal 严酷的考验,痛苦的经验 | innovative 创新的,革新(主义)的 |
| dictate 口述,口授,使听写,指令 | concise 简明的,简练的 |
| codify 编成法典,使法律成文化 | medieval 中世纪的,仿中世纪的 |

# Unit 4 王羲之 Wang Xizhi

## Key Sentences 流畅精句

1. Wang Xizhi, whose courtesy name was Yishao, was acelebrated writer and calligrapher during the Eastern Jin Dynasty.
   王羲之,字逸少,东晋著名书法家和文学家。
2. A critic later commented on his style as "light as a floating cloud, vigorous as a startled dragon."
   后来有位评论家评论他的书法风格是:"飘若游云,矫若惊龙"。
3. His most famous calligraphic work is the Preface to the Poems Composed at the Orchid Pavilion (Lanting Xu).
   他的书法作品中,行楷《兰亭序》最具有代表性。
4. Wang Xizhi's preface turned out to be outstanding both by standards of literature and calligraphy. The Song Dynasty calligrapher Mi Fu even called it the world's best work written in running script.
   王羲之的这篇序言不仅文采斐然,书法艺术更精美绝伦,宋代书法家米芾称之为"天下行书第一"。
5. It is said that Emperor Taizong of the Tang Dynasty treasured the work (Lanting Xu) so much that he had it buried with him in his tomb.
   传说唐太宗李世民对《兰亭序》十分珍爱,死时将其殉葬于自己的陵墓之中。
6. Although the original has long been lost, there are still a number of high-quality tracing copies and rubbings in existance.
   尽管真迹已经散失,当今仍有很多临摹本存在。

用英语说中国——古今名人
Introduce China in English—Eminent Persons

## Wonderful Paragraph
精彩片段

**Paragraph 1**

# W 王羲之
ang Xizhi

Wang Xizhi (321—379 or 303—361 or 307—365) was a Chinese calligrapher, traditionally referred to as the "Sage of Calligraphy".

Born in Linyi, Shandong, he spent most of his life in the present-day Shaoxing, Zhejiang. He learned the art of calligraphy from Wei Shuo. He excelled in every script but particularly in the semi-cursive script. Unfortunately, none of his original works remains today.

His most famous work is the "Preface to the Poems Composed at the Orchid Pavilion", the preface of a collection of poems written by a number of poets when gathering at Lanting near the town of Shaoxing for the Spring Purification Festival. The original is lost, but there are a number of fine tracing copies and rubbings.

Wang Xizhi is particularly remembered for one of his hobbies - rearing geese. Legend has it that he learnt the key of how to turn his wrist while writing by observing how the geese move their necks.

Wang Xizhi had seven children, all of whom were notable calligraphers. The most distinguished one was his youngest son, Wang Xianzhi.

**Paragraph 2**

# T "二王"
he Two Wangs

Wang Xizhi, "the Calligraphy Saint" and Wang Xianzhi, his son, are called "the Two Wangs (Kings)." Their calligraphies of the Cursive Hand are characterized by extreme beauty, elegance and prominence. Their calligraphies exerted a great impact on those of later generations.

Chinese calligraphy has had a great influence on Chinese art and communication through its many systems and schools. With a long history and tradition, it has been prosperous, getting more and more popular among today's numerous art forms. The reason why people enjoy Chinese calligraphy is that they can both develop skills and mold their temperament through learning and appreciating calligraphy. Chinese calligraphy, with its unique beauty and irresistible charms, is stepping out of the country and into the world.

## Cultural Links
## 文化链接

### 东床坦腹

晋太尉郗鉴想选女婿。他知道王导门下的几个子弟都是俊才,便想从中选一个做他的乘龙快婿,写了一函给王导,说明了他的意思。王导复信,同意让郗鉴派人去选,并通知了几个小伙子准备一番。届时,几个小伙子都收拾打扮停当,准备迎接挑选,惟王羲之没有打扮,仍是原先自在随便的样子。选婿的人来了,个个目测过,见王羲之还敞开衣服,露出肚皮,坐在胡床上吃胡饼,根本没把能不能入选当回事。结果郗鉴派出的差使如实回禀,出人意料之外,郗鉴听后很高兴地说,此正吾佳婿也!差使问看中的是哪一个,得到回答,选中的是王羲之。现在我们使用的成语"东床坦腹"、"东床骄婿"、"东床骄客",故事就来自王羲之的东床坦腹吃胡饼之事。

## Vocabulary
## 妙词连珠

| | |
|---|---|
| calligrapher 书法家 | orchid [植] 兰,兰花,淡紫色 |
| Sage of calligraphy 书经 | pavilion 大帐篷,亭,阁 |
| excell 胜过,超过,优于,超越 | purfication 镶边,花边 |
| script 手稿,手迹,剧本,考生的笔试卷,原本 | tracing 追踪,追查,描摹,摹图,显迹 |

rubbing 摹拓,摹拓品
rear 后面,背后,后方,屁股;培养, 饲养,举起,树立,栽种
elegance 高雅,典雅,优雅,雅致
prominence 突出,显著,突出物
temperament 气质,性情,易激动, 急躁
irresistible 不可抵抗的,不能压制的

# 文化名人
# Eminent Literati

# Unit 5  玄奘 Xuanzang

## Key Sentences
## 流畅精句

1. Xuanzang, whose trivial name was Chen Yi, was a native of Goushi, Luozhou (now Yanshi, in Henan Province). Xuanzang was his Buddhist monastic name. He was also called Master Sanzang.
   玄奘俗名陈祎,洛州缑氏(今河南偃师)人。玄奘是他的法号,又称三藏法师。

2. He had an unusual power of understanding and a preference for Buddhist scriptures. When he was 15 years old, he could recite The Nirvana Sutra very fluently.
   他对佛经有一种超乎常人的悟性和偏爱,15岁就能流利地背诵《涅槃经》了。

3. In order to understand the true essence of the Buddhist philosphy, he decided to go to India—the hometown of Sakyamuni, founder of Buddhism—to seek Buddhist scrptures and doctrines, and to be a disciple of Sakyamuni by direct line.
   为了了解佛学经典的真谛,他决心到佛教创始人释迦牟尼的故乡——天竺(今印度)去取经求法,做一个释迦牟尼的"嫡传"弟子。

4. In order to have a complete picture of Indian Buddhism, Xuanzang left Nalanda temporarily and went to study in South India. He traveled to more than 100 small states successively, visiting famous monks and temples.
   为了了解天竺佛学的全貌,玄奘暂离那烂陀寺,到南天竺游学,他先后走了百余个小国,遍访名僧、名寺。

5. From then on, Xuanzang was recognized as the highest authority of Buddhism in the Buddhist Holyland.
此后,玄奘在佛教圣地的佛教界被公认为是佛学的最高权威。
6. In the 17th year of Zhenguan, although the Indians tried to persuade him into staying in India, Xuanzang started on his journey back to China, taking with him 657 Buddhist Scriptures which were carried by elephants and horses.
贞观十七年,玄奘谢绝了天竺各界的诚恳挽留,用大象、马驮着657部佛经,启程回国。
7. After returning to China, Xuanzang raced against time to translate the Buddhist Scriptures and compose Records of the Western Regions of the Great Tang Empire (Da Tang Xi Yu Ji). Within 19 years he translated 74 Buddhist scriptures, 1 335 volumes in all.
回国后,玄奘只争朝夕地投入佛经的翻译和《大唐西域记》的撰写工作。19年中,共译出佛经74部,1 335卷。

## Wonderful Paragraph
### 精彩片段

**Paragraph 1**

# 玄奘 Xuanzang

Xuanzang (Wade-Giles: Hsüan-tsang) (599-664) was a famous Chinese Buddhist monk.

Xuanzang was born near Luoyang, Henan in 599 as Chen Yi and died 664 in Yu Hua Gong. He came from a scholarly family. He became famous for his seventeen year-long trip to India, during which he studied with many famous Buddhist masters, especially at the famous center of Buddhist learning in Nālanda. When he returned, he brought with him some 657 Sanskrit texts. With the emperor's support, he set up a large translation bureau in Chang'an (present-day Xi'an), drawing students and collaborators from all over East Asia. He is credited with the translation of some 1 330 fascicles of scriptures into Chinese. His strongest personal interest in Buddhism was in the field of Yogācāra（瑜伽行派）or Consciousness-only（唯识）.

The force of his own study, translation and commentary of the texts of these traditions initiated the development of the Faxiang school（法相宗）in East Asia. Although the school itself did not thrive for a long time, its theories regarding perception, consciousness, karma, rebirth, etc. found their way into the doctrines of other more successful schools. Xuanzang's closest and most eminent student was Kuiji（窥基）who became recognized as the first patriarch of the Faxiang school.

**Paragraph 2**

# N 名字 ames

Xuanzang is also known by the Cantonese transcription of his title, Táng Sānzàng（唐三藏）, as Tong Sam Jong. Less common romanizations of Xuanzang include Hhuen Kwan, Hiouen Thsang, Hiuen Tsiang, Hsientsang, Hsuan Chwang, Hsuan Tsiang, Hwen Thsang, Xuan Cang, Xuan Zang, Shuen Shang, Yuan Chang, Yuan Chwang, and Yuen Chwang. In Japanese, he is known as Genjō or Sanzō.

**Paragraph 3**

# L 遗产 egacy

In 646, under the Emperor's request, Xuanzang completed his book Records of the Western Regions of the Great Tang Empire（大唐西域记）, which has become one of the primary sources for the study of medieval history in India. This book was first translated into French by Sinologist Stanislas Julien in 1857. There was also a biography of Xuanzang written by the monk Huili. Both books were first translated into English by Samuel Beal, in 1884 and 1911 respectively. An English translation with copious notes by

Thomas Watters was edited by T. S. Rhys Dadivds and S. W. Bushell, and published posthumously in London in 1905.

Xuanzang's journey along the so-called Silk Roads, and the legends that grew up around it, inspired the Ming novel Journey to the West, one of the great classics of Chinese literature. The Xuanzang of the novel is the reincarnation of a disciple of Gautama Buddha, and is protected on his journey by three notorious monsters. One of them, the monkey, was a popular favourite and profoundly influenced Chinese culture and contemporary Japanese manga (including the popular Dragon Ball series), and became well known in the West by Arthur Waley's translation and later the cult TV series Monkey.

## Cultural Links 文化链接

### 《西游记》

《西游记》取材于唐太宗时僧人玄奘往天竺(印度)取经的故事,而加以神魔化的发挥,被称为至奇至幻之书,书中以丰富瑰奇的想象描写了师徒四众在迢遥的西方途上和穷山恶水冒险斗争的历程,并将所经历的千难万险形象化为妖魔鬼怪所设置的八十一难,以动物幻化的有情的精怪生动地表现了无情的山川的险阻,并以降妖服怪歌颂了取经人排除艰难的战斗精神,小说是人战胜自然的凯歌。几百年来,一直以其高度的浪漫主义成就,积极向上的抗争精神,绚丽多彩、汪洋恣肆的笔调,受到人们的喜爱。

## Vocabulary 妙词连珠

Buddhist 佛教徒
Sanskirt 梵语
collaborator 合作者
posthumously 后来解

fascicle [解]肌束,[植](花,叶等的)束,簇,丛
thrive 兴旺,繁荣,茁壮成长,旺盛
doctrine 教条,学说

eminent 显赫的,杰出的,有名的,优良的
romanization 古罗马化,皈依天主教
copious 很多的,广识的,丰富的
reincarnation 再投胎,化身,再生
notorious 声名狼籍的
profoundly 深深地,哀心地
contemporary 同时代的人
cult 礼拜,祭仪,一群信徒,礼拜式

# Unit 6  李白 / Li Bai

## Key Sentences
## 流畅精句

1. The High Tang period was the golden age of Chinese poetry, and Li Bai was the greatest poet of this period.
   盛唐是中国诗歌的黄金时代,而李白就是这一时代最伟大的代表诗人。
2. The charm of Li Bai's poems lies in his masterful conveyance of the splendor of the Tang Dynasty through his unique artistry.
   李白诗作的魅力在于他通过自己独特的艺术个性传递了盛唐气象。
3. His bold vision and unbridted tree spirit wondertully reved the youth and vitality of the Chinese nation during the prime of the Tang Dynasty.
   他恢宏的气魄和无拘无束的自由精神,集中体现了盛唐时期整个民族青春勃发的力量。
4. Li Bai's artistic gift and temperament are unparalleled in the history of Chinese poetery.
   李白的艺术天才和气质使他在中国诗史上独一无二。
5. His artistic style is unprecedented, his poems filled with unusual imagination and bold hyperbole.
   他的艺术风格是前无古人的,他的诗歌中充满奇特的想像和大胆的夸张。
6. Li Bai's poetic creations reflect his untrammeled, romantic spirit.
   李白的创作反映了他狂放不羁、浪漫自由的精神气质。

7. Li Bai's contemporaries and people of later generations produced many legendary anecdotes to commemorate him.
这使时人和后人营造了许多关于诗人的传奇。

## Wonderful Paragraph 精彩片段

### Paragraph 1

## Li Bai 李白

Li Bai (701—762), Chinese style name Taibai (太白), was a List of Chinese poet living in Tang Dynasty.

Renowned as the Poet Immortal, Li Bai was among the most well-respected poets in China's literary history. Approximately 1 100 poems of his remain today.

Li Bai is best known for the extravagant imagination and striking Taoismimagery in his poetry, as well as for his great love for liquor.

### Paragraph 2

## Early Life 早年生涯

Li Bai was the son of a rich merchant; his birthplace is uncertain. His family moved to Jiangyou, near modern Chengdu in Sichuan province, when he was 5 years old. He was influenced by Confucianism and Taoism thought, but ultimately his family heritage did not provide him with much opportunity in the aristocratic Tang dynasty. Though he expressed the wish to become an official, he did not sit for the Chinese civil service examination. Instead, beginning at age 25, he travelled around China, affecting a wild and free persona very much contrary to the prevailing ideas of a proper Confucian gentleman. This portrayal fascinated the aristocrats and common people alike and he was introduced to the Emperor Xuanzong of Tang around 742.

He was given a post at the Hanlin Academy, which served to provide a source of scholarly expertise for the emperor. Li Bai remained less than two years as a poet in the Emperor's service before he was dismissed for an unknown indiscretion. Thereafter he wandered throughout China for the rest of his life.

*Paragraph 3*

## P 诗歌 oetry

Over a thousand poems are attributed to him, but the authenticity of many of these is uncertain. He is best known for his yue fu poems, which are intense and often fantastic. He is often associated with Taoism: there is a strong element of this in his works, both in the sentiments they express and in their spontaneous tone. Nevertheless, his gufeng ("ancient airs") often adopt the perspective of the Confucian moralist, and many of his occasional verses are fairly conventional.

Much like the genius of Mozart there exist many legends on how effortlessly Li Bai composed his poetry, even (or some say, especially) when drunk; his favorite form is the jueju (five- or seven-character quatrain), of which he composed some 160 pieces. Using striking, unconventional imagery, Li Bai is able to create exquisite pieces to utilize fully the elements of the language. His use of language is not as erudite as Du Fu's but equally effective, impressing through an extravagance of imagination and a direct connection of a free-spirited persona with the reader. Li Bai's interactions with nature, friendship, and his acute observations of life inform his best poems. Some of the rest, like Changgan xing, records the hardships or emotions of common people. Like the best Chinese poets, Li Bai often evades translation.

One of Li Bai's most famous poems is "Drinking Alone under the Moon", which is a good example of some of the most famous aspects of his poetry—a very spontaneous poem, full of natural imagery and anthropomorphism.

文化名人
Eminent Literati

## Cultural Links 文化链接

### 只要功夫深铁杵磨成针

有一个流传很广的传说,是讲李白小时候的事。他曾经在昌隆县的象耳山中读书,有一天,读书遇到了难处时,屋外传来一阵欢笑声。李白走到窗前一看,原来是小伙伴在做游戏。他立刻丢下书,奔了出去。

春天里,野花满山,蜂飞蝶舞。李白一边采野花一边扑蝴蝶,来到一条小溪旁,看见一位满头白发的老奶奶正在溪边的石头上磨一根铁棒。他走上前去,好奇地问:"您磨这个做什么呀?"

老奶奶头也不抬地回答说:"做针呐。"

"做针?这么粗的铁棒怎么能磨成针呢?"李白惊讶地问。

"孩子,这铁棒虽然粗,可我今天磨明天磨,一直磨下去,总有一天能磨成针的。"老奶奶说完,又埋头磨起来。

李白摸了摸脑袋想,老奶奶说得对啊!只要功夫深,铁棒磨成针。读书不也是这样吗?不下功夫,怎么能学到丰富的知识呢?于是,他立刻跑回家,读起书来。

## Vocabulary 妙词连珠

immortal 不朽的
extravagant 奢侈的
ultimately 最后,终于,根本,基本上
heritage 遗产,继承权,传统
persona 人,角色
prevail 流行,盛行,获胜,成功
portrayal 描画,描写
fascinat 使着迷,使神魂颠倒
expertise 专家的意见,专门技术
indiscretion 不慎重,轻率
authenticity 确实性,真实性

sentiment 情操,情感,情绪
spontaneous 自发的,自然产生的
perspective 观点,观察
effortlessly 容易的,不费力气的
quatrain 四行诗
exquisite 优美的,高雅的
utilize 利用
erudite 博学的
interaction 交互作用,交感
acute 敏锐的,[医]急性的,剧烈
evade 规避,逃避,躲避

# Unit 7  杜甫 Du Fu

## Key Sentences
流畅精句

1. When we discuss Tang-dynasty poetry, people often list the names of both Li Bai and Du Fu.
   谈及唐诗,人们常常"李杜"并举。
2. Du Fu is credited as the greatest realist poet of ancient China.
   杜甫被称为中国古代最伟大的现实主义诗人。
3. His poems mostly came into being during and after the rebellion led by An Lushan and Shi Siming.
   他的诗作大都成于安史之乱以及乱后时期。
4. Du Fu fell victim to this social upheaval. He suffered the bitterness of homelessness and drifted from one place to another, experiencing fully the hardships of survival in a time of upheaval.
   杜甫本人就是社会动乱的受害者,他饱尝流离之苦,感受到了乱世生存的艰难。
5. His son died of hunger.
   他自己的幼子因无食而饿死。
6. From the perspective of a poet and an individual, Du Fu provides an accurate and insightful record of significant historical events and real lives of his time, hence garmering his poetry the title "Lyrical History."
   杜甫以诗人的视角,从个人的独特体验出发,忠实、敏锐地记录了他那个时代的重要历史事件和生活现实,使其作品赢得了"诗史"的称号。

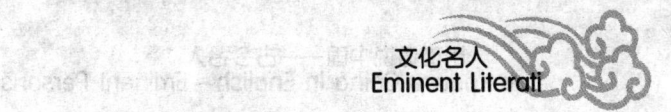

7. Unlike Li Bai's free and natural style, Du Fu was particularly concerned with minute detail and careful wording.
和李白的飘逸自然不同,杜甫作诗讲究细腻锤炼。

## Wonderful Paragraph 精彩片段

### Paragraph 1

# Du Fu 杜甫

Du Fu or Tu Fu (712—770) was a prominent Chinese poet of the Tang Dynasty. Along with Li Bai, he is frequently called the greatest of the Chinese poets. His own greatest ambition was to help his country by becoming a successful civil servant, but he proved unable to make the necessary accommodations. His life, like the whole country, was devastated by the An Lushan Rebellion of 755, and the last 15 years of his life were a time of almost constant unrest.

Initially unpopular, his works came to be hugely influential in both Chinese and Japanese culture. He has been called Poet-Historian and the Poet-Sage by Chinese critics, while the range of his work has allowed him to be introduced to Western readers as "the Chinese Virgil, Horace, Ovid, Shakespeare, Milton, Burns, Wordsworth, Béranger, Hugo or Baudelaire".

### Paragraph 2

# Poet Sage "诗圣"

A second favourite epithet of Chinese critics is that of "poet sage", a counterpart to the philosophical sage, Confucius. One of the earliest surviving works, The Song of the Wagons (from around 750), gives voice to the sufferings of a conscript soldier in the imperial army, even before the beginning of the rebellion; this poem brings out the tension between the need of acceptance and fulfilment of one's duties, and a clear-sighted consciousness of the suffering which this can involve. These themes are continuously articulated in the poems on the lives of both soldiers and civilians which Du Fu produced throughout his life.

Du Fu's compassion, for himself and for others, was part of his general broadening of the scope of poetry: he devoted many works to topics which had previously been considered unsuitable for poetic treatment. And he wrote extensively on subjects such as domestic life, calligraphy, paintings, animals and other poems.

**Paragraph 3**

## 诗技精湛
## Technical Excellence

Du Fu's work is notable above all for its range. Chinese critics traditionally used the term complete symphony(集大成), a reference to Mencius' description of Confucius.

Although he wrote in all poetic forms, Du Fu is best known for his lùshi, a type of poem with strict constraints on the form and content of the work. About two thirds of his 1 500 extant works are in this form, and he is generally considered to be its leading exponent. His best lùshi use the parallelisms required by the form to add expressive content rather than as mere technical restrictions.

**Paragraph 4**

## 著作译版
## Translation

There have been a number of notable translations of Du Fu's work into English. The translators have each had to contend with the same problems of bringing out the formal constraints of the original without sounding laboured to the western ear (particularly when translating lǜshi), and of dealing with the allusions contained particularly in the later works. One extreme on each issue is represented by Kenneth Rexroth's One Hundred Poems From the Chinese. His are free translations, which seek to conceal the parallelisms through enjambement and expansion and contraction of the content; his responses to the allusions are firstly to omit most of these poems from his selection, and secondly to "translate out" the references in those works which he does select.

An example of the opposite approach is Burton Watson's The Selected Poems of Du Fu. Watson follows the parallelisms quite strictly, persuading the western reader to adapt to the poems rather than vice versa. Similarly, he deals with the allusion of the later works by combining literal translation with extensive annotation.

## Cultural Links 文化链接

### 杜甫草堂

公元759年,为避"安史之乱",杜甫由甘肃来成都建茅屋居住,即"万里桥西一草堂",诗人在草堂先后居住近5年,写诗240余首。原草堂早已不存在,以后历史均有修葺,现存主要建筑有大廨、法史堂、柴门、工部祠、少陵草堂、碑亭等。草堂博物馆内,有3万余件珍贵文物,是研究杜甫的珍贵史料。

草堂总面积为300亩,其间檐廊结构布局紧凑,位于史法堂中的铜色杜甫像,恢宏古朴,工部祠堂内供奉有杜甫的泥塑像,栩栩如生,让人顿生敬穆之情。草堂内,小桥、流水、梅园、竹林交错庭中,另有春之梅,夏之荷,秋之菊,冬之兰可赏,置身其中,让人既有发古之幽思,又享大自然之浪漫。

## Vocabulary 妙词连珠

accommodation 住处,膳宿,(社会集团间的)迁就融合
devaste 毁坏
unrest 不安的状态,动荡的局面
initially 最初,开头
range 山脉,行列,范围,射程
epithet 绰号,称号
counterpart 副本,极相似的人或物
articulate 有关节的,发音清晰的
scope (活动)范围,机会,余地
exponent 解释者,说明者,代表者,典型,指数
parallelism [数]平行,对应,类似
restriction 限制,约束
allusion 提及,暗示
enjambement (诗句之)跨行连续
omit 省略,疏忽,遗漏
annotation 注解,评注;注解,注释

# Unit 8　白居易　Bai Juyi

## Key Sentences
## 流畅精句

1. Bai Juyi was the most prolific poet of the Tang Dynasty, with nearly 3 000 poems to his name still extant today.
   白居易是唐代最为高产的诗人,他的诗歌现存近三千首。
2. His poems are rich in contents, reflecting not only social problems in the hopes of waking up the ruling class, but also meticulously recording his personal life and feelings.
   白居易的创作内容极为丰富,他不仅用诗歌反映社会问题以警醒统治者,同时也在词句中详细记录了个人的情感和生活。
3. Bai Juyi attached great importance to his allegorical poems, which relate daily events in very ordinary language and reflect social problems in an extensive way, embodying the Confucian concept of poetry serving practical purposes.
   白居易非常重视自己的讽喻诗。这些诗作以通俗的语言书写时事,广泛反映社会问题,儒家注重实用的诗歌观念充分体现于其中。
4. "The Eternal Regret" and "Song of the Lute" are the most popular narrative poems composed by Bai Juyi.
   白居易的两首叙事长诗《长恨歌》和《琵琶行》是其流传最广的诗作。
5. Bai Juyi aspired after a simple, easy-to-understand language in his poems and seldom used literary allusions.
   白居易自觉追求浅显平易的语言风格,少用典故。

6. His poems were widely circulated both at home and abroad during his lifetime, and the easy-to-understand language constitutes one of the important reasons behind this fact.
他的作品在其生前就被广为传抄，且流播海外，语言上的明白易懂是一个重要原因。

## Wonderful Paragraph
## 精彩片段

### Paragraph 1

# Bai Juyi 白居易

Bai Juyi or Po Chü-i (772 — 846) was a Chinese poet of the Tang dynasty. His poems are not cheerful, and were themed around his responsibilities as a governor of several small provinces to sympathise with his people.

### Paragraph 2

# Life 生平

He was born in Xinzheng to a poor but scholarly family. At the age of ten he was sent away from his family to be educated near Chang'an. He passed the jinshi degree in 800. His official career was initially successful: he was a Member of the Hanlin Academy and Reminder of the Left from 807 until 815, when he was exiled for remonstrating too forcefully. His career resumed when he was made Prefect of Hangzhou (822—825) and then Suzhou (825—827).

文化名人
Eminent Literati

**Paragraph 3**

# W著作
orks

He wrote over 2 800 poems, which he had copied and distributed to ensure their survival.

He is most notable for the accessibility of his work. It is said that he rewrote any part of a poem which one of his servants was unable to understand. He tried to use simple language and direct themes. Two of his most famous works are the long narrative poems The Eternal Regret, which tells the story of Yang Guifei, and song of the Lute. Like Du Fu, he also had a strong sense of social responsibility, and he is also well-known for his satirical poems, such as The Elderly Charcoal Seller. Bai Juyi's accessibility made him extremely popular in his lifetime in both China and Japan, and he continues to be so today.

## Cultural Links
文化链接

### 叙事长诗《长恨歌》

白居易的诗歌中最为出名是叙事长诗《长恨歌》,堪称中国古代诗歌杰作。该诗是他35岁为周至县尉时所作。该诗以民间流传唐玄宗和杨贵妃的故事为题材,加以虚构,写得有声有色,生动动人,被评论家认为是唐代歌行体长诗中最好的一首,在我国诗歌史上占有突出地位。在这首诗里,他敢于批评唐玄宗的荒淫,至有"汉皇重色思倾国"、"从此君王不早朝"等语。后面描写两人之深情,既微有讽刺,又饱含哀怜。说及生离死别的情形,笔锋颇带感情。全诗从曲曲折折的故事中兴起层层波澜,感情充沛复杂,读之给人以极大的感染力。

# 用英语说中国——古今名人
## Introduce China in English—Eminent Persons

### Vocabulary 妙词连珠

theme(谈话,写作等的)题目,主题,学生的作文,作文题,[音乐]主题,主题曲,主旋律
exile 放逐,充军,流放,流犯,被放逐者
remonstrate 抗议
forcefully 强有力地,激烈地
resume 摘要,概略,<美>履历
survival 生存,幸存,残存,幸存者,残存物
accessibility 易接近,可到达的
narrative 叙述性的
satirical 好讽刺的,爱挖苦人的
charcoal 木炭
accessibility 易接近,可到达的

文化名人
Eminent Literati

# Unit 9  Su Shi
苏轼

## Key Sentences
流畅精句

1. After Ouyang Xiu, Su Shi became the second master of literature in the Song Dynasty.
   苏轼继欧阳修之后,成为北宋又一代文学宗师。
2. Su Shi claimed top distinctions in the literary creation of poetry, ci poetry and prose and was recognized for the highest literary standards during the Song Dynasty.
   苏轼在诗、词、文创作上都独领风骚,代表了北宋文坛的最高水平。
3. He aslo excelled at calligraphy and painting, and was one of the four Song-dynasty master calligraphers. His calligraphic works were much sought after even in his own time.
   同时,他精通书法、绘画,是宋代四大书法家之一,其作品当时就为人争购。
4. With a Confucian sense of social responsibility and mission, as well as a Taoist and Buddhist complaisance, understanding and aloofness existed harmoniously in him and formed his personality and spiritual world.
   他将儒家的社会责任感、使命感与道、佛两家的圆融通达和超然物外结合起来,构筑了自己的人格与精神境界。
5. Su Shi made the greatest contribution to the development of ci poetry.
   苏轼对词的发展贡献最大。

6. He broke through the subtle and decadent style popular since the Late Tang and, by adding a masculine power to it, broadened its scope to form a free and powerful ci style of his own.
他打破了晚唐以来婉约柔靡的词风,将阳刚之气注入词坛,从而开拓了词的境界,开创了另成一家的豪放词派。

## Wonderful Paragraph 精彩片段

### Paragraph 1

# S 苏轼
u Shi

Su Shi(1037—1101) was a writer, poet, artist, calligrapher and statesman of the Song Dynasty, one of the major poets of the Song era. His zi or courtesy name is Zizhan(子瞻) and his hao or pseudonym Dongpo Jushi(东坡居士), and he is often referred to as Su Dongpo(苏东坡).

### Paragraph 2

# L 生平
ife

Su Shi was born in Meishan, near Mount Emei in what is now Sichuan province. His brother Su Che(苏辙) and his father Su Xun(苏洵) were both famous literati. In 1057, he and his brother passed the municipal (highest-level) civil service examinations to attain the degree of jinshi, a prerequisite for high government office at that time. Throughout the next twenty years, he held a variety of government positions throughout China; most notably in Hangzhou, where he was responsible for constructing a pedestrian causeway across the West Lake that still bears his name: sudi(苏堤).

He was often at odds with a political faction headed by Wang Anshi. This faction's rise to power eventually resulted in Su Shi being exiled twice to remote places; first (1080—1084) to Huangzhou (now in Hubei province), and the second time (1094-1100) to Huizhou (now in Guangdong province) and Hainan island. The Dongpo Academy in Hainan was built on the site of his residence in exile. In Huangzhou, Su Shi lived at a farm called Dongpo ('Eastern Slope'), from which he took his literary pseudonym. He died in Changzhou, Jiangsu province.

## Paragraph 3

## W著作
orks

Su Dongpo excelled in the shi, ci and fu forms, as well as prose, calligraphy and painting; some of his notable poems include the First and Second Chibifu (赤壁赋 The Red Cliffs, written during his first exile), Nian Nu Jiao: Chibi Huai Gu (念奴娇·赤壁怀古 Remembering Chibi, to the tune of Nian Nu Jiao) and Shui diao ge tou (水调歌头 Remembering Su Che on the Mid-Autumn Festival). The bulk of his poems (around 2 400) are shi, but his poetic fame rests largely on his 350 ci. He founded the haofang school, which cultivated an attitude of heroic abandon. In both his written works and his visual art, he combined spontaneity, objectivity and vivid descriptions of natural phenomena. He also wrote essays on politics and governance such as Liuhou Lun.

## Cultural Links
文化链接

### "东坡肉"的来历

苏东坡曾两度到杭州为官。公元 1088 年时,西湖久无整治日见颓败,官府花了大钱整治西湖却未见成效。时任太守竟欲废湖造田。危急时刻苏东坡再度到杭州任太守。他带领杭州民众疏浚西湖,终使西湖重返青春。杭州百姓感激不尽,纷纷敲锣打鼓、抬猪担酒送到太守府。苏东坡推辞不掉,只好收下。面对成堆猪肉,他叫府上厨师把肉切成方块,用自己家

用英语说中国——古今名人
Introduce China in English—Eminent Persons

乡四川眉山炖肘子的方法,结合杭州人的口味特点,加入姜、葱、红糖、料酒、酱油,用文火焖得香嫩酥烂,然后再按疏浚西湖的民工花名册,每户一块,将肉分送出去。

民工们品尝着苏太守送来的红烧肉,顿感味道不同寻常,纷纷称其为"东坡肉"。有家饭馆老板灵机一动,设法请来太守府的厨师,按照苏东坡的方法制成"东坡肉",于是饭店从早到晚顾客不断,生意格外兴隆。别的饭馆一见也纷纷效仿,一时间,大小饭馆都卖起了"东坡肉","东坡肉"于是成了杭州第一大菜。

## Vocabulary 妙词连珠

pseudonym 假名,笔名
municipal 市政的,市立的,地方性的,地方自治的
prerequisite 先决条件
construct 建造,构造,创立
pedestrain 步行者
causeway 堤道,铺道
faction 派别,小集团,派系斗争,小派系,内讧
slope 斜坡,斜面,倾斜

bulk 大小,体积,大批,大多数,散装
visual 看的,视觉的,形象的,栩栩如生的
spontaneity 自发性
objectivity 客观性,客观现实
vivid 生动的,鲜明的,鲜艳的,大胆的,清晰的,活泼的,逼真的
phenomena 现象
goverance 可统治的,可控制的,可支配的

# Unit 10  Lu You
## 陆游

## Key Sentences
### 流畅精句

1. Throughout Lu You's lifetime, there were two obsessions he could not free himself from. One was his ambition to restore his conquered country and the other his yearning for his ex-wife Tang Wan.
   在陆游的一生中,有两个难以排解的情结,一是收复故地的报国之志,一是对前妻唐婉的终生怀恋。

2. What impresses readers most is a sense of desolation stemming from his failure to realize his lofty ideals.
   陆诗中让人体味最深的是他壮志难酬的悲凉情绪。

3. He created a great numbr of poems recording his dreams, a phenomenon never found among his predecessors.
   陆游创作了大批记梦诗,这在以往的作家中是绝无仅有的。

4. These poems mostly expressed his longing to join in the fight to safeguard his country. Through these poems we can touch the soul of a patriotic poet.
   这些诗歌大部分表达的是对参战报国的渴望,通过它们,我们能够触摸到诗人矢志爱国的灵魂。

5. It's said that Lu You died in a dream of fighting the enemy.
   据说陆游是做着从军杀敌之梦离开人世的。

# 用英语说中国——古今名人
## Introduce China in English—Eminent Persons

### Wonderful Paragraph
### 精彩片段

**Paragraph 1**

# 早年职业
## Early Career

Lu You (1125—1210), was a Chinese poet of the southern Song dynasty.

Lu You came from a family in which there were some government officials. At that time the southern Song dynasty was frequently invaded by the Jin Dynasty (金国). When he was one, Kaifeng (开封), the capital of Northern Song dynasty had been captured by the troops of Jin Dynasty. Lu You, who was still an infane, fled with his family. Because of the family influence and social turbulence in childhood, Lu You was committed to save the nation by outing the Jurchens.

**Paragraph 2**

# 官场生涯
## Official Career

He passed the civil service examination, but was unsuccessful in his official career: he adopted a patriotic stance, advocating the expulsion of the Jurchen from northern China, but this position was out of tune with the times. He retired to Shaoxing (绍兴) in frustration.

**Paragraph 3**

# 风格
## Style

Lu You wrote over ten thousand poems, in both the shi and ci forms, plus a number of prose works. In his poetry he continues to articulate the beliefs which cost him his official career, calling for reconquest of the north. Watson identifies these works as part of the legacy of Du Fu. Watson compares a second body of work, poems on country life and growing old, to those of Bai Juyi and Tao Qian. Lu You had written a lot of poem in his whole life, more than 10 000, still having 9 300 after erasing some of them by Lu You himself.

## Cultural Links
## 文化链接

### 钗头凤·陆游与唐婉

　　红酥手,黄滕酒,满城春色宫墙柳。东风恶,欢情薄,一杯愁绪,几年离索。错,错,错!

　　春如旧,人空瘦,泪痕红浥鲛绡透。桃花落,闲池阁,山盟虽在,锦书难托。莫,莫,莫!

　　陆游的《钗头凤》词,是一篇"风流千古"的佳作,它描述了一个动人的爱情悲剧。据《历代诗馀》载,陆游年轻时娶表妹唐婉为妻,感情深厚。但因陆母不喜欢唐婉,威逼二人各自另行嫁娶。十年之后的一天,陆游在沈园春游,与唐婉不期而遇。此情此景,陆游"怅然久之,为赋《钗头凤》一词,题园壁间。"这便是这首词的来历。传说,唐婉见了这首《钗头凤》词后,感慨万端,亦提笔和《钗头凤·世情薄》词一首。不久,唐婉竟因愁怨而死。又过了四十年,陆游七十多岁了,仍怀念唐婉,重游沈园,并作成《沈园》诗二首。

## Vocabulary
## 妙词连珠

| | |
|---|---|
| turbulence 骚乱,动荡,(液体或气体的)紊乱 | expulsion 逐出,开除 |
| | frustration 挫败,挫折,受挫 |
| Jurchen 女真人 | reconquest 再征服,夺回 |
| patriotic 爱国的,有爱国心的 | erase 抹去,擦掉,消磁,<俚>杀死 |

# Unit 11　Xin Qiji 辛弃疾

## Key Sentences
### 流畅精句

1. The Southern-Song-dynasty poet Xin Qiji is a great talent in the history of Chiense poetry.
   南宋词人辛弃疾是诗歌史上的怪杰。
2. He not only wanted to lay down his life for his country but also possessed a profound talent for military strategy. Thus he was not simply a customary literate or a popular hero but both.
   他不仅胸怀报国之志，而且有武略和才干，是一位非同一般文人的英雄豪杰之士。
3. Born in Shandong, which was occupied by the Jin troops, he became a fervent patriot under the influence of his family.
   辛弃疾出生于被金兵占领的山东，自幼受到家庭影响，具有强烈的爱国志愿。
4. Xin Qiji repeatedly submitted memorials to the Southern Song emperor, offering his knowledge of the enemy as well as political and military strategies, but his proposals never received a response.
   辛弃疾曾多次将自己对敌情的了解和政治军事谋略上书南宋朝廷，但一直不被采纳。
5. Poetry became the only way for him to express his thoughts and sorrow.
   因此诗歌成了他抒发壮怀与寄托悲慨的惟一方式。
6. He left to later generations more than 600 poems, the largest number among all the Song-dynasty poets.
   他一生留给我们词作六百多首，数量为宋朝词人中的第一。

## 文化名人
## Eminent Literati

7. Xin Qiji's poems are mostly solemn yet fervent songs filled with patriotism. He was another poet writing in the free and powerful style of Su Shi.
辛词中多是出于爱国忧时情怀的慷慨悲歌,他是继苏轼之后又一位成大气候的豪放词人。

## Wonderful Paragraph
## 精彩片段

### Paragraph 1

# 辛弃疾
# Xin Qiji

Xin Qiji (28 May, 1140—1207) was a Chinese poet and military leader during the Southern Song dynasty.

At the time of his life, northern China was occupied by the Jurchens, a people from what is now north-east China then regarded as barbarians but later to become the Manchus. Only southern China was ruled by the Han Chinese Southern Song dynasty. Xin Qiji was born in the north, and in his childhood his grandfather told him about the time when the Han Chinese ruled the north and told him to be a honorable man and reverage againsts the barbarian for the nation. It was then when he developed his patriotic feelings.

Xin Qiji start his rebel against Jurchens at age 20. With merely 50 men, he fought the way into Jurchens' camp and killed the traitor. He then led his men to the South Song. He then was given the position as a governor. He had many victories but was forced to give up his plan when the South negotiated a peace treaty in 1164. Despite of his great ability and experience in military and politics, he was soon forced to resign by the Consul.

In his late years, the war between the North and South intensified. The Consul had no choice but to use him again, but without trust. Xin Qiji retired in 1194 and built a retreat in the Shang-jao countryside. There he studied and perfected his famous ci form of poetry. He died in 1207, at the same time that war was restarted again between Song China and the Jurchens.

## Cultural Links
## 文化链接

### 大呼"杀贼"离世

辛弃疾在镇江知府任上仅短短1年,就被韩侂胄以荐举不当为由,把辛弃疾由镇江改派隆兴府(今江西南昌市)。还没有上任,又编造理由弹劾,把知隆兴府的任命也撤消了,只留下一个提举冲佑观的虚衔。辛弃疾在镇江的一切设想、安排,连同他的理想和希望都付诸东流了。他在接到免去镇江知府令时,写了一首《瑞鹧鸪》:"随缘道理应须会,过分功名莫强求。先自一身愁不了,那堪愁上更添愁。"

1205年7月,北伐壮志再次落空的辛弃疾,怀着满腔悲愤郁郁离开了镇江,回到江西铅山。1207年秋,辛弃疾大呼数声"杀贼",忧愤而终,享年68岁。他的爱国情怀,留在了他的词中,激励着后世的人们,成为爱国主义不竭的精神力量。

## Vocabulary
## 妙词连珠

| | |
|---|---|
| barbarian 粗鲁无礼的人,野蛮人 | negotiate(与某人)商议,谈判,磋商,买卖,让渡(支票、债券等),通过,越过 |
| manchu 满人 | |
| honorable 可敬的,荣誉的,光荣的 | treaty 条约,谈判 |
| patriotic 爱国的,有爱国心的 | consul 领事,(古罗马的)两执政官之一 |
| rebel 造反者,叛逆者,反抗者,叛乱者 | intensify 加强,强化 |
| traitor 叛逆者,叛国者 | retreat 撤退,退却 |

文化名人
Eminent Literati

# Unit 12 郑和 Zheng He

## Key Sentences
流畅精句

1. In order to look for Zhu Yunwen as well as to demonstrate the power of the Ming Empire, Chengzu decided to send envoys to the Western Seas.
   为了显示大明的强盛国力,顺便打探朱允炆的下落,明成祖决定派人出使西洋。
2. From 1405 to 1433, the Ming fleet made seven long journeys under Zheng He's command. They visited more than 30 countries along the coastline of the Indian Ocean and at their farthest reached Somalia on the eastern coast of Africa.
   从1405年到1433年的近三十年中,郑和先后七次出海远航,历经印度洋沿岸三十多个国家,最远到达了东部非洲的索马里。
3. Zheng He's voyages greatly promoted economic and cultural exchanges between China and many other countries in Asia and Africa.
   郑和的航行大大促进了中国和其他亚非国家的经济和文化交流。
4. Zheng He made his voyages more than half a century earlier than Christopher Columbus and later Vasco da Gama made theirs.
   郑和下西洋比哥伦布和达·伽马的远洋航行要早半个多世纪。
5. It was regrettable that the Ming court changed its exploration policy after Zheng He's death and the nautical records he left behind were lost.
   可惜明王朝在郑和死后便改变了航海政策,郑和的航行档案也下落不明。

用英语说中国——古今名人
Introduce China in English—Eminent Persons

## Wonderful Paragraph
精彩片段

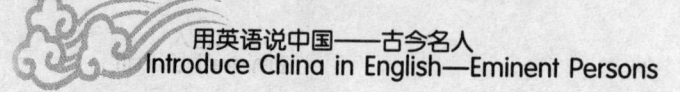

**Paragraph 1**

# Zheng He and His Voyages
郑和及他的航程

Zheng He or Cheng Ho in Wade-Giles(1371-1435), was a famous Chinese mariner and explorer who made the voyages collectively referred to as the "Eunuch Sanbao to the Western Ocean"(三保太监下西洋) or "Zheng He to the Western Ocean", from 1405 to 1433.

The Western Ocean" refers to the Asian and African places he explored, including: Southeast Asia, Sumatra, Java, Ceylon, India, Persia, the Persian Gulf, Arabia, the Red Sea as far north as Egypt, and Africa as far south as the Mozambique Channel.

The number of his voyages vary depending on method of division, but he explored at least seven times to "The Western Ocean" with his fleet. The fleet comprised 30 000 men and seventy ships at its height. He brought back to China many trophies and envoys from more than thirty kingdoms—including King Alagonakkara of Ceylon, who came to China to apologize to the Emperor.

**Paragraph 2**

# Biography
简介

Zheng He was a eunuch and close confidant of the Yongle Emperor of China, the third emperor of the Ming Dynasty. His original name was Ma Sanbao, born in Yunnan. The name Zheng He was given by the emperor. His missions were impressive demonstrations of organizational capability and technological might, but did not lead to significant trade, since Zheng He was an admiral and an official, not a merchant. Drawn by Shen Du (沈度), a giraffe brought from Africa in the twelfth year of Yongle (1414 AD).

文化名人
Eminent Literati

In 1424 the Yongle Emperor died. His successor, the Hongxi, decided to curb influence of the eunuchs at court. Zheng He made one more voyage under the Xuande Emperor, but after that, Chinese treasure ship fleets ended.

*Paragraph 3*

## 与中国晚期封建历史的关系
## Connection to the History of Late Imperial China

One popular belief is that after Zheng He's voyages, China turned away from the seas and underwent a period of technological stagnation. This view of history has been used to support the notion of investment into space exploration. Although this view was popularized by historians such as John Fairbanks and Joseph Needham in the 1950s, most current historians of China question its accuracy. They point out that Chinese maritime commerce did not stop after Zheng He, and that Chinese ships continued to dominate Southeast Asian commerce until the 19th century and that there was active Chinese trading with India and East Africa long after Zheng He. Although the Ming Dynasty did ban shipping with the Haijin for a few decades, this ban was eventually lifted.

### Cultural Links
文化链接

### 郑和的名字

郑和,本姓马,小名三宝,1385年洪武皇帝朱元璋出兵平定云南,郑和的父亲不幸蒙难,11岁的马三保成为无数被俘、并成为被立刻阉割的儿童之一。后进入燕王府,成为朱棣的一名侍卫。

1399年8月,明王朝爆发了长达四年之久的"靖难之役"中,他跟随朱棣出生入死,立下大功,为朱棣后来的胜利奠定基础。1402年7月,朱棣登基当上了皇帝,马三保也被封官,任内官监太监,相当于正四品,在经历二十多年艰苦生活后,他成了地位显赫的大内太监。1404年,又被赐姓"郑"。

## 用英语说中国——古今名人
## Introduce China in English—Eminent Persons

中国历来有"马不入宫殿"的说法，马三保在郑村立下他最大的战功，所以赐姓"郑"；三保出生时父母为祈求真主保佑，世道平和，小孩能平安成长，所以给他取名为和；从此他改名为郑和，原来的名字慢慢被遗忘了。在中国古代，赐姓是至高无上的荣耀，而宦官被赐姓则是绝无仅有，可见永乐皇帝是多么倚重与信任郑和。

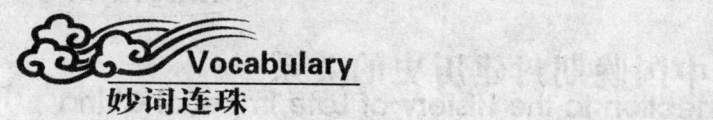

### Vocabulary 妙词连珠

collectively 全体地，共同地
eunuch 太监，宦官
referred 牵涉性痛，不在痛源处的疼痛
Sumatra 苏门答腊岛（在印尼西部）
Java 爪哇
Ceylon 锡兰（印）度以南一岛国，现以更名为斯里兰卡 Srilanka 首都为科伦坡 Colombo）
Persia 波斯（西南亚国家，现在伊朗）
Arabia 阿拉伯半岛
Mozambique 莫桑比克（非洲东南部国家）

fleet 舰队（尤指有固定活动地区的舰队），港湾，小河
comprise 包含，由……组成
confidant 心腹朋友，知己
curb 路边
stagnation 停滞
notion 概念，观念，想法，意见，打算，主张，（复数）＜美语＞小饰物
accuracy 精确性，正确度
maritime 海上的，海事的，海运的，海员的

# Unit 13　Cao Xueqin
曹雪芹

## Key Sentences
流畅精句

1. The Chinese classic A Dream of Red Mansions is perhaps the only novel to have become a specialized field of study.
   中国古典小说《红楼梦》是惟一一部在学术界成为专学的小说。
2. The author Cao Xueqin creates a comprehensive world that depicts life in the final days of feudal society, and his feelings on its vicissitudes and its disillusionment.
   它的作者曹雪芹为我们创造了一个完整的世界,这个世界既呈现了封建末世的生活面貌,又饱含着作者在人世中的沧桑感和空幻感。
3. With A Dream of Red Mansions, Cao Xueqin bequathed people with the tragic experiences of his life, his deep insight into humankind's inner worlds, and his great mastery of language.
   借助于《红楼梦》,曹雪芹将他对人生深切的悲剧体验,对人类心灵的深刻洞察,以及对汉语语言的纯熟运用一并留给了世人。
4. His ancestral home was Liaoyang, and later was received as member of the Orthodox White Banner of the "Eight Banners" of the Man nationality in the Qing Dynasty.
   他的先世本是辽阳汉人,清朝后入满洲正白旗。
5. From Cao Xueqin's great-grandfather to his father's generation, four persons of three generations of the Cao successively held the post of Jiangning Zhizao, ca post in charge of satin-weaving for the use of the emperor or officials, for as long as 60 years.
   从曹雪芹曾祖到父辈,曹家祖孙3代4人历任江宁织造达60年之久。

6. Cao Xueqin endured all kinds of frustrations and tribulations in his lifetime, getting a full taste of misery and bitterness.
   曹雪芹从繁华坠入贫困,一生历尽坎坷与苦难,饱尝了人世的辛酸与悲痛。
7. A Dream of Red Mansions was originally entitled The Story of the Stone. It took the author 10 years to read over marginalia and make additions and deletions five times.
   《红楼梦》初名《石头记》,披阅十载,增删五次。

## Wonderful Paragraph 精彩片段

**Paragraph 1**

### 曹雪芹 Cao Xueqin

Cao Xueqin (1716—1763) is the author of famous Chinese work A Dream of Red Mansions. His given name was Cao Zhan. A Han Chinese clan assimilated into Manchurian ethnicity, Cao's family had become so rich as to be able to play host four times to the Emperor Kangxi in his itinerant trips down south in Nanjing. For three generations the family held the office of Commissioner of Imperial Textiles in Jiangning. Cao Xueqin's grandfather, Cao Yin, was playmate and confidante to the Emperor Kangxi, and the family's fortunes lasted until Kangxi's death and the ascension of Emperor Yongzheng to the throne. In 1727 they suffered the first of a series of reversals to their fortunes in a political purge that saw the family properties confiscated and the family forced to relocate to Beijing a year later.

Most of what we know about Cao was passed down from his contemporaries and friends. Cao himself eventually settled in the rural areas around Western Beijing where he lived through the larger part of his late years in poverty selling off his paintings. Friends and acquaintances reported an intelligent, highly talented man who spent a decade working diligently on a work that must have been A Dream of Red Mansions. Extant handwritten copies of this work-some 80 chapters-had been in circulation in Beijing shortly after Cao's death before Chen Weiyuan and Gao E, who claimed to have access to the former's working papers, published a complete 120-chapter version in 1791. The 120-chapter version is the most printed version.

## Cultural Links 文化链接

### 曹雪芹妙联骂贪官

有一次,江苏句容县令叶仲秋适庆五十大寿,不料城北民宅着火,谁知这位平时聚敛贪狠、鱼肉人民的"父母官"却不予理睬,仍在酒宴上举杯痛饮。恰在这时,生性耿直而好抱不平的曹雪芹游历此地,目睹毁焚之火情,又闻县令漠不关心之事,刹间怒上眉头,义愤填膺,欲直面谴责这不顾百姓生死的昏庸贪官。然而一想,自己素与县令无交往,怎能相见呢?略一沉思,他便有计了,即叫随从取出笔墨,写了副对联作为"贺礼"连同"拜帖"一并送往衙门府第。

叶仲秋接到家仆呈上的"拜帖",赶紧请之入上席。县太爷喜出望外地亲手把对联展开,只见联云:

火魔驾风,横行霸道,四野难容老叶;
焰妖遇酒,助桀为虐,万民皆怨仲秋。

叶老爷顿时感到当众丢了丑,直气得脸像猪肝,浑身打冷颤,却又奈何不得"江宁织造"之公子,只好挥手示意大家前去救火。

## Vocabulary 妙词连珠

| | |
|---|---|
| assimilate 吸收 | purge 净化,清除,泻药 |
| itinerant 巡回的 | confiscated 没收,充公,查抄,征用 |
| textile 纺织品 | relocate 重新部署 |
| playmate 玩伴,游伴 | contemporary 同时代的人 |
| reversal 颠倒,反转,反向,逆转,撤销 | acquaintance 相识,熟人 |

# Unit 14　Yan Fu 严复

## Key Sentences 流畅精句

1. Yan Fu was among the first to study in England.
   严复曾经作为中国第一批留学生留学英国。
2. He attributed the sticking point of the "Chinese Problem" to "the messy and chaotic internal affairs instead of bully and humiliation of foreign countries".
   他把"中国问题"的症结归结为"不在外国之欺凌,而在内政之不修"。
3. He translated large numbers of Western academic masterpieces such as introducing the modern Western society, politics, culture and ideology, especially Darwinism, establishing his status of "top translator of modern China".
   他翻译出版了大量西方学术名著,介绍西方近代的社会、政治、文化与思想,尤其是达尔文的进化论,从而奠定了他"近代中国第一译手"的地位。
4. He wanted to acquaint the Chinese with such biological evolutionist ideas as "organic evolution and natural selection" and "the survival of the fittest" and awaken them to the necessity of retaining the political consciousness of striving to become stronger, of competing with nature for supremacy.
   他的目的是使中国人知道"物竞天择,适者生存"的道理,唤醒中国人保种自强、与天争胜进而变法图存的政治意识。

5. He translated the British political economist Adam Smith's An Inquiry into the Nature and Causes of the Wealth of Nations, which was the most important of his translations and largest in scale.
他翻译了英国政治经济学家亚当·斯密的《原富》(今译《国民财富的性质及原因研究》,是分量最重,规模最大的一本译作。
6. Yan Fu devoted all his life to the publicity of the ideology of enlightenment. He was one of the most eminent thinkers of enlightenment in modern China.
严复毕生致力于启蒙思想的宣传,是近代中国最著名的启蒙思想家之一。

## Wonderful Paragraph 精彩片段

### Paragraph 1

# Yan Fu 严复

Yan Fu (courtesy name: 几道) (1854—1921) was a Chinese scholar, most famous for introducing Western thoughts, including Darwin's ideas of "natural selection" and "survival of the fittest", into China during the late 19th century. He was also involved in the Gong Zhe Shangshu movement.

He studied in the Naval Management School in Fuzhou, Fujian Province. From 1877—1879, he studied in the Navy Academy in Greenwich, England. Upon his return to China, he was unable to pass the Imperial Civil Service Examination. It was not until after the Chinese defeat in the First Sino-Japanese War that Yan Fu became famous for his works of the time period. He is well-known for his translation of works such as Thomas Huxley's Evolution and Ethics, Adam Smith's Wealth of Nations, and John Stuart Mill's On Liberty. He was also greatly influenced by the works of Herbert Spencer.

The ideas of "natural selection" and "survival of the fittest" were introduced to Chinese readers through Huxley's work; and were famously rendered as "物竞天择" and "适者生存". The phrases have become proverbial in the Chinese language, but are often misunderstood as the synonyms of "merciless competition".

He stated in his preface to Evolution and Ethics that "there are three difficulties in translation: faithfulness, understandability and elegance". He never set that three difficulties as a general standard for translation, and didn't mean that those three were independent of each other. However, since the publication of that work, "faithfulness, understandability and elegance" has been attributed to Yan Fu as a standard for any good translation, become a cliche in the Chinese academic circle, and raised numerous debates and theses. Some scholars argue that the dictum came from Tytler.

## Cultural Links
文化链接

### 中国近代最伟大的翻译家

严复是中国近代第一位系统介绍西方学术的启蒙思想家,在介绍西学的同时提出了翻译的标准——"信、达、雅",对中国现代的翻译实践和理论研究影响巨大。

在1898年"天演论"的例言中他写有,"译事三难:信、达、雅。"这就成了我们近百年来的翻译原则。现在一般对严复的"信达雅"三字原则做这样的理解:"信"就是对原文忠实;"达"就是译文明白晓畅;"雅"就是译文的文字要优美。因此,翻译时对于原文应当求"信",而对于译文则应当求"达"、求"雅"。

## Vocabulary 妙词连珠

naval 海军的
evolution 进展,发展,演变,进化
ethics 偶尔,道德规范
Evolution and Ethics 天演论
proverbial 谚语的,谚语式的,众所周知的,公认的
synonyms 同义字
merciless 无慈悲心的,残忍的
faithfulness 忠诚,正确,诚实
understandability 易懂
elegance 高雅,典雅,优雅,雅致
cliche 陈词滥调,铅版
academic 学院的,理论的
theses [乐]指挥棒的朝下挥动
dictum 格言,[律]法官的附带意见

# Unit 15 梁启超 Liang Qichao

## Key Sentences 流畅精句

1. Liang Qichao is not only an important character in modern Chinese politics, but also a legendary figure in the modern history of Chinese culture.
   梁启超不仅是中国近代政坛上的风云人物,在近代文化史上也堪称奇人。

2. He introduced in quantity Western politics, economic theories and other academic ideas to China, and as such became one of the most influential enlightenment thinkers in modern Chinese history.
   他大量介绍西方政治、经济学说和其他学术,成为中国近代最具影响力的启蒙思想家之一。

3. In his later years, he withdrew from the political and devoted himself to teaching at the Qinghua Research Institute.
   晚年退出政界后,他讲学于清华研究院。

4. He was among those who first took a new attitude towards the study of ancient Chinese culture and opened up a new path for modern academic research.
   他较早以新学眼光研究中国古代文化,开启近代学术研究新风的先驱。

5. From the perspective of Liang Qichao's own writings, he made his greatest achievements in the "revolution in the field of essay."
   从梁启超自己的创作实践看,他在"文界革命"内取得的成绩最大。

6. Liang Qichao's theoretical contribution to the "revolution in the field of fiction" should not be underestimated.
梁启超对"小说界革命"的理论贡献也不容低估。
7. In 1902 he founded an important magazine called New Stories, the first of its kind in 20th-century China.
1902 年,他创办了 20 世纪中国第一份重要的小说杂志《新小说》。

## Wonderful Paragraph
精彩片段

**Paragraph 1**

# R"百日维新"变法运动
# eform Movements

Liang Qichao (Courtesy:卓如; Pseudonym:任公) (1873—1929) was a Chinese scholar, journalist, philosopher and reformist during the Qing Dynasty (1644 –1911), who inspired Chinese scholars with his writings and reform movements. He died of illness in Beijing at the age of 55.

As an advocate of constitutional monarchy, Liang was unhappy with the governance of the Qing Government and wanted to change the status quo in China. He organised reforms with Kang Youwei (康有为) by putting their ideas on paper and sending them to Emperor Guangxu (光绪帝) of the Qing Dynasty. This movement is known as the Wuxu Reform or the Hundred Days' Reform. Their proposal asserted that China was in need of more than "self-strengthening", and called for many institutional and ideological changes such as getting rid of corruption and remodeling the state examination system.

This proposal soon ignited a frenzy of disagreements, and Liang became a wanted man by order of Empress Cixi (慈禧太后), the leader of the political conservative party who later took over the government as regent. Cixi strongly opposed reforms at that time and along with her supporters, condemned the "Hundred Days' Reform" as being too radical.

In 1898, the Conservative Coup ended all reforms and exiled Liang to Japan, where he stayed for the next fourteen years of his life. In Japan, he continued to actively advocate democratic notions and reforms by using his writings to raise support for the reformers' cause among overseas Chinese and foreign governments. In 1899, Liang went to Canada, where he met Dr. Sun Yat-Sen among others, then to Honolulu in Hawaii. During the Boxer Rebellion, Liang was back in Canada, where he formed the "Save the Emperor Society". This organization later became the Constitutionalist Party which advocated constitutional monarchy. While Sun promoted revolution, Liang preached reform.

*Paragraph 2*

## 早期报人 As a Journalist

Liang Qichao was the "most influential turn-of-the-century scholar-journalist," according to Levenson. Liang showed that newspapers and magazines could serve as an effective medium for communicating political ideas.

Liang, as a historian and a journalist, believed that both careers must have the same purpose and "moral commitment." Thus, he founded his first newspaper, called the Qing Yi Bao, named after a student movement of the Han Dynasty.

Liang's exile to Japan allowed him to speak freely and exercise his intellectual autonomy. During his career in journalism, he edited two premier newspapers, Zhongwai Gongbao and Shiwu Bao. He also published his moral and political ideals in Qing Yi Bao and New Citizen.

In addition, he used his literary works to further spread his views on republicanism both in China and across the world. Accordingly, he had become an influential journalist in terms of political and cultural aspects by writing new forms of periodical journals. Furthermore, journalism paved the way for him to express his patriotism.

文化名人
Eminent Literati

### Paragraph 3

## L 文学造诣
iterary Career

Liang Qichao was both a traditional Confucian scholar and a reformist. Liang Qichao contributed to the reform in late Qing by writing various articles interpreting non-Chinese ideas of history and government, with the intent of stimulating Chinese citizens' minds to build a new China. In his writings, he argued that China should protect the ancient teachings of Confucianism, but also learn from the successes of Western political life and not just Western technology. Therefore, he was regarded as the pioneer of political friction.

Liang shaped the ideas of democracy in China, using his writings as a medium to combine Western scientific methods with traditional Chinese historical studies. Liang's works were strongly influenced by the Japanese political scholar Katō Hiroyuki（加藤弘之，1836-1916）, who used methods of social Darwinism to promote the statist ideology in Japanese society. Liang drew from much of his work and subsequently influenced Korean nationalists in the 1900s.

### Paragraph 4

## H 史家思想
istoriographical Thought

Liang Qichao's historiographical thought represents the beginning of modern Chinese historiography and reveals some important directions of Chinese historiography in the twentieth century.

For Liang, the major flaw of "old historians"（旧史家）was their failure to foster the national awareness necessary for a strong and modern nation. Liang's call for new history not only pointed to a new orientation for historical writing in China, but also indicated the rise of modern historical consciousness among Chinese intellectuals.

During this period of Japan's challenge in the First Sino-Japanese War

(1894—1895), Liang was involved in protests in Beijing pushing for an increased participation in the governnance by the Chinese people. It was the first protest of its kind in modern Chinese history. This changing outlook on tradition was shown in the historiographical revolution launched by Liang Qichao in the early twentieth century. Frustrated by his failure at political reform, Liang embarked upon cultural reform. In 1902, while in exile in Japan, Liang wrote New History, launching attacks on traditional historiography.

*Paragraph 5*

## 翻译家
## Translator

Liang was head of the Translation Bureau and oversaw the training of students who were learning to translate Western works into Chinese. He believed that this task was "the most essential of all essential undertakings to accomplish" because he believed Westerners were successful - politically, technologically and economically.

*Paragraph 6*

## 诗人与小说家
## Poet and Novelist

Liang advocated reform in both the genres of poem and novel. Collected Works of Yinbingshi (《饮冰室合集》) are his representative works in literature which were collected and compiled into 148 volumes.

Liang also wrote fiction and scholarly essays on fiction, which included Fleeing to Japan after failure of Hundred Days' Reform (1898) and the essay On the Relationship Between Fiction and the Government of the People (1902). These novels emphasized modernization in the West and the call for reform.

文化名人
Eminent Literati

Paragraph 7

# Educator
**教育家**

In the late 1920s, Liang retired from politics and taught at the Tung-nan University in Shanghai and the Tsinghua Research Institute in Peking as a tutor. He founded Chiang-hsüeh She (Chinese Lecture Association) and brought many intellectual figures to China, including Driesch and Tagore. Academically he was a renowned scholar of his time, introducing Western learning and ideology, and making extensive studies of ancient Chinese culture.

During this last decade of his life, he wrote many books documenting Chinese cultural history, Chinese literary history and historiography. He also had a strong interest in Buddhism and wrote numerous historical and political articles on its influence in China. Liang influenced many of his students in producing their own literary works. They included Xu Zhimo, renowned modern poet, and Wang Li, an accomplished poet and founder of Chinese linguistics as a modern discipline.

## Cultural Links
文化链接

### 花事对联轶事

梁启超十岁那年,随父亲到朋友家做客。一进家门,他便被院子里一株蓓蕾初绽的杏树迷住了,并偷偷地折下一枝,遮掩在宽阔的袖筒里。谁知,他的这一微妙之举,恰恰被教子甚严的父亲和朋友的家人看在眼里。

筵席上,父亲总为儿子这件事惴惴不安,一心想不露声色暗示儿子一番。为活跃气氛,父亲便当众对启超说:"开宴前,我先出一副上联,如能对好,方可举杯,否则,只能为长辈斟酒沏茶,不准落座。"小启超不知父亲用意,毫无思想准备,但凭腹中才学,自信不会出丑,于是满口答应。父亲略加思索,作出上联:"袖里笼花,小子暗藏春色"。小启超听后恍然大悟,但未显失色,随口对来:"堂前悬镜,大人明察秋毫"。对联一经出口,堂前喝彩不已。

## Vocabulary 妙词连珠

| | |
|---|---|
| monarchy 君主政体,君主政治 | radical 根本的,基本的,激进的 |
| assert 断言,声称 | preach 鼓吹 |
| institutional 制度上的 | intellectual 智力的,有智力的 |
| ideological 意识形态的 | autonomy 自治 |
| corruption 腐败,贪污,堕落 | patriotism 爱国心,爱国精神 |
| remodeling 重新塑造,改造,改变 | statist 统计学者,中央经济统制论者 |
| ignite 点火,点燃 | foster 养育,抚育,培养,鼓励 |
| frenzy 狂暴,狂怒 | orientation 方向,方位,定位,倾向性,向东方 |
| conservative 保守的,守旧的 | |
| regent 摄政者,董事 | |
| condemn 判刑,处刑,声讨,谴责 | |

# Unit 16  Lu Xun 鲁迅

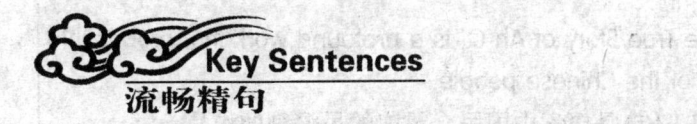

## Key Sentences
流畅精句

1. He made unremitting efforts in creating a multiplicity of literary forms for modern Chinese literature and displayed his artistic maturity in his early literary creations, thus launching new literature at a relatively high starting point.
   他经过不懈努力创造了中国现代文学的多种崭新样式,并在其创作之初就显现出艺术上的成熟,使得新文学创作有相当高的起点。
2. Lu Xun had laid down the basic tone for modern Chinese literature as fighting the ills found in real life.
   鲁迅为中国现代文学奠定了现实战斗精神的基调。
3. Lu Xun's experience of giving up medical studies for literature could perhaps elucidate the objective of his literary creation as "remolding the souls of the Chinese people."
   鲁迅弃医从文的经历或许能够注解他"改造国民的灵魂"的创作方向。
4. In 1918 Lu Xun published the first vernacular story in modern Chinese literanture, "A Madman's Diary". Through the mouth of the "madman," the writer discloss the "maneating" essence of a feudal history of several thousand years.
   1918 年,鲁迅发表了中国现代文学史上第一篇白话小说《狂人日记》,借"狂人"之口,揭示了旧中国几千年封建历史的"吃人"本质。
5. Lu Xun also created a new literary form, zawen, or the satirical essay.
   此外,鲁迅还创造了中国新文学另一种新形式:杂文。

6. Lu Xun's satirical essays not only condemned the social maladies of his time, but with wisdom and insight penetrated into every aspect of people's lives.
鲁迅的杂文不仅针砭时弊,而且涉及了现代中国人生活的各个方面,充满了智慧和洞见。

7. Lu Xun's "The True Story of Ah Q" is a profound work that probes into the very soul of the Chinese people.
鲁迅的《阿Q正传》是探索中国民众灵魂的最深刻的作品。

8. Ah Q can be looked at as "any ordinary person" in the countryside of China, a general image of the populace.
阿Q可被视为中国农村的"普通一人",是一个概括的大众形象。

9. Ah Q's "spiritual victory" therapy has long been considered the most profound summary of the inherent weakness of the Chinese nation.
阿Q的精神胜利法历来被认为是对国民劣根性最深刻的总结。

## Wonderful Paragraph
精彩片段

**Paragraph 1**

# 鲁迅及其青年时代
## Lu Xun and His Youth

Lu Xun or Lu Hsün (Wade-Giles) (September 25, 1881 ~ October 19, 1936), the pen name of Zhou Shuren (周树人), has been considered one of the most influential Chinese writers of the 20th century and the founder of modern vernacular literature. Highly influential in 20th century Chinese history, his literary works exerted a substantial influence after the May Fourth Movement. He was also a noted translator.

Born in Shaoxing, Zhejiang province, Lu Xun was first named Zhou Zhangshu and later renamed Shuren, literally, "to nurture a person". His family was well-educated and of the gentry class, yet somehow the family ended up being poor by the time he was born. His father's chronic illness and death in his adolescence persuaded Zhou to take up medical science. Distrusting traditional Chinese medicine (which in his time was often practiced by charlatans), he set out to study Westernized medicine in Tohoku High Medical Institute (nowadays part of Tohoku University) in Sendai, Japan.

Quitting his studies and returning to China in 1909, he became a lecturer in the Peking University and began writing.

Paragraph 2

## C职业生涯
## Career

In May 1918, he used his pen name for the first time and published the first major baihua short story A Madman's Diary, which was to become one of his two most famed works. With its criticism of many old Chinese traditions and family rules, it became a cornerstone of the May Fourth Movement. Another of his well-known longer stories, The True Story of Ah Q, was published in the 1920s. The latter became his most famous work. Both works were included in his short story collection Na Han (呐喊) or Call to Arms, published in 1923.

Between 1924 to 1926, Lu wrote his masterpiece of ironic reminiscences, Zhaohua Xishi (朝花夕拾, published 1928), as well as the prose poem collection Ye Cao (野草, published 1927). Lu Xun also wrote some of the stories to be published in his second short story collection Pang Huang (彷徨) in 1926. In 1930 Lu Xun published Zhongguo Xiaoshuo Shilue (中国小说史略), a comprehensive overview of Chinese fiction and one of the landmark pieces of twentieth-century Chinese literary criticism.

His other important works include volumes of translations—notably from Russian (he particularly admired Nikolai Gogol and made a translation of Dead Souls, and his own first story is inspired by Gogol)—discursive writings like Re Feng (热风), and many other works such as prose essays, which number around 20 volumes or more. As a left-wing writer, Lu played an important role in the history of Chinese literature. His books were and remain highly influential and popular even today, particularly amongst youths. Lu Xun's works also appear in high school textbooks in Japan. He is known to Japanese by the name Rojin.

Lu Xun was also the editor of several left-wing magazines such as New Youth (新青年) and Sprouts (萌芽). He was the brother of another important Chinese political figure and essayist Zhou Zuoren (周作人). Though highly sympathetic of the Chinese Communist movement, Lu Xun never joined the Communist Party of China. Because of his leanings, and of the role his works played in the subsequent history of the People's Republic of China, Lu Xun's works were banned in Taiwan until late 1980s. He was among the early supporters of the Esperanto movement in China.

*Paragraph 3*

## S风格与遗产
## tyle and Legacy

Lu Xun's style is wry, incisive and often sardonic in his societal commentary. His mastery of the vernacular language, coupled with his expertise with tone—often refusing to occupy any easy position—make some of his works (阿Q正传) truly difficult to translate. Lu Xun's importance to modern Chinese literature lies in the fact that he contributed significantly to every modern literary genre except the novel during his lifetime.

*Paragraph 4*

## T思想
## hought

Lu Xun, hailed as "commander of China's cultural revolution" by Mao Zedong, is typically regarded as the most influential Chinese writer who was associated with the May Fourth Movement. He produced harsh criticism of social problems in China, particularly in his analysis of the "Chinese national character." He has often been considered to have had leftist leanings. Called by some a "champion of common humanity," he helped bring many fellow writers to support communist thought, though he never took the step of actually joining the Communist Party. It should be remarked, however, that throughout his work the individual is given more emphasis over collectivistic concerns.

## Cultural Links 文化链接

### 鲁迅与国宝级图书

今天，国家图书馆珍藏的国宝级图书——《永乐大典》和文津阁《四库全书》，是经鲁迅当年力争才得以入藏的。

《永乐大典》22 877 卷。光绪二十六年（1900 年），八国联年占领北京时，此书一部分被焚毁，一部分被入侵军劫走，仅残余 64 册，原在翰林院保存，后又被陆润庠（状元出身，后曾为帝师）留存，经鲁迅与其联系收回馆中。

《四库全书》是清代最大的丛书，收入图书 3 503 种，79 339 卷，共缮写七部。宣统元年（1909 年）曾决定将承德文津阁收藏的《四库全书》移交当时筹办中的京师图书馆，但一直没有办成。民国成立后，鲁迅多次催办，但热河当局以"留存热河图书馆，以为纪念"为由，迟迟不肯移交，后虽运到北京但又被内务部运交故宫文华殿的古物陈列所。鲁迅据理力争，才终于 1912 年 9 月 1 日与内务部商妥，并于 9 月 6 日开始清点移交。京师图书馆于 1912 年 8 月 27 日在广化寺开馆。但因其时交通不便，读者不多，鲁迅又为寻觅适当新址奔波，经过数年努力，该馆迁方家胡同国子监南学房舍旧址（今方家胡同 17 号），1917 年 1 月 26 日再次开馆。

## Vocabulary 妙词连珠

| | |
|---|---|
| vernacular 本国的 | imminent 即将来临的，逼近的 |
| exert 尽（力），施加（压力等，努力 | execution 实行，完成，执行，死刑 |
| substantial 坚固的，实质的，真实的 | alleged 声称的，所谓的 |
| chronic 慢性的，延续根长的 | apathy 缺乏感情或兴趣，冷漠 |

reminiscence 回想,记忆力,怀旧
landmark 里程碑,划时代的事
discursive 散漫的,不得要领的
essayist 小品作者,随笔作家,
　评论家
wry 扭歪的,歪曲的,歪斜的
incisive 深刻的,尖锐的,激烈的
sardonic 讽刺的
genre 类型,流派
hail 冰雹,致敬,招呼,一阵
leftist 左翼的人,左派,左撇子

# Unit 17　Guo Moruo
### 郭沫若

## Key Sentences
### 流畅精句

1. It was not until the 1921 publication of Guo Moruo's collection of poems, Goddess, that a boundless domain was opened up for new poetry.
   直到1921年郭沫若的诗集——《女神》出现,才为新诗开辟了一个广阔的天地。
2. The romantic, bold style and the free form evident in the Goddess collection are reminiscent of the US poet Walt Whitman.
   《女神》浪漫奔放的风格和自由体形式都让人想到惠特曼。
3. The artistic appeal of the collected poems is deeply rooted in the volcanic eruptions of emotions.
   《女神》的艺术表现力深深植根于其火山爆发般的情感力量中。
4. Once the collection was published, it rocked the poetry world with the momentum of an avalanche. Thousands of youth felt inspired and impassioned.
   诗集一出版,就以排山倒海的气势震撼了诗坛,尤其令成千上万的青年人感到振奋和激动。
5. Guo Moruo was not only an outstanding poet and historical playwright in the hisotry of modern Chinese literature, but also a famous historian, a philologist, an archaeologist, and a social activist.
   郭沫若不仅是现代文学史上杰出的诗人和历史剧作家,还是著名的历史学家、古文学学家、考古学家和社会活动家。

6. His historical dramas had sublime tragic beauty, incisive historical opinions and passionate personal emotions, which reflected his strong sense of social responsibility and political participation.

他的历史剧含有精辟的史识与强烈的主观抒情色彩,具有明显的指导性和战斗性,体现了作者强烈的社会责任感和政治参与意识。

## Wonderful Paragraph
精彩片段

### Paragraph 1

# Guo Moruo
郭沫若

Guo Moruo (Wade-Giles: Kuo Mo-jo, courtesy name 鼎堂) (November 16, 1892 - June 12, 1978) was a Chinese author, poet, historian, archaeologist, and government official.

In 1914, after receiving Chinese traditional education, he left China, and his arranged bride, to study medicine at Kyushu Imperial University (九州帝国大学) in Japan. There he fell in love with a Japanese woman who became his common-law wife. His studies at this time focused on foreign language and literature, namely that of: Spinoza, Goethe, Walt Whitman, and the Bengali poet Tagore. Along with numerous translations, he published his first poem anthology, titled The Goddesses. He was one of the co-founder of the Chuang-tsao She ("Creation Society") in Shanghai, which promoted modern and vernacular literature. He joined the Communist Party of China in 1927. He was involved in the communist Nanchang Uprising and fled to Japan after its failure. He stayed there for 10 years studying Chinese ancient history until he returned in 1937 to join the anti-Japanese resistance.

Along with holding important government offices in the People's Republic of China, he was a prolific writer, not just of poetry but also fiction, plays, autobiographies, translations, and historical and philosophical treatises. He was the first President of the Chinese Academy of Social Sciences and remained so from its founding in 1949 until his death in 1978. He also produced his study of inscriptions on oracle bones and bronze vessels, Corpus of Inscriptions on Bronzes from the Two Chou Dynasties. In this work, he attempted to demonstrate, according to Communist doctrine, the "slave society" nature of ancient China.

In 1966 he was one of the first to be attacked in the Great Proletarian Cultural Revolution. He confessed that he had not properly understood the thought of Mao Zedong, and agreed that his works should be burned. Unlike the others similarly attacked, Guo Moruo was not stripped of all his official positions and had regained much of his powers by the seventies.

Guo Moruo was awarded the Lenin Peace Prize in 1951.

## Cultural Links
## 文化链接

### 钱瘦铁"智救"郭沫若

日寇侵华前夕，钱瘦铁与郭沫若同在日本，因郭老联络留学生进行革命活动，日警准备拘捕，被瘦铁探知，并买好船票，备好西装，约郭老穿了浴衣在门口闲眺，当预约的小汽车开到门口，乘人不备就把郭老带走，换上西装，辗转乘加拿大邮船，化名杨伯勉回国。日警后来怀凝钱瘦铁而拘禁了他，他在法庭上坚决不下跪，并抓起铜墨盒向法警掷去，为此被判刑五年。由于日本友人相助，三年半后提早释放归国。他在狱中作画、刻印，他的画风深受日本艺坛人士喜爱，因而他的画名在日本大振。一九六三年国庆前夕，瘦铁应邀到北京郭老家作客，故人重逢，瘦铁欣然为郭老刻印二方，其中"鼎堂"一印由郭老篆字，瘦铁刻石，成为二老数十年友谊的结晶。

## Vocabulary 妙词连珠

archaeologist 考古学家
anthology 诗选,文选
resistance 反抗,抵抗,抵抗力,阻力,电阻,阻抗
prolific 多产的,丰富的,大量繁殖的
autobiography 自传
philosophical 哲学的
oracle [宗](古希腊)神谕,预言,神谕处,神使,哲人,圣贤
vessel 船,容器,器皿脉,管,导管
strip 剥,剥去

# Unit 18  林语堂 Lin Yutang

## Key Sentences 流畅精句

1. In the 1920s, Lin suggested that the English word "humor" be translated into "幽默".
   20 世纪 20 年代，林语堂主张将英语中的 humour 直译为"幽默"。
2. In the 1930s, he founded the magazines Language and Human World, in which he advocated humorous, light essays. He appreciated humor as both an aesthetic pursuit and an attitude toward life. As "humor" became fashionable, Lin earned the reputation, "master of humor."
   30 年代，他创办了《论语》、《人间世》等刊物，大力提倡幽默、闲适的小品文，并且将幽默作为一种美学追求和人生姿态加以赞赏，一时间使幽默成为一种时尚，而他本人也被冠以"幽默大师"的称号。
3. Lin Yutang's essays present a unique moment in modern prose history.
   林语堂的小品文构成了现代散文史上一道独特的风景。
4. Many of his works pursue a sense of humor, with strong individual color.
   他的多数作品都追求幽默的情调，有很强的个性色彩。
5. In 1936 My Country and My People was published in New York, and reprinted six times in less than four months.
   1936 年，他的《吾国与吾民》(My Country and My People) 在纽约刊行，不到四个月就印了七次。

6. With the learnedness of a literary master and his gentle, humorous style, Lin Yutang completed this work in English, breaking the language barrier and deepening Western understanding of Chinese culture.

   林语堂以大师级的学养与温和幽默的笔锋,用英文完成了这部著作,使其能越过语言的隔膜,加深外国人对中国文化的了解。

7. Lin Yutang became one of the few Chinese writers that people in the West were familiar with.

   林语堂也成为西方人所熟悉的少数几位中国作家之一。

## Wonderful Paragraph 精彩片段

### Paragraph 1

## 林语堂 Lin Yutang

Lin Yutang (October 10, 1895 ~ March 26, 1976) was a Chinese writer and inventor whose original works and translations of classic Chinese texts became very popular in the West.

Lin was born in Fujian province in southeastern China, near Xiamen. This mountainous region made a deep impression on his consciousness, and thereafter he would constantly consider himself a child of the mountains (in one of his books he commented that his idea of hell was a city apartment). His father was a Christian minister.

Lin studied for his bachelor's degree at Saint John's University in Shanghai, then received a half-scholarship to continue study for a doctoral degree at Harvard University. He left Harvard early however, moving to France and eventually to Germany, where he completed his requirements for a doctoral degree (in Chinese) at the University of Leipzig. From 1923 to 1926 he taught English literature at Peking University.

Dr. Lin was very active in the popularization of classical Chinese literature in the West, as well as the general Chinese attitude towards life. He worked to formulate a new method of romanizing the Chinese language, and created an indexing system for Chinese characters. He was interested in mechanics, he has invented and patented a Chinese typewriter, and several lesser inventions such as a tootbrush with toothpaste dispensing. After 1928 he lived mainly in the United States, where his translations of Chinese texts remained popular for many years. His many works represent an attempt to bridge the cultural gap between the East and the West. He was frequently nominated for the Nobel Prize in Literature.

His first two books, My Country and My People (1935) and The Importance of Living (生活的艺术) (1937), written in English in a charming and witty style, brought him international fame. Others include Between Tears and Laughter (啼笑皆非) (1943), The Importance of Understanding (1960, a book of translated Chinese literary passages and short pieces), The Chinese Theory of Art (1967), and the novels Moment in Peking (1939) and The Vermillion Gate (朱门) (1953), Chinese-English Dictionary of Modern Usage (1973). His wife, Lin Tsuifeng (a.k.a. Mrs. Lin Yutang) was a cookbook author whose authentic recipes did a great deal to popularize the art of Chinese cookery in America. Dr. Lin wrote an introduction to one of her collections of Chinese recipes. Dr. Lin was buried at his home in Yangmingshan, Taipei, Taiwan. His home has been turned into a museum, which is operated by Taipei-based Soochow University.

## Cultural Links
文化链接

## 林语堂谈英文学习要诀

一、学英文时须学全句,勿专念单字。学时须把全句语法、语音及腔调整个读出来。

二、学时不可以识字为足。识之必然兼用之。凡遇新字,必至少学得该字之一种正确用法。以后见有多种用法,便多记住。

三、识字不可强记。得其句中用法,自然容易记得。

四、读英文时须耳目口手并到。耳闻、目见、口讲、手抄,缺一不可。四者备,字句自然记得。

五、"四到"中以口到为主要。英语便是英国话,如果不肯开口,如何学得说话?

六、口讲必须重叠练习,凡习一字一句必须反复习诵十数次至数十次,到口音纯熟为止。学外国语与学古文同一道理,须以背诵为入门捷径。每谋取一二句背诵之。日久必有大进。

七、口讲练习有二忌。(一)忌怕羞。学者在课堂上怕羞,则他处更无练习机会。(二)忌想分数。一想到分数,便怕说错,怕说错,便开口不得。最后的胜利者,还是不怕羞、不怕错、充分练习的学生。若得教员随时指正,自然可由多错而少错,由少错而纯正,由纯正而流利,甚至由流利而精通。此是先苦后甘之法。

八、读书要精。读音拼写,皆须注意。马马虎虎,糊涂了事,不但英文学不好,任何学问也学不好。

## Vocabulary 妙词连珠

| | |
|---|---|
| mountainous 多山的,山一般的,巨大的 | indexing 标定指数 |
| consciousness 意识,知觉,自觉,觉悟,个人思想 | patent 专利权,执照,专利品 |
| | nominate 提名,推荐,任命,命名 |
| | witty 富于机智的,诙谐的 |
| popularization 普及 | recipe 处方 |

# Unit 19  Mao Dun
## 茅盾

## Key Sentences
### 流畅精句

1. Mao Dun's works signaled a new literary ear.
   茅盾的创作开启了又一个文学时代。
2. His novels, based on close observation and analysis of society, reproduce a panorama of life of that time, with an epic grandeur, marking the maturity of novel creation, and providing new possiblities for the development of the modern Chinese novel.
   他的小说以对社会的精细观察和分析为基础,全景式地再现了时代生活,有宏伟的史诗气魄,不仅标志着长篇小说创作的成熟,也为中国现代小说的发展提供了新的可能性。
3. Mao Dun was not only an active participant in literary revolution, but also a practitioner of social revolution.
   茅盾不仅是文学革命的积极参与者,同时也是社会革命的实践者。
4. He was one of the first modern writers to accept Marxist theories and was among the first-generation members of the Communist Party of China.
   他是较早接受马克思主义学说的现代作家、中国共产党的第一批党员。
5. The most acclaimed work of Mao Dun's is Midnight, published in 1933. With Shanghai as its backdrop, the novel describes the complex contradictions and struggles between all forces of the society, and successfully portrays a typical national capitalist named Wu Sunfu.
   茅盾最受赞誉的作品是1933年出版的《子夜》。小说以上海为背景,展开了社会各方面势力错综复杂的矛盾斗争,出色地塑造了吴荪甫这个民族资本家的典型形象。

6. In order to truthfully reflect the situation of Chinese society, Mao Dun had painstakingly collected and studied many documents and material about the financial community of Shanghai.
为了真实全面地反映中国社会的现状,茅盾细心搜集和研究了有关上海金融社会的大量文献和材料。
7. Mao Dun's novels have likewise bequeathed us a chronicle of Chinese society in the first half of the 20th century.
茅盾自己以他的小说创作为我们提供了一部20世纪上半叶中国社会的编年史。

## Wonderful Paragraph 精彩片段

### Paragraph 1

## Mao Dun 茅盾

Mao Dun (July 4, 1896 ~ March 27, 1981) was the pen name of Shen Dehong, a 20th century Chinese novelist, cultural critic, and journalist. He was also the Minister of Culture of China. He is currently renowned for being one of the best modern novelists in China. His most famous work is Midnight, a grand novel depicting life in Shanghai, and Spring Silk Worms and Other Stories. He adopted "Mao Dun" (矛盾), meaning "contradiction", as his pen name to express his sigh for the contradicting revolutionary ideology in China in the unstable 1920s. His friend Ye Shengtao changed the first word from 矛 to 茅, which literally means "thatch", to prevent him from political persecution.

### Paragraph 2

## Early Life 早年生涯

Mao Dun was born in Tongxiang County, Zhejiang Province, China.

His father taught and designed the curriculum for his son, but he died when Mao Dun was ten. Mao Dun's mother then became his teacher. He mentioned in his memoirs that "my first instructor is my mother". Through learning from his parents, Mao Dun developed great interest in writing during his childhood.

Mao Dun had already started to develop his writing skills when he was still in primary school. While Mao Dun was studying in secondary school in Hangzhou, extensive reading and strict writing skills training filled his life. Mao Dun entered the three-year foundation school offered by Peking University in 1913, in which he studied Chinese and Western literature. Due to financial difficulties, he had to quit in the summer of 1916, before his graduation.

The trainings in Chinese and English as well as knowledge of Chinese and Western literature provided by the fifteen years' education Mao Dun received had prepared him to show up in the limelight of the Chinese journalistic and literary arena.

### Paragraph 3

## 报刊从业者
## Journalistic Career

After graduation, Mao Dun soon got his first job in the English editing and translation sections of the Commercial Press, Shanghai branch. At the age of 21, he was invitied to be the assistant editor of Students' Magazine under the Commercial Press, which had published many articles about the new ideologies that had emerged in China at that time.

Apart from editing, Mao Dun also started to write about his social thoughts and criticisms. To some extent, he was inspired by the famous magazine New Youths. Like in 1917 and 1918, he wrote two editorials for Students and Society and The Students of 1918, those were significant in stimulating political consciousness among the young educated Chinese.

At 24 years of age, Mao Dun was already renowned as a novelist by the community in general, and in 1920, he and a group of young writers took over the magazine Xiaoshuo Yuebao (小说月报) to publish literature by western authors, such as Tolstoy, Chekhov, Balzac, Flaubert, Zola, Byron, Keats, Shaw, etc., and make new theories of literature more well known. Despite the fact that he was a naturalistic novelist, he admired writers like Leo Tolstoy, for their great artistic style.

In 1920, he was invited to edit a new column: Xiaoshuo Xinchao (小说新潮) (The Fiction-New-Waves) in Xiaoshuo Yuebao. He even took up the post of Chief Editor of the Monthly in the same year and was obliged to reform it thoroughly, in response to the New Cultural Movement (新文化运动). His young writer friends in Beijing supported him by submitting their creative writings, translating Western literature and their views on new literature theories and techniques to the magazines. Literature Study Group was formed partly because of this. The reformed Monthly was proved to be a success. It had facilitated the continuation of the New Cultural Movement by selling ten thousand copies a month and more importantly by introducing literature for life, a brand new realistic approach to Chinese literature. In this period, Mao Dun had become a leading figure of the movement in the southern part of China.

On the notion of content reformation, both the innovative and conservative parties in the Commercial Press could not make a compromise. Mao Dun resigned from the Chief Editor of Fiction Monthly in 1923, but in 1927 he became the chief columnist of the Minguo yuebao. He wrote more than 30 editorials for this newspaper to criticize Chiang Kai-shek, and to support revolutions.

*Paragraph 4*

## P政治生涯
## olitical Life

Inspired by the October Revolution of 1917 in Russia, Mao Dun took part in the May Fourth Movement in China. In 1920, he joined the Shanghai Communist Team, and helped to establish the Chinese Communist Party in 1921. At first, he worked as a liaison for the party. He also wrote for the party magazine "The Communist Party" (共产党).

At the same time, Mao Dun participated in Chiang Kai-shek's Northern Expedition (1926—1928), the main purpose was to unite the country. He quit, however, when Chiang's Kuomintang broke with the Communists. In July 1928, he went to Japan in order to take refuge. As he returned to China in 1930, he joined the League of the Left-Wing Writers. Later, China went to war with Japan and he actively engaged in resisting the Japanese attack in 1937. In 1949, the communist government took over and he was responsible for working as Mao Zedong's secretary and Culture Minister until 1964.

## Paragraph 5

## As a Literary Man 文学家

Xiaoshuo Yuebao Reform was Mao Dun's first contribution to Chinese literature. The magazine then became a place where "New Literature" circulated. Many famous writers like Lu Xun, Xu Dishan, Bing Xin, Ye Shengtao, had their works published through it. Mao Dun supported movements such as "New Literature" and "New Thinking". He believed that Chinese literature should have a place in the world.

The experience of political conflict broadened his horizon in literature, therefore the theme of his later writing was mostly based on this. He then helped to found the League of Left-Wing Writers in 1930. After that, he worked together with Lu Xun to fight for the right of the society and the revolutionary movement in literature. The harvest period of Mao Dun's writing is considered to have been from 1927 to 1937.

Shi, the first actual novel written by Mao Dun, was composed of three volumes, Huanmie (1927), Dongyao (1928), and Zhuiqiu (1928). It is the story of a generation of young intellectuals, who are caught up in the world of revolutionary fervor without a true understanding of the nature of social change. In 1933 came his next grand work, Midnight, which gained great popularity, to a point that it was also published in French and English, and it allowed to develop a sense of revolutionary realism. He left a work unfinished, the trilogy Shuangye Hongsi Eryuehua (1942). After the initiation of the Sino-Japanese War War in 1937, Mao traveled to many places and started a literary magazine in Wuhan. He edited the periodical Literary Front and the literary page of the newspaper Libao in Hong Kong and worked as a teacher. After 1943 Mao Dun did not produce any major works, but still wrote some articles and essays. In 1946 he visited the Soviet Union.

When the people's Republic of china was established by the communist Party of China in 1949, he started the monthly literary journal Chinese Literature, which became the most popular for western readers. He was dismissed from his position as minister in 1964 due to the ideological upheavals. Despite this fact, Mao Dun survived the Cultural Revolution and was afterwards rehabilitated. In the 1970s he became an editor of a children's magazine, and began working on his memoirs, which were serialized in the Party publication, the quarterly Xinwenxue Shiliao (新文学史料), but he died in March 27, 1981 before he could finish it. His influence on Chinese literature continues to the present day because he used his savings to set up a fund called the Mao Dun Literature Scholarship to promote an atmosphere for writing fiction.

Mao Dun's influence and achievements in the literary field were witnessed. On the other hand, he was twice elected as the chairman and then once elected as the vice-chairman of the China Literary Arts Representative Assembly. His status in the literary field has been highly recognized. Although he suffered great pain from illness in his old age, he still kept writing his memories, called The Road I Walked (我走过的路).

## Cultural Links
## 文化链接

### 茅盾文学奖

茅盾文学奖由中国作家协会主办,根据茅盾先生生前遗愿于1981年设立,茅盾捐资 25 万元,当时决定由巴金担任评委会主任。此奖项的设立旨在推出和褒奖长篇小说作家和作品,是我国目前具有最高荣誉的文学大奖之一。当时规定每三年评选一次,参与首评而未获奖的作品,在下一届以至将来历届评选中仍可获奖。首届评选在 1982 年确定,评选范围限于 1977 年至 1981 年的长篇小说。

## Vocabulary 妙词连珠

depict 描述.描写
sigh 叹息,叹息,声
thatch 盖屋的材料,茅草屋顶,浓密的头发
persecution 迫害,烦扰
curriculum 课程
memoir 论文集
limelight 引人注目的中心
arena 竞技场,舞台
Commercial Press 商务印书馆
editorial 社论;编辑上的,主笔的,社论的
horizon 地平线

naturalistic 自然的,自然主义的,博物学的
oblige 迫使,责成
innovative 创新的,革新(主义)的
columnist 专栏作家
liaison 联络,(语音)连音
refuge 庇护,避难,避难所
fervor 热情,热烈,炽热
realism 现实主义
unheavals 未被注意的,被忽视的
rehabilitated 使(身体)康复,使复职,使恢复名誉,使复原

# 6 巾帼风范
## *Famous Chinese Women*

## Unit 1  王昭君 Wang Zhaojun

### Key Sentences
### 流畅精句

1. Since King Huhanye had suffered losses in the struggles between the different groups, he accepted the proposal of his subordinates to ally with the Western Han Dynasty.
   名叫呼韩邪的匈奴王在内斗中吃了亏,就接受大臣的建议与西汉交好。
2. In 33 BC, King Huhanye came to Chan'an again to ask the throne, now filled by Emperor Yuan, for the hand of a Han woman. Emperor Yuan selected Wang Zhaojun, a palace maid, to be the Hun king's wife.
   公元前33年,呼韩邪再次朝见汉皇并请求和亲,当时在位的汉元帝就把宫女王昭君赐给他做妻子。
3. Legend has it that Emperor Yuan had never seen Wang Zhaojun before.
   传说汉元帝此前没有见过王昭君。
4. When he saw Wang Zhaojun in person before her marriage, Emperor Yuan regretted his decision because she was so beautiful.

在决定把她赐给呼韩邪之后,他才知道王昭君实在是非常美丽。

5. Wang Zhaojun was thus described as a stunning beauty, and more than 500 poems have been attributed to her by later poets.

王昭君因此成了中国历史上著名的美女。而这段故事也广为传诵,后代文人为此所作的诗歌超过 500 首。

6. This marriage for peace has been lauded by later generations because it was a choice on the part of the Western Han government rather than a forced concession.

这次和亲得到后代的赞颂,因为它不是被迫的权宜之计,而是居于优势地位的西汉政府促进和平的积极行动。

7. The Huns and Western Han enjoyed a long period of peace after Zhaojun's marriage. She has therefore been praised as an envoy of peace and exchange.

王昭君远嫁匈奴之后,西汉与匈奴之间出现了长时期的和平,因此她又被人们看作是促进和平与交流的使者。

## Wonderful Paragraph
精彩片段

### Paragraph 1

## 历史上的王昭君
## Wang Zhaojun in History

Wang Qiang (王嫱), more commonly known by her style name Wang Zhaojun was the consort of the Xiongnu shanyu Huhanye. She is famed as one of the Four Beauties of ancient China.

Wang Zhaojun was born to a prominent family of Zigui county, Nan county (now Xingshan county, Hubei) in the south of the Western Han empire. She entered the harem of Emperor Yuan probably after 40 BC. During her time in the Lateral Courts, Wang Qiang was never visited by the emperor and remained as a palace lady-in-waiting.

In 33 BC, Huhanye visited Chang'an on a homage trip, as part of the tributary system between the Han and Xiongnu. He took the opportunity to ask to be allowed to become an imperial son-in-law. Instead of honouring the chanyu with a princess, Huhanye was presented with five women from the imperial harem, one of them who was Wang Zhaojun.

A story from the Hou Han Shu relates that Wang Zhaojun volunteered to join the chanyu. When summoned to court, her beauty astonished the emperor's courtiers and made the emperor reconsider his decision to send her to the Xiongnu.

Wang Zhaojun became a favourite of the Huhanye chanyu, giving birth to two sons. They also had at least one daughter who was created Princess Yimuo and who would later become a powerful figure in Xiongnu politics. When Huhanye died in 31 BC, Wang Zhaojun requested to return to China. Emperor Cheng, however, ordered that she follow Xiongnu levirate custom and become the wife of the next chanyu, the oldest son of her husband. In her new marriage she had two daughters.

Wang was honoured as Ninghu Yanzhi ("Hu-Pacifying Chief-Consort").

### Paragraph 2

## 传说中的王昭君
## Wang Zhaojun in Legend

According to other legends, she commits suicide after her husband's death as her only resort in order to avoid marrying her son.

Her life became the story of "Zhaojun Departs the Frontier" (昭君出塞). Peace was maintained for over 60 years between China and the Xiongnu. However, China eventually lost touch with her and her descendants.

Since the 3rd century the story of Zhaojun had been elaborated upon and she had been touted as a tragic heroine. People uses her as a symbol of the integration of Han Chinese and ethnic minorities. Zhaojun Tomb still exists today in Inner Mongolia.

## Cultural Links
文化链接

### 王昭君的传奇故事

玉太守的女儿王昭君天生丽质,被汉元帝征召入宫。然而,王昭君却钟情于书生刘文龙,更赠金予刘文龙助他上京赴考。相国毛延寿为迫王昭君入宫,竟然设计诬害王太守。王昭君为救父亲,答允入宫。毛延寿私下更改王昭君的肖像,令汉元帝误以为王昭君实非大美人。后来,汉元帝无意中听到王昭君弹奏琵琶,终得见王昭君的真正容貌。毛延寿自知奸计败露,随即逃到番邦,并怂恿番王起兵攻打中原,迫汉元帝献上王昭君。王昭君为拯救国家,最终出塞和番。刘文龙虽则高中状元,但亦只得目送爱人远去。

## Vocabulary
妙词连珠

| | |
|---|---|
| prominent 卓越的,显著的,突出的 | elaborate 精心制作的,详细阐述的,精细精心制作,详细阐述;详细描述 |
| harem 后宫 | |
| homage 敬意 | |
| courtier 朝臣,奉承者,拍马屁的人 | tout 吹捧 |

# Unit 2  Princess Wencheng
## 文成公主

## Key Sentences
### 流畅精句

1. In terms of the dynasty's relations with different ethnic peoples, the marriage between a Tang princess and the King of Tubo was most significant and influential.
   在唐朝对各少数民族的安抚政策中,影响最为深远的是与吐蕃的和亲。
2. Out of his admiration for the Tang culture, Songtsan Gambo sent an envoy to Chang'an in AD 634 to convey his wishes for good relations with Tang and to ask for the hand of a Tang princess.
   松赞干布仰慕唐朝的文化,于公元634年派使者到长安,希望与唐朝建立友好关系,后来又请求与唐通婚。
3. Emperor Taizong answered with a counterattack, at which Songtsan Gambo called for a truce and requested a Tang princess once more.
   唐太宗答应了他的请求,决定把皇室中的文成公主嫁给他。
4. Emperor Taizong eventually married Princess Wencheng of the imperial family to him. Princess Wencheng arrived in Tubo in AD 641, bringing with her various grains, vegetables, and fruit seeds. She also brought a large number of books on medicine, engineering, technology, astronomy and calendars.
   公元641年,文成公主嫁到吐蕃,跟她一起去到那里的还有许多吐蕃没有的粮食和蔬果种子、药材、蚕种以及大批医药、工程技术、天文历法等方面的书籍。
5. The marriage bound together Tang and Tubo as "one family."
   唐朝和吐蕃自此"和同为一家"。

6. The marriage between Princess Wencheng and King Songtsan Gambo strengthened the good relations between the Han and the Tibetan peoples. It also contributed to the economic and cultural development of the Tibetan peoples.

文成公主入藏加强了汉藏两族人民的友好联系,促进了藏族经济、文化的发展,具有重要的历史意义。

7. To this day, people still pay homage to the royal couple before their statues enshrined in the Jokhang Temple and Potala Palace in Lhasa.

直到今天,西藏的大昭寺和布达拉宫中还供奉着松赞干布和文成公主的塑像。

## Wonderful Paragraph 精彩片段

### Paragraph 1

## 文成公主
## Princess Wencheng

Some 1 300 years ago, Princess Wencheng of the Tang Dynasty (618-907) left Chang'an (present-day Xi'an in Shanxi Province) to marry Songtsan gambo, king of the Tubo kingdom, which was located about 3 000 km to the west. This pioneered amicable relations between the Tang and the Tubo, and the story of the marriage is still much talked about in areas inhabited by the Han and Tibetan peoples.

In the early 7th century, Songtsan Gambo gain control of the highland area in the west. Beginning in 634, he twice dispatched Gar Tongtsan to Chang'an, where the Tubo minister informed the Tang of Songtsan Gambo's desire for a daughter of the Tang emperor. Tang Emperor Taizong agreed to let Wencheng Marry the Tubo king. Accompanied by the Tubo minister, Princess Wencheng set out for the farway Tubo Kingdom. This segment of history was later turned into tales which remain an important part of Tibetan folklore.

## 用英语说中国——古今名人
## Introduce China in English—Eminent Persons

When the couple moved to Yushu (in present-day Qinghai Province), they were much taken with the local landscapes and pleasant weather, and spent one month in a mountain valley for their honeymoon. Princess Wencheng had carried crop and vegetable seeds to Tibet, and joined her entourage in teaching the local people how to grow crops and vegetables, grind wheat flour and make wine. Seeing that Buddhism, which was at its height of influence in Tang areas, had not been spread into the Tubo Kingdom, Princess Wencheng brought out Buddhist pagodas, scriptures and statues of Buddha which she had brought into the Tubo area for construction of monasteries. Goats were mobilized to carry earth to fill in a pond for the construction of the Jokhang Monastery. Upon complete of the monastery. Princess Wencheng and her husband, Songtsan Gambo, planted willow tree in front of the monastery, which later was dubbed the Tang Willow, as the Uncle-Nephew Alliance Tablet (erected in 823 to mark the alliance between the Tang and the Tubo) was placed next to the tree.

Princess Wencheng also had the Ramoche Monastery built. She named the eight surrouding mountains the Eight Treasures, a name which is still in use today. All these paved the way for the spread of Buddhism into Tubo Kingdom.

While making efforts to propagate Buddhism and pray for blessings for the Tibetans, Princess Wencheng taught them how to grow crops and vegetables. Maize, potatoes, soybeans and rape proved adaptable to the highland enviroment, while wheat mutated into highland barley known in Tibetan as qingke. Princess Wencheng also brought into the Tubo Kingdom carriages, horses, donkeys and camels, as well as medical works and various kinds of farming and industrial techniques. Under her direction, the Tubo Kingdom experienced fast social progress.

*Paragraph 2*

## 布达拉宫
## Potala Palace

Songtsan Gambo loved Princess Wencheng so much that he had the

Potala Palace built for his talented and beautiful wife. The majestic Potala Palace, with 1 000 chambers, was partially damaged by thunderbolts and wars. It twice underwent repairs and expansions in the 17th century, reaching its present size, with the 13-story main structure standing 117 meters high and covering a land area of 360 000 square meters. Frescos of the Potala Palace record historical events, including Tang Emperor Taizong asking Gar Tongtsan to perform five difficult tasks before acceding to the envoy's request for his master to marry a Tang princess, the hardships Princess Wencheng endured on way to the Tubo Kingdom, and how warmly she was greeted at Lhasa. The ruins of the Tubo period behind the Potala Palace includes a chamber for Songtsan Gambo to meditate and practice Buddhism. On the four walls of the chamber hang colored statues of Songtsan Gambo, Princess Wencheng and Gar Tongtsan.

**Paragraph 3**

## 中原与西藏的密切关系
## Close Relations between Central Plains and Tibet

After Princess Wencheng married into the Tubo Kingdom, the Central Plains and the Tubo area maintained close relations for more than 200 years, a period almost free from wars and most notable for its varied cultural and commerical exchanges.

Songtsan Gambo unified Tibet, promoted political, economic and cultural development of his Tubo Kingdom, and strengthened ties between Tibet and Central Plains. In so doing he made outstanding contributions to the unification of the Chinese nation. Princess Wencheng, who married into the Tubo Kingdom and worked to promote economic and cultural exchanges between the Central Plains and the Tubo area, left a historic legacy of friendship and cooperation between the Han and the Tibetan peoples. All these events have been recorded in history books and lie embedded in the minds of the Han and the Tibetan peoples.

用英语说中国——古今名人
Introduce China in English—Eminent Persons

## Cultural Links
文化链接

### 文成公主与大昭寺的传说

　　大昭寺开始动工的时候困难重重，当时根本建不起墙，修了就倒，在尺尊公主没有办法的时候，协助尺尊公主建大昭寺的文成公主谙熟星象和五行说，她夜观天象，日察地形，提出只有填平卧塘湖，庙才能建起来。

　　文成公主又推算出如果不用山羊驮土，那土就永远不能把湖填平。有趣的是"羊驮土"这件事还形成了拉萨城市的名字：藏语里面"白山羊"发"热"音，"土"发"萨"音，为了纪念全称白山羊的功绩，佛殿最初名为"惹萨"，后改称"祖拉康"（经堂），又称"觉康"（佛堂），意即由山羊驮土而建的。

　　久而久之，"热萨"演变为"拉萨"，其意义，也由"白山羊驮土"转为"圣地"了。当年修建大昭寺，白山羊驮土立了功劳，匠师们塑了一只白山羊的像，供奉在寺庙一楼西南角，现在还可以看到。

## Vocabulary
妙词连珠

| | |
|---|---|
| amicable 友善的，和平的 | maize 玉米 |
| tale 故事，传说 | soybean 大豆 |
| folklore 民间传说 | rape 油菜 |
| wheat 小麦 | mutate 变异 |
| scripture 手稿，文件 | barley 大麦 |
| monastery 修道院，僧侣 | bestow 给予，安放 |
| dub 授予称号 | fresco 壁画作壁画于 |
| enshrine 入庙祀奉，铭记 | envoy 外交使节，特使 |
| incessant 不断的，不停的 | felt 毡，毡制品，（造纸用的）毛布， |
| worshiper 参加礼拜者，崇拜者 | 把……制成毡，使粘结 |

# Unit 3  李清照 Li Qingzhao

## Key Sentences 流畅精句

1. Indeed, Li's works overshadowed many of the ci poems composed by male poets.

   李清照的作品确实有压倒须眉之势。

2. Not catering to an ornate style and often using ordinary language, her ci works are original in artistic conception and her language is powerful and admirably expressive and creative.

   她的词不尚雕琢,常以寻常语入诗,但却创意新颖,使语言的运用富于表现力和创造性,为人称叹。

3. What merits attention is that Li Qingzhao in her ci poems repeatedly expressed her love for her husband in a forthright, sincere yet refined way. Touching and beautiful, her lyrics surpassed those written by literati taking on the persona of women, and advanced the development of ci poetry in a subtle and implicit style to a new level.

   尤其值得注意的是,李清照在诗歌中反复抒发了对丈夫的相思之情,真率细腻,缠绵婉丽,以一己的真实情感,超越了那些代女子抒情的士大夫们,使婉约词的发展进入到一个新的天地。

4. These miserable experiences in her middle age filled Li Qingzhao's ci poems of this later period with blood and tears, sadness and loneliness that arose out of the vicissitudes of life she could not free herself from.

   中年后的痛苦遭遇使李清照的后期作品充满了血泪,表达了她在饱经忧患后难以排解的悲愁和凄苦。

5. Li Qingzhao's ci poems are a record of her life and emotional experiences, through which readers may understand the greatest woman poet in the history of ancient Chinese literature.
李清照的词铭刻了她的生命与情感历程,透过它们,读者得以理解这位古代文学史上最伟大的女性。

## Wonderful Paragraph
精彩片段

*Paragraph 1*

# 李清照
# Li Qingzhao

Li Qingzhao (old spelling: Li Ch'ing-chao) was born into a Chinese family known for literary talent and service to the emperor. Her poetry was well known even before her marriage in 1101 to a student, Zhao Mingching (1081—1129). In 1103, her husband began his official career; from 1108 the couple lived in Shandong province. From 1121, he spent much time traveling around the province; his periodic absences may have provided the occasion for some of Li's love poems. Throughout their married life, the couple collected antiquities; this, combined with the political upheavals of the time, explains the relative poverty in which they lived.

In 1126, the Song dynasty capital, Kaifeng, fell to the Jin people from the north; Shandong province was in their path and considerable fighting took place there. In the fighting, the home of Li and Zhao was burnt. In 1127, the emperors were captured by the Jin; the Han loyalists named a new emperor, and the entire court moved slowly to the south, to establish a new "Southern Song" court in Hangzhou. During this period Zhao died, and Li was left to try to save their collection. Li describes her married life and the turmoil that ended it in Hou hsu.

Li Qingzhao finally arrived at Hangzhou, to spend the rest of her life and to publish her husband's work, Jin shi lu (Records on metal and stone), a 30-volume collection of inscriptions that Zhao had copied over the years. She continued to write poetry; we know that she was writing for the court in the 1140s.

The last official mention of her is in 1149. In the same year a contemporary wrote that she had remarried and then divorced; a letter exists that has Li Qingzhao describing that experience. Attribution of the letter is not certain: for centuries neo-Confucian writers said it was a forgery and that a "proper lady" wouldn't have done such a thing; most modern scholars appear to accept the letter as genuine.

Li Qingzhao's poetry was originally published in seven volumes of shi (traditional poetry) and prose, plus six volumes of ci (lyrics composed to be set to existing popular music). About 50 ci (tz'u in the old spelling) and 17 shi survive. Also extant are brief prose works: Hou hsu, an epilogue that she added in 1132 to her husband's book; Cilun (or Lun ci: On lyrics), a study of the ci form of poetry; and the disputed letter.

## Cultural Links 文化链接

### 传世之作《漱玉词》

"寻寻觅觅,冷冷清清,凄凄惨惨戚戚。乍暖还寒时节,最难将息。三杯两盏淡酒,怎敌他,晚来风急。雁过也,正伤心,却是旧时相识。

满地黄花堆积,憔悴损,如今有谁堪摘?守着窗儿,独自怎生得黑。梧桐更兼细雨,到黄昏,点点滴滴。这次第,怎一个愁字了得!"

李清照的传世之作是《漱玉词》,基本属婉约派,由于她一生经历比晏几道、秦观等更艰苦曲折,加上她在艺术上的力求专精和在文艺上的多方面才能,词的成就超过了他们,她后期的词还兼有豪放之长。她的《思项羽》诗和"南渡衣冠思王导,北来消息少刘琨。"的诗句反映出她忧国忧民的情怀。

# 用英语说中国——古今名人
## Introduce China in English—Eminent Persons

### Vocabulary
### 妙词连珠

| | |
|---|---|
| antiquitiy 古代，古老，古代的遗物 | inscription 题字，碑铭 |
| upheaval 剧变 | forgery 伪造物，伪造罪，伪造 |
| turmoil 骚动，混乱 | epilogue 结语，尾声 |

# Unit 4　Qiu Jin

## Key Sentences
### 流畅精句

1. Unhappily married, Qiu found herself in contact with new ideas which led her to decide to travel overseas, eventually leaving her two children behind to study in Japan.

   婚姻的不幸福,与新思潮接触,使秋瑾最终决定抛下两个孩子远渡日本学习。

2. In 1905, Qiu joined Guangfuhui led by Cai Yuanpei, and the Tokyo-based Tongmenghui led by Sun Yat-sen.

   1905年,秋瑾加入了蔡元培组织的光复会和孙中山在日本东京发起的同盟会。

3. However Qiu Jin did not succumb, and she was publicly executed at 32 years old in her home village.

   然而她并没有屈服,年仅32岁的秋瑾在她的家乡被当众杀害。

4. She went calmly to the execution ground the second day of her captivity.

   被捕的第二天她平静地走向刑场。

5. She was an eloquent orator who spoke out for women's rights, such as the freedom to marry, freedom of education, and abolishment of bound feet.

   她是一位高呼女权的雄辩家,提出婚姻自由,教育解放,废除裹脚的思想。

# 用英语说中国——古今名人
## Introduce China in English—Eminent Persons

## Wonderful Paragraph
### 精彩片段

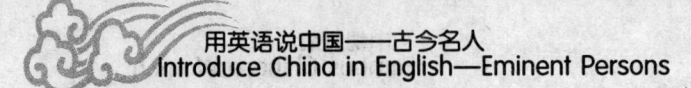

**Paragraph 1**

# Q秋瑾
## iu Jin

Qiu Jin (November 8, 1875 ~ July 15, 1907) was a Chinese female anti-Qing Empire revolutionary killed after a failed uprising.
- Courtesy names: Xuanqing (璿卿) and Jingxiong (竞雄)
- Sobriquet: The Woman-knight of Mirror Lake (鉴湖女侠)

Born in Minhou, Fujian Province, Qiu grew up in Shanyin Village, Shaoxing Subprefecture, Zhejiang Province. Unhappily married, Qiu found herself in contact with new ideas which led her to decide to travel overseas, eventually leaving her two children behind to study in Japan. She was known by her acquaintances for wearing Western male dress (very unusual for the time) and for her left-wing ideology. She joined the Triads, who at the time advocated the overthrow of the Qing dynasty and return of Chinese government to the Chinese people. In 1905, Qiu joined Guangfuhui led by Cai Yuanpei, and the Tokyo-based Tongmenghui led by Sun Yat-sen. After the Xu Gao-led uprising failed, Qiu was tortured by Qing officials in order to make her reveal secrets. However she did not succumb, and she was publicly executed at 32 years old in her home village, Shanyīn. She wrote down the line on the paper provided for her writing of confession and revealed the names of other revolutionaries: "Qiufeng qiuyu chousharen—the autumn wind and autumn rain agonizes human being to death" and went calmly to the execution ground the second day of her captivity. Her name "Qiu Jin" literally meant "autumn caution". She was an eloquent orator who spoke out for women's rights, such as the freedom to marry, freedom of education, and abolishment of bound feet (her own feet being bound).

Qiu was immortalized in Republican China's popular consciousness and literature after her death.

Qiu is now buried beside West Lake in Hangzhou, people established a museum for her in Shaoxing City.

## Cultural Links
### 文化链接

## 吴芝瑛与秋瑾的生死之谊

晚清女革命家秋瑾是一位有名的才女。一次,她路过浙江天姥山动石夫人府,听僧人讲述金兵征宋时,秋瑾有感而发撰留一联:"如斯巾帼女儿,有志复仇能动石;多少须眉男子,无人倡议敢排金。"此联对仗工稳,可见才女的确多才。当时吴芝瑛女士一直支持秋瑾从事妇女解放和反清斗争。在一次聚会中,她挥毫题写了一副对联赠与秋瑾:"今日何年,共诸君几许头颅,来此一堂痛饮;万方多难,与四海同胞手足,竞雄世纪新元。"绍兴秋瑾故居有副对联,也是出自吴女士之手,联语云:"英雄尚毅力;志士多苦心。"光绪三十三年,秋瑾被害,吴芝瑛将其遗骨葬于杭州西泠桥畔,吴芝瑛夫君廉泉请无锡著名画家吴观岱描画了《西泠寒食图》,并在秋瑾就义处轩亭口建立"风雨亭",在杭州南湖小万柳堂别墅内建立"悲秋阁",以志哀悼。清廷为此欲加害于他们夫妇,后迫于舆论的压力未敢下手。

## Vocabulary
### 妙词连珠

uprising 起义,升起
acquaintance 相识,熟人
ideology 意识形态
succumb 屈服,屈从,死
confession 供认,承认,招供
agonize 使极度痛苦,折磨 感到极度痛苦
captivity 囚禁,俘虏

eloquent 雄辩的,有口才的,动人的,意味深长的
orator 演说者,演讲者,雄辩家
abolishment 废止,革除,取消
immortalize 使不灭,使不朽,使名垂千古
consciousness 意识,知觉,自觉,觉悟,个人思想

用英语说中国——古今名人
Introduce China in English—Eminent Persons

# Unit 5　宋庆龄　Soong Ching-ling

## Key Sentences 流畅精句

1. Soong Ching-ling went to America in 1907, then she studied at Wesleyan College for Women, and finished school in 1913.
   1907年宋庆龄赴美,后考入威斯里安女子学院,1913年毕业。
2. In 1915, she was married to Sun Yat-sen in Tokyo.
   1915年她与孙中山在日本东京结婚。
3. After Sun Yat-sen died in 1925, she endorsed Sun Yat-sen's Three People's Princinles; in 1938, she sponsored the China Defense League in Hongkong.
   1925年孙中山先生逝世后,她坚持和维护孙中山先生的三民主义思想,于1938年在香港组织发起了"保卫中国同盟"。
4. After the war of resistance against Japan ended, she continued to support the Peopel's Liberation War.
   抗战胜利后,她继续支持中国人民的解放斗争。
5. In 1949, she was invited to attend Chinese Peopel's Political Consultative Conference by Mao Zedong, Zhou Enlai, and elected vice chairwoman of the Central People's Government, vice chairwoman of the People's Republic of China, vice chairwoman of the Standing Committee of the National People's Congress and honorary chairwoman of the People's Republic of China.
   1949年应毛泽东、周恩来之邀,她参加了全国人民政治协商会议并被选为人民政府副主席;历任中华人民共和国副主席、全国人民代表大会常务委员会副委员长、中华人民共和国名誉主席等职务。
6. In 1981, Soong Ching-ling died in Beijing.
   1981年,宋庆龄在北京逝世。

巾帼风范
Famous Chinese Women

## Wonderful Paragraph
精彩片段

**Paragraph 1**

# S宋庆龄
### oong Ching-ling

Soong Ching-ling (Wade-Giles: Sung Ch'ing-ling) (January 27, 1893 ~ May 29, 1981) was born to the wealthy businessman and missionary Charlie Soong in Kunshan, Jiangsu, attended high school in Shanghai, and graduated from Wesleyan College in Macon, Georgia, United States.

She married Sun Yat-sen in Japan on October 25, 1915. Ching-ling's parents greatly opposed the marriage, as Dr. Sun was 28 years her senior. After Sun's death in 1925, she was elected to the Kuomintang Central Executive Committee in 1926. However, she exiled herself to Moscow after the expulsion of the Communists from the KMT in 1927.

Although she reconciled with the KMT during the Sino-Japanese War (1937-1945), she sided with the Communist Party of China. She did not join the party but rather was part of the united front heading up the Revolutionary Committee of the Kuomintang.

After the establishment of the People's Republic of China, she became the Vice Chair of the People's Republic of China (now translated as "Vice President"), Head of the Sino-Soviet Friendship Association and Honorary President of the All-China Women's Federation. In 1951 she was awarded the Stalin Peace Prize, and in 1953 a collection of her writings, Struggle for New China, was published. From 1968 to 1972 she acted jointly with Dong Biwu as head of state.

On May 16, 1981, two weeks before her death, she was admitted to the Communist Party and was named Honorary President of the People's Republic of China.

Unlike her younger sister Soong May-ling, who sided with her husband Chiang Kai-shek and fled to Taiwan, Soong Ching-ling is greatly revered in

用英语说中国——古今名人
# Introduce China in English—Eminent Persons

mainland China.

## Cultural Links
## 文化链接

### 孙中山与宋庆龄

志同道合最容易成就伴侣,孙中山与宋庆龄就是一个很好的例子。1913年8月,"二次革命"失败,革命派在国内失去了立足之地,大多追随孙中山流亡日本,宋耀如一家更是举家迁避扶桑。从美国读书归来的宋庆龄到日本与家人会面,终于见到了她所敬仰的孙中山,并开始接替父亲和姐姐的工作,于1914年9月起正式担任孙中山的英文秘书。这是在患难中生长出来的爱情:革命失败,心灵的创伤和流亡海外生活的孤寂,孙中山都从宋庆龄的帮助和抚慰中得到补偿;而宋庆龄追随孙中山革命的愿望得到了满足,并发出了这样的肺腑之言:"我的快乐,我惟一的快乐是与孙先生在一起。"这遭到宋庆龄父母尤其是母亲的坚决反对:他们的年龄相差28岁!1915年10月,在得知孙中山已与前妻离婚的消息后,22岁的宋庆龄冲破父母的"软禁",赴东京与孙中山成婚。

## Vocabulary
## 妙词连珠

| | |
|---|---|
| missionary 传教士 | reconcile 使和解,使和谐,使顺从 |
| revere 尊敬,敬畏,崇敬 | vice 恶习,恶行,坏脾气,罪恶堕落, |
| admit to 加入 | 老虎钳,缺点,缺陷 |
| oppose 反对,使对立,使对抗,抗争 | expulsion 驱逐,开除 |
| exile 放逐,充军,流放,流犯被 | federation 同盟,联盟,联合会 |
| 放逐者 | KMT 中国国民党 |

# Unit 6　Bing Xin
冰心

## Key Sentences
流畅精句

1. In 1923 Bing Xin published two collections, entitled respectively Stars and Spring Water, which compiled more than 300 short poems.
   1923年,冰心出版了诗集《繁星》和《春水》。这两本诗集共收录了三百余首小诗。
2. A child's heart, a mother's love, and nature—these are the most moving melodies Bing Xin sang of in her poems, stories and prose works during the May Fourth Movement.
   童心、母爱、自然,是冰心在"五四"时代所咏唱的最动人的旋律,贯穿于她的诗歌、小说和散文创作中。
3. Under Bing Xin's pen, maternal love is endowed with an absolute, almost religious power, and becomes the source of love and the refuge of human souls.
   在冰心笔下,母爱已具有某种宗教般的力量,成为爱的源泉和人类灵魂的安顿之所。
4. Bing Xin's essays made great contributions to the standardization of modern Chinese language.
   冰心的散文对建立现代汉语的典范卓有贡献。
5. Her language, based on the varnacular mixed with classical Chinese, dialects and imported Western words, is concise and elegant, yet flexible and natural.
   她的语言在白话的基础上融入古文、方言、欧化的种种成分,不仅典雅凝练,而且灵活自然。

6. Since the 1920s, her essays have continuously been incorporated into textbooks.

从20世纪20年代起,她的散文作品就被学校竞相选入课本。

## Wonderful Paragraph 精彩片段

### Paragraph 1

### 冰心及其生平
### Bing Xin and Her Life

Bing Xin, (1900—1999) whose real given name is Xie Wanying, is one of the most prolific and esteemed Chinese writers of the 20th Century, as much beloved as the male literary giants of her time.

A native of Fuzhou, Fujian Province, Bing Xin finished her higher education at Yanjing University in Peking, where she graduated with a degree in literature. Later, she went to the United States for further education in Wellesley College, where she gained an MA in English Literature. She returned to China in 1926 and taught at Yanjing University, Qinghua University and Peking Women's Wenli College thereafter. She also spent a year in Tokyo (1949—1950) as a visit scholar.

### Paragraph 2

### 著作
### Works

Bing Xin began writing during the May Fourth Movement and published her first piece of writing in 1919 in Chenbao (Morning Paper). That year also marked the beginning of her literary career that were to span a century. From the 1920s to the 1990s, Bing Xin had many works of prose and poetry, as well as translations, published during her lifetime.

Early works of Bing Xin, advocated "the philosophy of love" and expressed a strong individualism.

She was deft at constructing gentle, beautiful, and visionary concepts in her writings. Works of this kind are found in her collections Past Events and To My Young Readers. The prose pieces in Past Events are mostly reminiscences. To My Young Readers documented her life and thoughts in foreign countries for young Chinese readers in the form of correspondences.

Works in both collections express the author's inner feelings and praise of nature and motherhood through descriptions of past and current events. These works are in fact lyrical prose. Bing Xin's prose is written in exquisite and beautiful language with a vibrant tone. Her works are both flowing and concise.

Bing Xin's prose published after 1949 include the collections An Orange-peel Lamp, Shi Sui Xiao Zha—A Collection of Bing Xin's Prose, and To My Young Readers III. Among these prose works, "An Orange-peel Lamp," "We Have No Winter," and "Cherry Blossoms and Friendship" are the most representative pieces. These works maintain her usual fresh and beautiful artistic style but replace misty and melancholy sentiments with a bright and optimistic tone. Some of Bing Xin's short writings published in recent years are emotionally inspiring and much loved by readers.

While her literary achievements cover a wide spectrum, from novels to poems, she is best remembered for her Letters to Young Readers series, which have stimulated and educated generations of young readers. Bing Xin is well known for her beliefs in maternal love as a cure for various social problems and the importance she placed on mother's role in family and society.

### Paragraph 3

## 文学影响
## Influences on Literature

Bing Xin, who witnessed the twists and turns of the twentieth century, always kept pace with the times and engaged herself in writing for 75 years. Her writing career was a vivid representation of the development Chinese literature, namely, from the "May Fourth" literary revolution to modern and contemporary Chinese literature. As the initiator of several "Bing Xin-style" literature forms, she was also a firm practitioner of literature modernization. Besides being an outstanding writer of children's literature, Bing Xin is also a well known modern novelist, proser, poet, and translator. Many of her translations, such as The Prophet by Lebanese poet Kahlil Gibran and The Gardener by Indian poet Rabindrnanth Tagore, have been recognized as masterpieces among literary translations. In 1995, Bing Xin was conferred the Nation-level Snow-pine Badge signed by president of The Republic of Lebanon. Her literary works have also been translated into several foreign languages, winning readers' admiration from home and abroad.

A famous social activist, Bing Xin held several official positions, including that of vice-chairwoman of the Federation of Literary and Art Circles, and was a delegate to the National People's Congress.

## Cultural Links
## 文化链接

### 冰心——可爱的小书迷

冰心自小是个聪颖异常的女孩子,四岁的时候,就跟着母亲认字片。但是,单个的字片,满足不了冰心的求知欲,她更感兴趣的,是那些有人物、有情节、悲欢离合的故事。于是,在刮风下雨的天气,她不到海边去的时候,就纠缠住母亲或奶娘,请她们讲故事。

1906年,冰心的舅舅杨子敬先生担任她的启蒙教师。杨子敬先生是同盟会员,他的思想很开明。冰心从舅舅的嘴里,第一次听到了美国女作家斯陀夫人的小说《黑奴吁天录》,也是从舅舅的嘴里,第一次听到了《三国志》的故事。为了讨得舅舅的欢心,她对白天的功课做得加倍勤奋。可是舅舅公务一忙,晚上就顾不上给外甥女儿讲故事。每逢这种时候,小冰心就急得像热锅上的蚂蚁一样,没办法,只得自己拿起《三国志》来,边猜边看。她就这样又猜又看,又看又猜,囫囵吞枣,一知半解地读下去,居然把偌大的一本《三国志》,一口气看完了。

这一年,小冰心只有七岁。从此开了头,她看完了《三国志》,又拿起

《水浒传》,看完了《水浒传》,又拿起《聊斋志异》,就这样,一本接一本地看下去了。

## Vocabulary 妙词连珠

prolific 多产的,丰富的,大量繁殖的
esteem 把……看作,尊敬,尊重,认为
span 跨度,跨距,范围
prose 散文
philosophy 哲学,哲学体系,达观,冷静
deft 敏捷熟练的,灵巧的
visionary 幻影的,幻想的,梦想的
reminiscence 回想,记忆力,怀旧
motherhood 母性,为母之道,母亲身份,母亲们(集合称)
lyrical 抒情诗调的,充满感情的,热情的

exquisite 优美的,精致的,细腻的,敏锐的
practitioner 从业者,开业者
individualism 个人主义,利己主义
construct 建造,构造,创立
correspondence 相应,通信,信件
vibrant 振动
concise 简明的,简练的
misty 有薄雾的
melancho 精神忧郁症
sentiment 情操,情感,情绪,观点,多愁善感,感情
spectrum 光,光谱,型谱频谱
delegate 代表

图书在版编目(CIP)数据

古今名人/浩瀚,李生禄主编.-北京:科学技术文献出版社,2008.2
(用英语说中国)
ISBN 978-7-5023-5892-1

Ⅰ.古… Ⅱ.①浩… ②李… Ⅲ.①英语-语言读物 ②名人-生平事迹-中国 Ⅳ.H319.4:K

中国版本图书馆CIP数据核字(2007)第193763号

| | |
|---|---|
| 出　版　者 | 科学技术文献出版社 |
| 地　　　址 | 北京市复兴路15号(中央电视台西侧)/100038 |
| 图书编务部电话 | (010)51501739 |
| 图书发行部电话 | (010)51501720,(010)51501722(传真) |
| 邮购部电话 | (010)51501729 |
| 网　　　址 | http://www.stdph.com |
| E-mail: | stdph@istic.ac.cn |
| 策划编辑 | 李洁　崔岩 |
| 责任编辑 | 崔岩 |
| 责任校对 | 唐炜 |
| 责任出版 | 王杰馨 |
| 发　行　者 | 科学技术文献出版社发行　全国各地新华书店经销 |
| 印　刷　者 | 富华印刷包装有限公司 |
| 版（印）次 | 2008年2月第1版第1次印刷 |
| 开　　　本 | 880×1230　32开 |
| 字　　　数 | 280千 |
| 印　　　张 | 9.75 |
| 印　　　数 | 1～8000册 |
| 定　　　价 | 15.00元 |

ⓒ 版权所有　　违法必究

购买本社图书,凡字迹不清、缺页、倒页、脱页者,本社发行部负责调换。